A Transnational History of the Modern Caribbean

D1715261

Kirwin Shaffer

A Transnational History of the Modern Caribbean

Popular Resistance across Borders

Kirwin Shaffer
Humanities, Arts, & Social Sciences
Penn State Berks
Reading, PA, USA

ISBN 978-3-030-93011-0   ISBN 978-3-030-93012-7   (eBook)
https://doi.org/10.1007/978-3-030-93012-7

Cover Credit: Lost Horizon Images / GettyImages

This Palgrave Macmillan imprint is published by the registered company Springer Nature Switzerland AG.
The registered company address is: Gewerbestrasse 11, 6330 Cham, Switzerland

For Zohra

ACKNOWLEDGMENTS

I must acknowledge the support of the editors at Palgrave who encouraged me to conceive of and run with this idea for a narrative "textbook" on transnational modern Caribbean history. Anonymous readers were vital with their ideas for constructing the narrative, pitfalls to avoid, ideas for revisions, and suggestions for sources. And to those sources: well, this book would have been impossible without them. Here is a hearty "thank you" to my fellow historians past and present whose work I have relied on to write this book. Finally, a thank you to the never-ending joy and inspiration from our children (Hannah, Imane, Malick, Nathaniel, and Sarra) and the fast-rising number of grandchildren (Ada, Harper, Hattie-Anne, Kilian, Lucía, and Zeno). Cheers!

CONTENTS

ABOUT THE AUTHOR

Kirwin Shaffer is Professor of Latin American Studies at Penn State University—Berks College. He teaches courses on Latin American and Caribbean History, Latin American Studies, Global Terrorism, Tyranny and Freedom, Globalization, and Global Cinema. Shaffer has received multiple teaching awards, including being named a Penn State University Teaching Fellow. When not teaching, he continues research on transnational anarchism in the Americas. He has published four books on anarchist politics and culture in the Caribbean and Latin America: *Anarchism and Countercultural Politics in Early Twentieth-Century Cuba* (University Press of Florida, 2005) and reissued as *Anarchist Cuba: Countercultural Politics in the Early Twentieth Century* (PM Press, 2019); *Black Flag Boricuas: Anarchism, Antiauthoritarianism, and the Left in Puerto Rico, 1897–1921* (University of Illinois Press, 2013/2020); *In Defiance of Boundaries: Anarchism in Latin American History* (University Press of Florida 2015/2017) coedited with Geoffroy de Laforcade; and *Anarchists of the Caribbean: Countercultural Politics and Transnational Networks in the Age of US Expansion* (Cambridge University Press, 2020/2022.)

ABBREVIATIONS

ABB	African Blood Brotherhood, United States and Caribbean
ALBA	Alianza Bolivariana para los Pueblos de Nuestra América (Bolivarian Alliance for the Peoples of Our America), Caribbean
ANERC	Asociación de Nuevos Emigrados Revolucionarios Cubanos (Association of New Cuban Revolutionary Emigrants), Mexico
ANLC	American Negro Labor Congress, United States
ANR	Acción Nacional Revolucionaria (Revolutionary National Action), Cuba
BLM	Black Lives Matter
BWIR	British West Indian Regiment
CANF	Cuban-American National Foundation, United States
CARICOM	Caribbean Community
CIA	Central Intelligence Agency, United States
CPUSA	Communist Party of the United States of America
DR	Directorio Revolucionario (Revolutionary Directorate), Cuba
FARC	Fuerzas Armadas Revolucionarias de Colombia (Revolutionary Armed Forces of Colombia)
FBI	Federal Bureau of Investigation, United States
FBM	Free Beach Movement, US Virgin Islands
FMC	Federación de Mujeres Cubanas (Federation of Cuban Women)
FSLN	Frente Sandinista de Liberación Nacional (Sandinista Front for National Liberation), Nicaragua
ICAIC	Instituto Cubano del Arte e Industria Cinematográfica (Cuban Institute of Cinematographic Art and Industry)
IMF	International Monetary Fund
INTERPOL	International Criminal Police Organization
IWW	Industrial Workers of the World, United States and Caribbean
LGBTQ/I	Lesbian, Gay, Bisexual, Transexual, Queer/Intersexual
LKP	Lyannaj Kont Pwofitasyon (Alliance against Profiteering), Guadeloupe
M-26-7	Movimiento de 26 de Julio (26th of July Movement), Cuba
MBR—200	Movimiento Bolivariano Revolucionario—200 (Revolutionary Bolivarian Movement—200), Venezuela

MLCE	Movimiento Libertario Cubano en el Exilio (Cuban Libertarian Movement in Exile), United States
NAACP	National Association for the Advancement of Colored People, United States
NJAC	National Joint Action Committee, Trinidad
NJM	New Jewel Movement, Grenada
NUFF	National United Freedom Fighters, Trinidad
NWCSA	Negro Welfare Cultural and Social Association, Trinidad
PIC	Partido Independiente de Color (Independent Party of Color), Cuba
PPP	People's Progressive Party, Guyana
PRC	Partido Revolucionario Cubano (Cuban Revolutionary Party)
RBA	Red Barrial Afrodescendiente (Afrodescendant Neighborhood Network), Cuba
TWA	Trinidad Workingmen's Association
UDAD	Unión Democrática Antinazista Dominicana (Dominican Antinazi Democratic Union)
ULM	Unión Laborista de Mujeres (Union of Women Workers), Cuba
UMAP	Unidades Militares de Ayuda a la Producción (Military Units to Aid Production), Cuba
UNIA	Universal Negro Improvement Association, United States and Caribbean
UNICEF	United Nations Children's Emergency Fund
USSR	Union of Soviet Socialist Republics

LIST OF FIGURES

CHAPTER 1

A Popular History of Resistance across Borders

In the Caribbean—where history is filled with crimes of slavery, tyranny, exploitation, and colonialism—not everybody accepted the cultural, physical, and structural violence imposed on them. Some fought back using machetes and guns, others with religion, song, and verse. Many resisted by fleeing to different realms to start life anew. Still others used the structural mechanisms of repression to assert their rights in schools, courtrooms, and elections. "Resistance" is central to Caribbean history, deserving an elevated place in understanding its peoples' pasts. As Richard Gott notes, when we focus on resistance, we are "challenging not just the traditional, self-indulgent view of empire, but also the customary depiction of the colonized as *victims*, lacking in agency or political will" (Gott 2011, p. 3) (Fig. 1.1).

I deeply appreciate historians from around the Atlantic World who have studied Caribbean resistance. In this modest volume, I bring together this wealth of research to illustrate various forms of resistance since the eve of the Haitian Revolution to the early twenty-first century. People stood up against authoritarianism, exploitation, and injustice. Some fought to better their individual lives or the lives of their families. Others fought to free whole colonies or countries, to free whole races, or even to free humanity. In addition, many resisted revolutionary changes taking place in their societies either because they disagreed with radical changes or because they did not think that the radical changes went far enough.

This book also illustrates the transnational dimensions of resistance. "Transnational" here is different from "international." The latter generally reflects relations between countries and their governments. "Transnational" is broader, encompassing relations between states as well as the roles of nonstate actors agitating across geographical expanses. Men and women traveled across open seas and narrow passages between islands where they took up arms or spread revolutionary messages. Ideas about anti-imperialism, national liberation, racial or economic justice, and more traveled the seas too through

© The Author(s), under exclusive license to Springer Nature
Switzerland AG 2022
K. Shaffer, *A Transnational History of the Modern Caribbean*,
https://doi.org/10.1007/978-3-030-93012-7_1

Fig. 1.1 The Modern Caribbean Basin (United States Central Intelligence Agency (1990); Central America and the Caribbean [Washington, D.C.: Central Intelligence Agency] [Map]; retrieved from the Library of Congress, https://www.loc.gov/item/90683938/)

newspapers and pamphlets, via word of mouth from passengers and stowaways, among exiles, and from those fleeing rebellion or authoritarianism. People learned about acts of resistance elsewhere in the Caribbean, often replicating those acts in their own lands. Individuals engaged in these pursuits might be government emissaries or militaries, but just as often they were nonstate actors like enslaved peoples fleeing servitude to other lands, political radicals engaged in cross-border acts of rebellion, or activists sending messages, images, and stories about resistance around the region that inspired people in different lands. In short, acts of resistance rarely happened in isolation and had implications beyond local settings.

There is a larger mission to this transnational approach: to see the Caribbean as more than a collection of linguistic or imperial "silos" where one studies the Francophone, Anglophone, Hispanophone, and so on Caribbean. Such a silo approach privileges the dominating empires. A transnational focus on resistance illustrates the commonalities of experiences across linguistic and imperial boundaries, while showcasing the sharing and influencing of ideas around the Caribbean Basin.

So, how should we understand what comprises the "Caribbean"? A university search committee once asked me about teaching Caribbean history. I talked about the importance of understanding the Caribbean as more than just the islands and as more than just the English-speaking West Indies (the job was at an English-speaking Caribbean university). One interviewer said that students would only be interested in the English-speaking islands. I did not get the job. That conversation shaped how I encourage people to think about the Caribbean—or what some more accurately call the "Greater Caribbean." This includes the islands stretching from Cuba in the north to Trinidad and Tobago in the south, from Jamaica and the Cayman Islands in the west to Barbados in the east. Yet, the Caribbean is more than its islands and includes lands where Caribbean waters touch their shores: the Yucatán Peninsula of Mexico, the eastern shores of Central America, and the northern coasts of Colombia and Venezuela. Too often, these Latin American regions are overlooked in discussions of the Caribbean, but a transnational approach illustrates how the islands and these mainland cousins impacted each other's histories. For instance, Mexican revolutionaries sought to free Cuba from Spanish control in the 1820s; the Haitian Revolution sparked conspiracies and revolts by enslaved peoples across the Greater Caribbean; privateers (think of them as government-funded pirates) from Haiti, Guadeloupe, and Cartagena sailed the region, attacking Spanish and British vessels; South American revolutionary Simón Bolívar depended on aid from revolutionary Haiti; West Indian laborers joined a global workforce building the Panama Canal; Cuba assisted revolutionaries in Grenada and Nicaragua; several island nations joined Venezuela to form a regional political and economic challenge to the United States and globalization. Plus, the Caribbean is more than those places touched by the Caribbean Sea. After all, Caribbean waves do not touch the Guianas of South America, Barbados, or Havana. Yet, historically we think of all these as "Caribbean" locations—and rightly so as their histories are interconnected. Lastly, we cannot forget that when people migrated to Europe and North America, they created new Caribbean communities, so it is also reasonable to think of New York, Miami, and more as "Caribbean" cities. Thus, I ask the reader to be generous in thinking about what comprises the "Caribbean."

THINKING ABOUT "RESISTANCE"

How do people imagine who they are? How do they imagine the world around them? How do they imagine a better world for which they are striving? Brian Meeks suggests resistance is "forged at the margins of the real and the imaginary" where people carve out "an alternative social universe" to shape and control their own lives and destinies. This might be done through a head-on confrontation with authority, or it might be something on the margins where people create an alternative world for themselves. This latter is not "an avenue of evasion" but "a powerful incubator to nurture and reshape" one's life in the here and now as well as to prepare for "frontal resistance, if and when it does come" (Meeks 2001, p. 94).

Not all resistance sought to demolish and replace institutions. After all, destroying oppressive cultural, economic, or political institutions takes a large, dedicated, and generally armed force. While we see attempts and successes in destroying institutions and creating new revolutionary alternatives throughout this book, we also see examples of people pursuing what some have referred to as "masterlessness" or "ungovernability." Individuals attempted "to fashion a life outside the scrutiny of Caribbean officialdom" (Julius Scott 2019, p. 37). Thus, people formed maroon communities, formerly enslaved people refused to work on plantations and instead pursued their own individual and small community endeavors, Rastafari worshippers organized communes, and more. The goal was to become one's own master.

Relatedly, some people resisted authority with the desire to become "ungovernable" and thus free from imposed authority. This often meant they sustained themselves on the margins of official society. For instance, ordinary people resisted the Haitian revolutionary state that abolished slavery. This was not because people liked slavery. Just the opposite. Recently freed people resisted Haitian government efforts to tie workers to newly revived sugar plantations. People had fought to gain and work their own lands and, in doing so, rejected their government's policies. Jean Casimir refers to this as the "counter plantation" and reflects what Michel Trouillot calls the "nation vs. the state," that is, the people resisted governmental authority—even in a revolutionary context—because they believed their resistance to the state continued the revolution's true essence (Trouillot 2000, pp. 44–5). The case of the Cuban Revolution is illustrative. The new revolutionary government that came to power in 1959 created new waves of animosity, violence, sabotage, and resistance by many Cubans who saw new Communist policies reaching unacceptably into people's personal and daily lives.

If It's Not Rebellion, Is it Just Another Form of Accommodation?

Some might argue that if people resisted without intending to overthrow the dominant order and create a more just world for everyone, then it was selfish, conservative, and even accommodating to those in power. Thus, using "passive" or everyday forms of resistance to be "ungovernable" did little to free the larger collective of people. From this viewpoint, "active resistance" uses violence to overturn an exploitative order (armed revolt being the best example), while "passive resistance" (cultural retention, music, temporary flight) merely aims to help people be "ungovernable," carve out some separate identity, or achieve better conditions in the short term while keeping the overall repressive system in place.

However, instead of thinking of "passive" and "active" resistance as opposites—an "either/or" dichotomy—it is more useful to envision a "sliding scale" of resistance with active and passive examples on the ends of a spectrum and other forms of resistance (sabotage, strikes, tax protests) in between. We might even consider how passive and active forms of violence were interlinked. For instance, everyday passive resistance laid the groundwork for the 1823 Demerara slave revolt. "It was in daily resistance that slaves' resentment grew, that bonds of solidarity were strengthened, that networks and leaders were formed, and individual acts of defiance were converted into collective protest" (da Costa 1994, p. 81). Similarly, resistance shy of full-fledged armed revolt might not have overturned empires, but it could disrupt how empires and states functioned.

If resistance were about "being free," then it could just as easily be about "feeling free." Throughout Caribbean history, people in dominant positions of economic, educational, political, and religious power created institutions and structures to control people. This structural violence did not erase peoples' desires to be free. As Natasha Lightfoot notes, "despite being mired in poverty, subject to coercion, and denied even the most basic rights," people "still found spaces in their ordinary lives to feel free" (Lightfoot 2015, p. 3).

In fact, we may wish to consider which is more effective: Organized, armed rebellion or quotidian forms of resistance? Aline Helg argues that in a repressive context "everyday forms of resistance can be more efficient" (Helg 1995, pp. 14–5). James Scott argues similarly. For him, rarely is resistance about revolution, but revolution could not happen without resistance. Most resistance did not overturn structures but instead carved out different levels of autonomy. Did any of these acts physically harm exploiters? Often, the answer was no, but that does not mean those who perpetrated such acts were accommodationists. Just because people resisted in "passive" ways did not mean they allowed exploitation to continue unchallenged. Rather, people used these "weapons of the weak," that is, "ordinary weapons of relatively powerless groups," to defend their "interests against both conservative and progressive orders." Such struggles effectively preserved one's freedom and autonomy more than uprisings and collective action (which were only sometimes successful). In fact, it was "the vast aggregation of petty acts" that was most successful. As Scott concludes, it "is no simple matter to determine where compliance ends and resistance begins, as the circumstances lead many of the poor to clothe their resistance in the public language of conformity" (James Scott 1985, pp. xvi–xvii and 289).

There is a related issue to consider. While this book explores the famous and not-so-famous people whose resistance shaped their lives and their communities, we should also consider a question that Robin Kelley asks: "If we are going to write a history of black working-class resistance, where do we place the vast majority of people who did not belong to either 'working-class' organizations or black political movements?" (Kelley 1996, p. 4). It is a great question and one with which historians grapple, even if the answer is not always satisfactory. After all, most people did not join unions, political parties, or organizations. Most did not go on strike, attack overseers, petition for redress of rights at the courthouse, call for women's suffrage, or pick up a gun to fight for liberation.

There is no shortage of possible reasons for why this was the case: fear, uncertainty, dislike of the goals, belief that nothing really could be accomplished, and so on and on.

Yet, just because many or even most people did not join organizations or movements does not mean they failed to resist in their own—often small—ways. This returns us to the issue of everyday resistance. Maybe people mistrusted those who wanted to lead them against authorities, but they still resisted by doing small things that empowered them with an element of autonomy to shape their lives—to say that we are more than simply cogs in this death machine of life. Bob Marley and Peter Tosh wrote, "Get Up, Stand Up. Stand up for your rights." Many people did, but more found ways to stand up for their interests than by joining organizations. So, when we think about organized opposition, we should remember that these forms of resistance might grab headlines, but they were not the only game in town. Being a menacing dragon during Carnival, reading a book on Black Power, giving money to a cause, practicing a religion outlawed by the state, fighting to keep your family intact during slavery, and more were equally resistant.

Culture and Resistance

People also resisted through culture such as Carnival and popular celebrations, religious expression, language, song, literature, and cinema. Residents and outsiders, scholars and tourists recognize that a central attractive feature of the Caribbean is the rich, diverse cultural expressions emanating from the region. Of course, such expression is more than fun and games—even if some of it today has become commercialized pap devoid of historical context and political symbolism. Yet, over the last two centuries, Caribbean peoples used cultural expressions as "weapons of the weak" in homes and on the streets. The imagination became a place for people "to cast off mental slavery" (as Bob Marley put it) and envision lives fighting oppression.

The ethnomusicologist Gage Averill notes, "Popular music…is a site at which power is enacted, acknowledged, accommodated, signified, contested, and resisted" (Averill 1997, p. xi). Caribbean armed resistance movements used sound throughout history. Uprisings in nineteenth-century Puerto Rico and Cuba are known as the Grito de Lares and Grito de Yara respectively—essentially, "shouts" or "cries" for freedom. As Tanya Saunders concludes, the "idea of insurrections being named after a sound or a yell in the public sphere that calls people to arms illustrates the importance of sound in mass mobilization, in hailing the subject, or a group of subjects" (Saunders 2015, p. 29). We see this intercourse of sound-song-resistance throughout the region's history: Haiti's *kilti libète* musical opposition to the Duvalier dictatorship; reggae musicians attacking racism and capitalism while promoting Pan-Africanism; maroons using conch shells to announce their enemies' arrival; the musical instrument known as abeng that Akan peoples used across the Caribbean during slavery—and which Black Power activists symbolically used when naming their 1969 newspaper *Abeng*; Trinidadian calypsonians singing political criticisms of colonial leaders while voicing support for nationalists; and Cuban hip-hop musicians lyrically challenging conservativism and lingering racism.

Culture is rarely, if ever, static; it always evolves. Not a radical concept to be sure. Yet, where it can get tricky and downright political is the nature and implications of this evolution. If cultures evolve, then that means they adapt to surrounding environments and the push and pull of external phenomena. People take what they inherit; they adopt parts of external cultural forces; they shape their lives with these ever-arriving influences and create hybrid forms of cultural expression. This gets political in discussions of "cultural imperialism." Simply, cultural imperialism asserts that outside, foreign cultures arrive, uproot native cultures, and replace those native cultures with the new arrival—the "Coca-Colaization" effect as we once called it. However, people are more than sponges mindlessly absorbing imposed culture. Rather, Caribbean peoples embraced cultural influences from India, Java, Africa, Europe, and the United States, shaped them to reflect their lives, and imbued them with new meanings. Caribbean peoples created hybrid forms of cultural expression to resist oppression. For instance, reggae music is a Caribbean form of cultural resistance, but its origins are rooted in the fusion of Western instrumentation and Ashanti drumming. The instrumentation became a global musical expression of the Afro-Caribbean religion Rastafari—a religious form of resistance rooted in a deeper history of religious resistance in Jamaica that blended West African and Judeo-Christian ideas.

Transnational Resistance and Alternative Geographies

Hybridization—whether cultural, economic, or political—reflects two important and interlocking aspects of Caribbean history: globalization and transnationalism. The modern era of capitalist globalization first appeared in the Caribbean when Europeans unleashed transnational, globalized forces through trade in sugar, coffee, and African peoples. European colonialism arose—eventually joined by US neocolonialism. European cultures interacted with African and Asian cultures in new tropical settings, merging language, music, politics, and religion to create an ever-evolving product of intermixing. As Vanessa Mongey puts it, the Greater Caribbean was "one of the earliest and most completely globalized regions in the world" and "was a fertile ground for the cross-pollination of goods, ideas, and peoples; it was a revolutionary rendezvous" (Mongey 2020, p. 4). Transnationalism and globalization merged in the Caribbean.

Consequently, resistance too was frequently transnational—crossing natural and human-made borders. Why did countries have colonies and neocolonies? To extract wealth. Yet, when governments created economic networks, they failed to appreciate how such networks also created communication networks for the spread of radicals and radical ideas. Both colonial and national governments worked to keep out radicalism. However, empires are rarely, if ever, solid fortresses. Instead, empires are porous, and empires whose colonial borders are mostly coastlines are especially porous. As a result, people and ideas slipped in and around clandestinely. Migrants expressed revolutionary ideas. People shipped books, money, and newspapers supportive of various causes across frontiers in cargo crates, suitcases, the mail, and their own pockets.

Transnationalism is about the transfer of people, money, resources, ideas, literature, and more across borders. There can be a two-way or even multidirectional movement of these in which events shape and are shaped by forces both local and from abroad. For instance, massive revolutionary change in Haiti in the early 1800s influenced events, people, and processes outside of Haiti. News of the revolution spread via white refugees, their relocated human property, and formerly enslaved men and women. People across the Caribbean sang songs praising Haiti. Haiti inspired slave conspiracies throughout the region, encouraged enslaved peoples elsewhere to travel to Haiti and become free Haitian citizens, led to Haitian-dominated privateering ships attacking vessels from slave-owning countries, and influenced free peoples of African descent abroad to pursue republican political goals.

Throughout the past 200 years, people used cross-regional connections to advance radical agendas. Anti-colonial fighters in the Dominican Republic moved to Cuba to help that island fight for freedom from Spain. Anarchists from around the Caribbean moved from locale to locale, shipped money and newspapers to each other, and generated a regional antiauthoritarian culture attacking capitalism, politics, religion, and imperialism. Exiles, black consciousness groups, and anti-imperialist leagues abroad attacked US military interventions and dictatorships. Rastafari might have arisen in Jamaica but leaders built their message on decades of black consciousness politics rooted in the islands, New York, and Europe before finding expression around the Caribbean.

These movements of rebels, radicals, and resistance fighters bring to light another important aspect of transnational resistance: the role of diasporas. As Jorge Giovannetti puts it, these centuries of "unsettled times triggered human mobility, with people from almost every Caribbean territory going elsewhere, either escaping (or at times seeking) political or social turmoil or searching for labor opportunities in foreign lands" (Giovannetti 2013, p. 77). Caribbean peoples long migrated to seats of colonial power in France, Great Britain, Spain, and the Netherlands. By the late nineteenth century, increasing numbers of Cubans and some Puerto Ricans arrived to work in cigar factories from Florida to New York. During construction of the Panama Canal from 1904 to 1914, thousands of Caribbean peoples (especially from the British West Indies) migrated to Central America. Likewise, migrants from the British Caribbean and Haiti moved to Cuba in large numbers in the 1910s to cut sugarcane on predominantly US-owned plantations. By the 1920s, Caribbean peoples from Puerto Rico, Cuba, and the British West Indies increasingly relocated to New York. In these diasporic communities, they met political allies from throughout the Caribbean. Sometimes this migration was unidirectional. Often, it was circular with migrants returning to their homelands.

Transnational resistance in the Caribbean often originated and thrived in these diasporas. For instance, many Cuban independence fighters in the 1890s came from the US state of Florida where radical workers raised money for and joined armed expeditions against Spanish rule. Marcus Garvey's United Negro Improvement Association (UNIA)—while launched in Jamaica—developed into a regional black consciousness and black empowerment force when Garvey moved to New York and from there organized chapters across the United States and the Caribbean Basin. The 1960s Black Power movements in the United States, Canada, and the Caribbean influenced each other while some of the key organizers in the north were themselves children of the Caribbean like Trinidad-born Stokely Carmichael. Much of the anti-Duvalier freedom culture movement in the 1970s and 1980s grew out of the Haitian diaspora.

Transnationalism focuses on the transfer of ideas, peoples, and resources. In short, it tends to focus on the lines that connect dots. However, we cannot forsake understanding the dots, that is, the local conditions, events, and peoples themselves whose actions influenced events elsewhere and who were themselves influenced by conditions, events, and people beyond their immediate contact. So, as we examine transnational resistance in this book, we spend equal time on the local and the linkages, always keeping in mind that local and national events had larger regional implications and regional or global processes impacted local and national environments. We may wish to consider what Aisha Finch has variably called "rival," "alternative," "insurgent," and "contested" geographies. Finch illustrates how enslaved people in Cuba created spaces to challenge authorities while imagining and practicing freedom. When transnational news of rebellion or antislavery campaigns arrived on the island, enslaved peoples already had local spaces across Cuba from where they received and acted on this transnational news (Finch 2005, pp. 221–2). Again, we should understand how resistance frequently interacted at the local and transnational levels to see the larger picture. As Giovannetti concludes, modern Caribbean history is often a "borderless story" (Giovannetti 2013, p. 83). Yet, many conditions that gave rise to that borderlessness were forged within those borders—and often shaped by transnational influences. The local shaped the transnational and vice versa.

Women and Resistance

Many people probably think—at least initially—of resistance and violence as "male-oriented" activity where men guided protests, armed struggle, and more. Yet, women performed various acts of resistance all along the sliding scale between active and passive, organized and quotidian. Sometimes, women played public leadership roles. Other times, their everyday actions set the stage for larger, more organized forms of resistance. During slavery, women like the famous Nanny of the Maroons in Jamaica and Nanny Grigg in Barbados led armed slave resistance. Female cooks and surgeons in plantation houses sometimes poisoned owners. Enslaved women dominated market day in many parts of the Caribbean, and when reformers tried to restrict market sellers, women protested. Some enslaved women practiced birth control, abortion, and infanticide to prevent oppressors from gaining control of their children, but even more enslaved women did all they could to keep children and families intact—the resistance of motherhood.

After slavery's abolition, women of African descent resisted efforts to control their labor. They fought alongside men as in Guadeloupe in 1802 during the struggle to prevent slavery's reimposition. They fled plantation labor. They joined anti-tax revolts and fought attempts to ban religious and cultural celebrations. They fought alongside and encouraged men to wage more violence in Jamaica's Morant Bay rebellion in 1865. They served as military leaders and in support positions in the Spanish Caribbean during anti-colonial wars in the 1800s.

Women also found themselves after slavery resisting another form of coercion—that arising from men of all races and ethnicities as patriarchal systems of domination continued from slavery to post-slavery eras and from colonial to postcolonial eras. For instance, while the Haitian Revolution abolished slavery, women encountered gender inequality in a system where free male laborers (but not themselves) were full citizens. When the British introduced indentured workers to the Caribbean in the mid-1800s, they brought mostly men, meaning there was a scarcity of East Indian women. Some women used their scarcity as bargaining chips to improve their lives, but they also risked honor killings and abuse from jealous lovers. When suffrage arrived throughout the Caribbean, male-controlled governments—as throughout the republican world—long denied women voting rights, leading women across the region to engage in feminist, pro-suffrage struggles.

Such acts of resistance—active, passive, and everything in between—enrich our understanding of modern Caribbean history and the complexities of Caribbean peoples' battles. While local factors conditioned women's resistance, women also heard about other women fighting back in neighboring lands. They might have met other women who engaged in acts of resistance as these women traveled (voluntarily or in exile) abroad. They read about, heard songs about, and even saw images of women resisting as media and cultural portrayals traveled the region. Thus, both local and transnational issues shaped women's resistance.

SOME CAUTIONARY ASIDES ABOUT HERO WORSHIP AND RESISTANCE

Many people have favorite historical characters—probably someone who inspires, or with whom we are in awe at the hurdles they overcame in the quest for freedom and justice, or maybe just someone we have heard about and been told of their "greatness" and how important they are in our past. Caribbean history is resplendent with such people—great men and women who have been canonized for their liberation struggles in the face of repression. We know many famous names who led such struggles: The Nannies, Toussaint, Dessalines, Christophe, Bogle, Luperón, Maceo, Martí, Garvey, Howell, Rodney, Fidel, Che, Marley, Bishop, and many others. Heroes can play a useful role. As nineteenth-century Dominican general Gregorio Luperón supposedly said, "God in his infinite wisdom has made heroes so that the memory of them might serve the oppressed as a lesson of triumph against their oppressors" (quoted in Derby 2009, p. 14).

However, Diana Paton urges caution in painting heroic images of resistance. As she writes, hero worship "can lead to false assumptions about both the ease with which opposition can be organized and the unproblematic nature of what might replace the status quo, and thus tends to produce a romantic and politically naïve version of history" (Paton 2011, p. 5). In many ways, we must confront that old bugaboo that official history is written by winners. Governments love to create "national heroes" for their own unifying political purposes that usually fall around some historically false claim that "all o' we is one" thanks to the efforts of these historical national heroes.

We cannot deny the often-awe-inspiring achievements of these people. After all, freeing the world's richest colony from the French empire in 1804 or overthrowing a dictator and creating the Western Hemisphere's first socialist society just 90 miles from the United States during the Cold War were no small feats. Yet, leaders alone did not accomplish such feats; rather, countless people whose names we barely (if ever) know did the dirty work. In addition, much resistance was not headline-worthy, and those events that were—tax protests, labor strikes, Black Power marches, armed resistance to occupiers, and so on—were generally waged by average people who never became well known, let alone "national heroes."

This book tells the stories of the famous, the marginally known, and that great heap of humanity that fought for their interests but whose names are generally lost to history. Beyond this, we can think about those resisters who have been elevated to national hero status. The reality is that governments canonize people to bring them into whatever national fold those in power wish, and, by so doing, they seek to co-opt the image of and sway the narrative about these "heroes" to fit a specific national and political perspective. Sometimes there is truth in these stories. Often the stories' messier features are omitted. Still, we should not denigrate people's achievements simply because they have been turned into national heroes by a government that has appropriated their histories for political statecraft. Rather, these men and women deserve our attention, but we should liberate them from state control and understand them in their original context alongside the forgotten men and women as well as those resistance fighters who now fail to fit into a neat nationalist project. So, let us be cautious, liberate symbols from state control, and illuminate the roles of nonstate actors.

The Chapters Ahead

This book takes a mostly chronological approach evolving around numerous themes. In Chap. 2, we examine Caribbean resistance on the eve of the 1791 Saint-Domingue slave revolt that launched the Haitian Revolution. We explore the key events and roles of revolutionaries until Jean-Jacques Dessalines declared independence in January 1804. Then, we investigate decisions made by new revolutionary governments that led many Haitians to resist and live removed from the reach of the state. The chapter also examines multiple trans-national impacts of the revolution throughout the Caribbean: a source of inspiration for enslaved peoples elsewhere, a source of fear for whites abroad, its influence on vessels that attacked ships of slave-owning colonies, its granting of freedom to enslaved individuals who arrived in Haiti, and its impact on free peoples of African descent in the region.

Chapter 3 analyzes nineteenth-century emancipation struggles. Legal abolition of slavery occurred at different times and in different ways across the region, but here we focus on the multiple ways enslaved peoples themselves fought for freedom. In the decades following the Haitian Revolution, enslaved Caribbean peoples rebelled—many invoking the symbolism of the Haitian revolt. In the British Caribbean, religion played a role, especially as Baptist and other nonconformist missionaries and African spiritual beliefs challenged slavery, leading to several uprisings until London passed the Slavery Abolition Act of 1833. Resistance in the French West Indies surged until France officially abolished slavery in 1848. In Spanish Cuba and Puerto Rico, enslaved peoples invoked the Haitian example, revolted, and established runaway communities.

Authorities outlawed slavery in Spanish Santo Domingo (first in 1801 and then again in 1822—both times by Haitian unifiers), between 1821 and 1824 in Mexico, Central America, and Gran Colombia, 1833–1834 in the British West Indies, 1848 in the French and Danish West Indies, 1863 in the Dutch West Indies, 1871 in Puerto Rico, and 1886 in Cuba. Yet, real freedom eluded men and women. Legality and reality were two very different things. Chapter 4 looks at the multiple ways people resisted new coercive measures imposed upon them after slavery. Workers in the British and Spanish Caribbean resisted newly imposed apprenticeship systems, protested new census counts, and used courts to pursue legal rights. Throughout the region, formerly enslaved people, plus those born after slavery, migrated to find work away from plantations. Indentured workers of Indian and Javanese descent in the British and Dutch Caribbean staged labor protests. Armed revolts arose as well, including the famous 1865 Morant Bay rebellion in Jamaica. Resistance took other forms besides direct physical confrontation. Individuals used various strategies to shape their lives under new forms of exploitation: theft, arson, refusing to send one's children to colonial schools, deciding what language to speak, and more. People also used culture and street resistance to challenge those in power. They invoked their Christian, Hindu, Muslim, Obeah, Santería, and Vodou religions to resist or survive repression. During religious festivals and annual celebrations, individuals and communities not only "let off steam" but also symbolically attacked their oppressors in song, dance, and masquerade.

Chapter 5 expands our focus to anti-colonial resistance from the 1820s to the early 1900s. By the 1820s, liberating forces on the Spanish Caribbean mainland won independence from Spain, but Madrid retained Puerto Rico and Cuba. Numerous movements arose. Some sought outright freedom for the islands, while others wanted to free Cuba and then annex it to the United States. On neighboring Hispaniola, the 1822 Haitian occupation unified the island under rule in Port-au-Prince. A generation later, though, the Spanish-speaking east broke away and then Spain recolonized the region—rule that Dominicans and Haitians fought against, leading ultimately to the Dominican Republic's independence in 1865. This victory impacted the region: it inspired independence leaders in Puerto Rico and led Dominican leaders to join Cuba's fight for independence in 1868. In the 1890s, Cuba's third war for independence became a transnational affair with organization and fundraising stretching to Florida, New York, Madrid, and Paris. In 1898, Washington intervened and defeated Spain, bringing Cuba and Puerto Rico under US oversight. The war also raised concerns in Washington about the need to rapidly sail ships between the Pacific and Atlantic Oceans. As a result, Washington aided a small Panamanian independence movement to break from Colombia. Panama's leaders then transferred land to Washington to build the Panama Canal.

Chapter 6 examines the worker-dominated resistance to colonialism and neocolonialism in the early 1900s. The United States rapidly became a dominant imperial force in the Caribbean. US military and corporate expansion in the region facilitated mass migration of Caribbean peoples to build the Panama Canal, cut sugarcane in Cuba, and find work in New York. Washington militarily intervened in Cuba, the Dominican Republic, Haiti, Mexico, Nicaragua, and Panama. US neocolonialism coincided with continued European imperial control in the British, French, and Dutch West Indies, sparking new resistance movements. Anarchists in Cuba, Puerto Rico, Florida, New York, and Panama coordinated local and transnational challenges against US neocolonialism. *Cacos* fought US marines occupying Haiti, *gavilleros* fought US occupiers and local colluders in the Dominican Republic, and people waged passive and cultural resistance against the occupations. In the British Caribbean, returning soldiers from the Great War's battlefields sparked labor, nationalist, and racial activism to challenge British colonial capitalism. In the 1910s and 1920s, Marcus Garvey's UNIA promoted black consciousness and served as a transnational resistance organization linking peoples of African descent from the United States through the Caribbean. Meanwhile, Marxist political parties and organizations formed anti-imperialist leagues and often allied with black consciousness organizations and individuals.

Imperialism continued to dominate the Caribbean in the mid-1900s. This led to a surge in often-violent resistance, as outlined in Chap. 7. Puerto Ricans formed the Nationalist Party, sought an independent homeland, and attacked US personnel and symbols on the island and in Washington. Meanwhile, tyrannical regimes dotted the Caribbean: Gerardo Machado and Fulgencio Batista in Cuba, François Duvalier in Haiti, Rafael Trujillo in the Dominican Republic, and other more-or-less unsavory figures. In Cuba, the political left, rebel soldiers, and students toppled Machado. Trujillo's brutality unleashed opposition movements on the island and among exiles in Cuba, New York, and Puerto Rico, leading to his assassination in 1961. These examples reflect that resistance to tyranny had larger transnational dimensions. We see this especially with the Caribbean Legion—pro-democracy radicals from the region in the late 1940s who tried to violently overthrow dictators. Meanwhile, pro-independence sentiment arose in the British Caribbean. In Jamaica, the 1938 rebellion started what Colin Palmer calls "the process of self-recovery for many, an assault on the bastions of racial mistreatment and denigration" for others (Palmer 2016, p. 23). In Curaçao in May 1969, a labor protest morphed into anti-colonial protests, reflecting growing challenges to the status of the Dutch Caribbean islands within the Kingdom of the Netherlands. In the French Caribbean, Martinican writer Aimé Césaire attacked French rule with the publication of *Discourse on Colonialism* in 1950, while pro-independence movements launched a series of bombings in Guadeloupe, Martinique, and France from the 1960s to 1980s. Still, political independence remains elusive for French, Dutch, US, and some British possessions.

Chapter 8 explores the rise of Caribbean black consciousness and Black Power. The Cuban constitution of 1902 promised equality for all Cubans. Again, reality and legality were quite different for African-descended peoples. Some Afro-Cubans created the Independent Party of Color calling for pride in being Afro-Cuban. The government saw it as racist, facilitated its destruction, and murdered thousands of supporters. Elsewhere, Afro-Caribbean peoples moved around the region and to the United States, establishing "solidarity and comradeship transcending national and colonial boundaries" (James 2011, p. 456). Caribbean peoples met abroad and worked together in the UNIA, the Industrial Workers of the World, and Marxist political parties, generating "a transnational black public possessed of an international optic that showed the global dimensions of local injustice" (Putnam 2013, p. 137). In the wake of the 1917 Bolshevik Revolution, new Marxist movements emerged that drew Afro- and Hispano-Caribbean support because these movements and parties preached both antiracism and anticapitalism. In the French Caribbean, new forms of race consciousness developed around the cultural movements of *négritude*, *indigénisme*, and *noirisme*. In Haiti, tension between supporters of black consciousness and Marxists increased as Haitian leaders gave space to black consciousness advocates while repressing Communists. In 1930s Jamaica, black consciousness activists created the Rastafari religion—a transnational creation inspired by Garvey's Pan-Africanism, the reality of poor Jamaicans' lives, biblical scripture, and the coronation of Haile Selassie I in Ethiopia. Rasta inspired Black Power advocates like Guyana-born Walter Rodney. Black Power movements sprouted around the region in the late 1960s and early 1970s.

In Chap. 9, we explore the Cuban revolution and its transnational impacts. Many people know the story of Fidel and comrades organizing in the mountains and fighting westward toward Havana until the dictator Batista fled in late 1958. That story of armed resistance by the *barbudos* (the bearded ones) is the Cuban government's official dominant storyline; there are others. Urban women, students, mothers, workers, anarchists, Catholics, and more fought the Batista dictatorship. Batista fell but resistance continued versus the emerging socialist regime in the 1960s. Some of this resistance was transnational: conservatives, Catholics, liberal democrats, and anarchists moved to Miami to challenge the regime. They used an array of weapons: armed assaults, radio, newspapers, US governmental assistance, and sabotage. Many stayed on the island and challenged the revolution for not going far enough to transform Cuban society into its egalitarian ideal. Meanwhile, the revolution's transnational dimensions appeared throughout the Caribbean. Official policy supported leftist movements in Venezuela and the Dominican Republic (1960s), Colombia (1960s–2000s), Grenada (1970s–1980s), Guatemala (1960s–1990s), and Nicaragua (1970s–1990s) as well as the Puerto Rican nationalist movement. Cuba also forged alliances with democratically elected leftist governments in Jamaica and Guyana.

In Chap. 10, we explore ongoing resistance across the region. We note everything from the role of the arts to armed struggle, maroon revolts to mobilizations in the wake of natural disasters, labor actions and general strikes to the rise of transnational state anti-imperialist efforts in Venezuela, ongoing efforts to fight against sexual harassment to campaigns for LGBTQ rights, and indigenous identity movements to struggles for slavery reparations.

Domination underlines much of modern Caribbean history. People fought this domination in multiple ways and with different levels of success. They still do. What Walter Rodney called the violence of oppression versus the violence of liberation has been one of the central historical engines in the region. This book attempts to understand the many ways people fought (culturally, physically, politically, and more) to shape their own destinies against capitalist, colonial, imperial, racist, and sexist domination. Just as the forces of domination operated transnationally, so too did men and women who struggled to be free and often influenced others around the Caribbean.

Works Cited and Further References[1]

G. Averill (1997) *A Day for the Hunter. A Day for the Prey* (University of Chicago Press).
E.V. da Costa (1994) *Crowns of Glory, Tears of Blood: The Demerara Slave Rebellion of 1823* (Oxford University Press).

---

[1] Each chapter concludes with a Works Cited and Further References list of sources used to inform this book. Readers can use these titles to pursue subjects more in-depth. All sources are in English—which in no way is to disparage the importance of historians publishing in Dutch, French, and Spanish. Rather, most readers of this book will be English-language readers primarily, and the sources are geared to those readers.

L. Derby (2009) *The Dictator's Seduction: Politics and the Popular Imagination in the Era of Trujillo* (Duke University Press).

A.K. Finch (2005) *Rethinking Slave Rebellion in Cuba: La Escalera and the Insurgencies of 1841–44* (University of North Carolina Press).

J. Giovannetti (2013) "Caribbean Studies as Practice: Insights from Border-Crossing Histories and Research," *Small Axe*, 17/2, 77–87.

R. Gott (2011). *Britain's Empire: Resistance, Repression and Revolt* (Verso).

L. Guerra (2012) *Visions of Power in Cuba: Revolution, Redemption, and Resistance, 1959–1971* (University of North Carolina Press).

A. Helg (1995) *Our Rightful Share: The Afro-Cuban Struggle for Equality, 1886–1912* (University of North Carolina Press).

W. James (2011) "Culture, Labor, and Race in the Shadow of US Capital" in Stephan Palmié and Francisco Scarano (eds.) *The Caribbean: A History of the Region and Its Peoples* (University of Chicago Press), 445–58.

R. Kelley (1996) *Race Rebels: Culture, Politics, and the Black Working Class* (Free Press).

N. Lightfoot (2015) *Troubling Freedom: Antigua and the Aftermath of British Emancipation* (Duke University Press).

A. McPherson (2003) *Yankee No! Anti-Americanism in U.S.-Latin American Relations* (Harvard University Press).

B. Meeks (2001) *Narratives of Resistance: Jamaica, Trinidad, and the Caribbean* (University of the West Indies Press).

V. Mongey (2020) *Rogue Revolutionaries: The Fight for Legitimacy in the Greater Caribbean* (University of Pennsylvania Press).

P. Morgan (2011) "Slave Cultures: Systems of Domination and Forms of Resistance" in Stephan Palmié and Francisco Scarano (eds.) *The Caribbean: A History of the Region and Its Peoples* (University of Chicago Press), 245–60.

C.A. Palmer (2016) *Inward Yearnings: Jamaica's Journey to Nationhood* (University of the West Indies Press).

D. Paton (2011) "The Abolition of Slavery in the Non-Hispanic Caribbean" in Stephan Palmié and Francisco Scarano (eds.) *The Caribbean: A History of the Region and Its Peoples* (University of Chicago Press), 289–301.

L. Putnam (2013) *Radical Moves: Caribbean Migrants and the Politics of Race in the Age of Jazz* (University of North Carolina Press).

T. Saunders (2015) *Cuban Underground Hip Hop: Black Thoughts, Black Revolution, Black Modernity* (University of Texas Press).

J. Scott (1985) *Weapons of the Weak* (Yale University Press).

J.S. Scott (2019) *The Common Wind: Afro-American Currents in the Age of the Haitian Revolution* (Verso).

K.R. Shaffer (2020) *Anarchists of the Caribbean: Countercultural Politics and Transnational Networks in the Age of US Expansion* (Cambridge University Press).

M.-R. Trouillot (2000). *Haiti: State against Nation* (Monthly Review).

W. Zips (1999) *Black Rebels: African Caribbean Freedom Fighters in Jamaica* (Marcus Wiener).

CHAPTER 2

Dèyè mòn gen mòn: The Haitian Revolution Throughout the Caribbean

Cuban novelist Alejo Carpentier told the story something like this: Gradually, they arrived in the prearranged meeting place in the Bois Caïman forest. It was a rainy mid-August night, 1791. Some 200 leaders of enslaved peoples from plantations around the northern plain of the French colony of Saint-Domingue initiated a Vodou ceremony. Then, Boukman rose. This respected enslaved man, Vodou priest, and rebel leader with a voice ranging widely and wildly between base and shrill, announced that whites on the other side of the ocean had proclaimed a revolution. They declared freedom for all, only to be rebuffed by white colonial leaders on the island who rejected the French Revolution's liberalism. Soon, a priestess stood and cut a black pig with her ritual blade, and rebels drank the blood—ceremoniously sealing their pact with the Vodou religion's *loas* (spiritual intermediaries). While later Christians viewed this blood-letting as a pact with Satan, participants understood it as a ritual sacrifice to Ezili Dantor—a mother figure in Vodou related to the Dahomey culture of West Africa and from where most of the ceremony's participants came. After the ceremony, most of the leaders returned to their plantations to launch an uprising.

We mark the beginning of the modern era of Caribbean history with the Haitian Revolution, and for good reason. This was the first rebellion to cast off the shackles of European colonial rule and thus begin the long era of anti-colonialism in the region. It also represents the first successful Caribbean effort by enslaved peoples to abolish slavery. Yet, the revolution was not the region's first example of resistance. We begin by surveying how indigenous and enslaved peoples long resisted their abusers. Then, we explore the complexities of the Haitian Revolution, conflicts surrounding the founding of the new country of Haiti, and transnational impacts of the revolution throughout the Caribbean.

© The Author(s), under exclusive license to Springer Nature Switzerland AG 2022
K. Shaffer, *A Transnational History of the Modern Caribbean*,
https://doi.org/10.1007/978-3-030-93012-7_2

Indigenous and Slave Resistance before the Haitian Revolution

Caribbean resistance began soon after Europeans arrived in 1492. The Taíno lived in the Greater Antilles of eastern Cuba, Hispaniola, Jamaica, and Puerto Rico. Spanish colonization quickly brought slavery and death to thousands of Taíno, prompting many to flee. In 1493, Columbus left Hispaniola, which Taíno called Quisqueya or Ayiti. Soon after, Taíno under their local leader Caonabo attacked soldiers that Columbus left behind, decimating the Spanish community of La Navidad. Following the capture of Caonabo, his wife Anacaona moved to her brother's part of the island. She became leader after his death, deciding to negotiate with Spaniards rather than engage in military confrontation. It did not go well. Spaniards soon arrested and hung her. When Spaniards brought 100 African men and women to Hispaniola in 1502, many ran away, aided by Taínos. Over the next decade, the Taíno waged armed resistance, but in 1508 Taíno leader Agüeybaná I in Puerto Rico (known as Borinquen to the Taíno) signed a peace treaty with Ponce de León—a treaty the Spaniards reneged on. Agüeybaná's brother then picked up the mantle. In 1511, Agüeybaná II in Borinquen and Hatuey in Quisqueya continued their anti-colonial war with Hatuey traveling to Cuba to warn and organize islanders.

In the end, though, Spaniards caught both leaders, executing Agüeybaná II in 1511 and Hatuey in 1512. In 1519, one of the last Taíno chieftains, Guarocuya (aka, Enriquillo—his Christian name), rebelled against continued Spanish abuses in Quisqueya. He led followers into a remote section of the island, forming a community that became a refuge for fleeing Africans and Taínos. From there for the next 13 years, his band raided Spanish settlements and fought off Spanish efforts to capture him until signing a peace agreement in 1533. By the 1600s, most indigenous islanders in the Greater Antilles had died, fled to mountain strongholds, or been assimilated. Those who fled to the interiors continued for centuries to preserve cultures and languages while sometimes joining in open armed conflict—as happened in Puerto Rico in the 1860s (see Chap. 5).

Elsewhere, indigenous peoples remained defiant. For the first centuries of colonization, Europeans neglected many islands in the Lesser Antilles. Indigenous peoples took refuge there. For instance, throughout the sixteenth and seventeenth centuries, Kalinago (aka Caribs) in the Lesser Antilles, and especially on St. Vincent (Hairouna as the Kalinago called it), lived autonomously as Europeans generally ignored the island. African peoples fleeing slavery in Barbados sailed as maritime maroons to St. Vincent and lived among the Kalinago. When France claimed the island in the 1700s, Kalinago cooperated with the French in exchange for continued autonomy. When France transferred the island to Great Britain in 1763, the Kalinago sought French residents' support to help oust British settlers. The Kalinago continued to fight the British in the 1790s as we see later in this chapter.

In response to the decline in native populations due to warfare and disease, Europeans imported Africans as enslaved labor to bring the region into full-scale sugar, coffee, indigo, and tobacco production to meet growing European demand. Demand for sugar caused short-term price spikes, prompting investors to bring more lands under production and necessitating more enslaved workers. As production increased, sugar prices in Europe fell. This meant average European workers increasingly could afford it. Thus, demand continued to rise, prompting more Caribbean sugar production and the demand for more African workers.

Slavery generated widespread and varied forms of resistance in the Caribbean. The most common resistance existed in cultural and everyday realms. New African arrivals meant new injections of different cultural traits from West Africa and Congo. New arrivals fought to maintain languages, cosmologies, religious rituals, medicinal practices, songs, and dances. Far from trivial, this signaled a rejection of European cultures as men and women refused to relinquish their identities. By retaining and practicing cultures and languages, enslaved peoples demonstrated agency in their own lives and refused to be mere victims.

Enslaved workers turned plantations into scenes of sabotage where they broke tools, feigned illness, and killed livestock. Enslaved women operated local markets where they made money to hopefully purchase freedom or at least buy items to make life easier, and where they kept abreast of local developments. Enslaved women working in white households overheard whites speak of revolts and abolition, then passed information to their communities. Serving as maids, they had access to rooms and white children. Household cooks had access to whites, and thus opportunities to poison them should the occasion arise. For instance, in French Guiana, a 55-year-old plantation cook and surgeon named Magdeleine poisoned the plantation's new manager. As Bernard Moitt puts it, "control of the pharmacy and the kitchen put Magdeleine in a strategic position" (Moitt 2011, p. 389). While such resistance did little to overthrow the slave system, it induced fear in whites while reflecting the agency of enslaved peoples defining their own lives.

Across the region, many people became fugitives from slavery. Some became maritime maroons. They rowed small boats to Cuba or Puerto Rico, where Spanish officials granted them freedom, or to St. Vincent, where Europeans focused little attention. These maritime maroons not only escaped slavery but also spread rumors, information, and political ideas from island to island. For instance, in 1768 some spread rumors that an African king had arrived in Martinique to free enslaved peoples.

Other enslaved peoples practiced *petit marronage* (short-term flight); they were less concerned about overthrowing the system and more about carving out a better life under hostile conditions. Enslaved men and women ran away from plantations and then returned for numerous reasons. Many left to visit family on neighboring plantations, intending to return to their plantations after a short visit. Sometimes they fled temporarily to improve their conditions such as when people ran away, engaged the plantation owner or manager through an intermediary, and negotiated their return. A frequent condition for returning included a guarantee of more free time to work their gardens, which they used to feed themselves or to sell food for cash at markets. Optimistically, one could save money to purchase their freedom or that of a family member, or money could buy items to make one's life more comfortable. Why would an owner or manager negotiate with a fugitive from slavery? From the enslaver's perspective, more provision ground time was a small price to pay versus permanently losing one's property. While enslaved peoples practiced *petit marronage* to improve their conditions, we know too that short-term flight could have more revolutionary implications. People sometimes fled the plantations to meet fellow conspirators from other estates to plot rebellion. The iconic meeting led by Boukman in Saint-Domingue illustrates how some left, met, conspired, returned, and ultimately engaged in armed conflict designed to overthrow the whole repressive system.

Meanwhile, *grand marronage* (permanent flight from plantations) could challenge long-term stability of plantation systems. Africans fleeing enslavement sometimes joined with surviving indigenous peoples in the hills and mountains of various colonies as they did with Taíno on Hispaniola and Puerto Rico or with Kalinago in Dominica and St. Vincent. Here, they might join forces to fight Europeans or share free spaces to preserve their cultures' languages and beliefs while adopting part of each other's cultures.

In Jamaica, self-emancipated men and women founded four large maroon towns across the island, offering refuge to future runaways. Liberated women in maroon towns supported their communities through cooking food, torching villages when forced to flee, and gathering the spoils of war. In Jamaica, Nanny led one such maroon town. Born among Ashanti people in modern-day Ghana, she arrived in Jamaica and immediately fled to the mountains where she and others built Nanny Town. Newly self-liberated people in Nanny Town fought off British assaults through well-camouflaged guerrilla attacks. Rumors spread about Nanny's supernatural abilities. People spoke of her powers to stop a bullet with her teeth. One told of Nanny catching a British cannon ball between her buttocks and farting it back toward the British. Across Saint-Domingue, fugitives from slavery formed maroon towns, including the large Kingdom of Les Platons in the south. Meanwhile, in the 1750s, François Makandal traversed Saint-Domingue, uniting maroons and coordinating with free market peddlers and itinerant merchants of African descent to organize plantation workers. Makandal created poisons that he gave followers to kill enslavers and their families. This wave of—let us call it what it was: assassination—lasted until authorities captured Makandal in 1758 and burned him at the stake.

Laurent Dubois asks us to consider the overall importance of maroons in a place like Saint-Domingue on the eve of revolution. Were they a precursor to the slave uprising of 1791; or, did enslaved men and women see maroon communities as too few, too small, and offering too few options so that armed rebellion rather than permanent flight became the better choice (Dubois 2005, pp. 52–6)? In addition, we should be cautious about romanticizing maroons. Sometimes maroons made strategic decisions that benefited them but not enslaved peoples. For instance, Windward maroons in Jamaica entered a 1739 treaty with the British, who agreed to stop attacking maroons if maroons returned future fugitives to their enslavers. In addition, when maroons raided plantations for food or supplies, they sometimes raided for women too. While one could argue that women perhaps were better off in maroon towns than on plantations—and this seems perfectly reasonable—these also usually were young women who might have been taken against their will and possibly stripped from parents or children.

The Saint-Domingue slave rebellion that became central to 13 years of revolutionary struggle also had its Caribbean precursors. Slave rebellions erupted in Martinique and Guadeloupe in 1789 and 1790 as word of the French Revolution arrived in these French colonies. In 1790, the free, mixed-race Vincent Ogé left France and returned to Saint-Domingue, where he led an armed uprising of free and enslaved peoples against entrenched royalist (i.e., anti-French Revolution) whites. Authorities arrested and executed Ogé. Whites used this as an excuse to intensify repression against free people of African descent while denying economic and political reforms granted them by the French revolutionary assembly. Then, in January 1791 on Dominica, Parcelle (a former rebel leader) and Jean-Louis Polinaire (a free person of African descent from Martinique) led a revolt of free peoples and maroons.

It is worth noting that many Saint-Domingue people of African descent—free and enslaved—had previous military experience. In the 1770s, hundreds of free men from Saint-Domingue served in French military units in North America. There, individuals like the future Haitian leader Henri Christophe—born in British-controlled Grenada—fought with French forces against British soldiers in the North American War for Independence. Many enslaved men too had military experience as large numbers were captured in warfare in Africa. Thus, many enslaved peoples came from societies with military traditions where they had also experienced freedom. This is vital when we consider the slave revolt in Saint-Domingue. In 1789, there were over 434,000 enslaved men, women, and children in the colony, two-thirds of whom had been born in Africa. The transnational slave trade inadvertently facilitated a transnational transfer of militaristic tradition and understanding of freedom just waiting for coordination and leadership by people like Boukman.

On the Eve of the Haitian Revolution

By 1789, Saint-Domingue provided around half the world's coffee and sugar, generating more wealth than any European colony at the time. Of course, enslaved workers produced this wealth. On the eve of revolution, enslaved peoples outnumbered whites by a ratio of 14:1 and the free population of African descent by a ratio of over 17:1. While most enslaved peoples worked in sugar, both white and nonwhite landowners owned people for things like work on coffee estates. Because French law prohibited free people of color from working in professions, many earned their income from landownership (and thus slave ownership).

When news about the French Revolution and its revolutionary laws arrived in Saint-Domingue, people had mixed reactions. One phrase associated with the revolution (not "Let them eat cake"!) was *Liberté, Egalité, Fraternité* (Freedom, Equality, Brotherhood). "Freedom" had different meanings for different sectors of Saint-Domingue life. Planters (white and nonwhite) could interpret it from an economic point of view: free trade, that is, the possibility to break from the French Empire's *Exclusif* trade system that required colonies to sell to and buy from France at prices determined in France. Planters and merchants hoped to take advantage of Adam Smith's new revolutionary ideas about free trade and seek the best prices on an open market. Free peoples of African descent understood the concept of freedom differently. New revolutionary laws overturned bans that prevented them from working in higher-status professional careers; plus, now they expected the right to vote and to serve in the colonial legislature. However, few free peoples advocated the end of slavery, and even fewer whites believed in racial equality between free peoples of European and African descent. Enslaved peoples also heard about the revolution. Drivers, servants, cooks, and others overheard owners talking about the revolution, and some enslaved peoples read French or spoke with free people who told them news about radical events transpiring across the sea. To them, freedom meant the end of enslavement on plantations and the ability to work their own lands.

When revolutionary decrees granting free people of color more economic and political rights arrived in Saint-Domingue, white legislators refused to implement these laws and talked of breaking away from France, that is, a war for independence led by counterrevolutionaries. Unamused, free people of color increasingly spoke of violence against whites. Enslaved peoples took advantage of the situation. As free peoples (European and African descended) armed their enslaved workers to fight for them, some 200 slave leaders met in Bois Caïman.

THE REVOLT OF THE ENSLAVED

In the first months of revolution, slave armies laid waste to the island, killing hundreds of whites and destroying thousands of sugar and coffee estates. However, by November 1791, the French had killed Boukman and many rebels grew tired of fighting. Until this point, one future key figure remained mostly in the shadows: Toussaint Louverture. Born into slavery, his free godfather provided him an education, teaching him French. In 1776, at age 33, his enslaver freed him. Toussaint then worked as a wage-earning employee on the plantation where he had been enslaved. In the early days of the revolt, Toussaint led a small rebel unit. By late 1791, with rebel zeal falling, Toussaint stepped forward to meet with newly arrived French ministers. He proposed a deal to stop the fighting. In return, rebels would return to enslavement on the plantations (but under improved conditions) and French authorities would not punish rebel leaders. After whites rejected the offer, Toussaint joined forces with the Spanish—enemies of the French, both royalist and revolutionary—on the eastern side of Hispaniola.

In 1792, French General Léger-Félicité Sonthonax arrived with 7000 French republican troops. He tried to diminish the power of whites, who he saw as counterrevolutionaries, and proclaimed that all free nonwhite people were French citizens. In August 1793, he abolished slavery in the north, followed soon after with proclamations abolishing slavery throughout Saint-Domingue. Some rebels joined the French, like Bramante Lazzary, who urged holdouts to abandon the Spanish and join him: "Without the error that Spanish barbarism and slavery has thrown you into, Saint-Domingue would already be peaceful and would enjoy the same happiness. The proof is our good father Sonthonax….There are no more slaves in Saint-Domingue: all men of all colors are free and equal in their rights and believe that this is the greatest of gifts" (quoted in Dubois and Garrigus 2006, p. 126). However, many rebel leaders refused to side with the French, including Toussaint. Then in February 1794, the French National Assembly formally abolished slavery in the empire, a move that led Toussaint to switch sides and ally with the French Republic.

The French appointed Toussaint as lieutenant governor of the colony. However, in 1796 and 1797, conflicts arose between Toussaint and Sonthonax. Toussaint wanted to bring whites back to the island and use their technical expertise to resurrect Saint-Domingue's devastated economy. Sonthonax saw whites as traitors and rejected this. Each man accused the other of nefarious skullduggery and being a counterrevolutionary. Then, in 1797, Toussaint wrote the government in France, declaring his loyalty but warning France to put an end to what he saw as a plot between Saint-Domingue whites in France and the governments of the United States and Great Britain to take over the island and reimpose slavery. Paris had to do everything to prevent that, and if they did not, then the newly freed people of Saint-Domingue would.

Rebel plots, interracial intrigues, international conspiracies—all shaped Toussaint's thinking and guided his actions, but Toussaint had other immediate concerns. London wanted this island. It was in Great Britain's economic interest to get the colony but also important to suppress the image of a successful slave rebellion. So, the British invaded Saint-Domingue and other French Caribbean colonies. Across the French islands, the British encountered heavy resistance from fighters of African descent who sometimes acted alone, sometimes fought with French military assistance. By 1798, Toussaint had routed the British in Saint-Domingue thanks in no small part to Toussaint's leadership against them and to the prevalence of mosquito-borne diseases that wiped out British troops (Fig. 2.1).

Fig. 2.1   Collage of the Haitian Revolution (WikiMedia Commons)

THREATS FROM NAPOLEON AND CITIZEN TOUSSAINT

Haitian Kreyol is resplendent with phrases and proverbs whose meanings serve the historian particularly well. Take *Dèye mòn gen mòn* (Behind mountains there are mountains). In short, just as one overcomes one test, one hurdle, one complication, a new one emerges. Few combinations of words more appropriately describe the Haitian Revolution: slave rebellion met by opposition from whites and sometimes free peoples of African descent or even sometimes enslaved peoples themselves; French efforts to repress or co-opt or deny;

Spanish cooperation or opposition; British invasion; internal conflicts between rebel leaders; and more. Just when one problem seemed solved (*dèye mòn*), another arose (*gen mòn*).

That was particularly the case from 1799 to 1802. In France, Napoleon Bonaparte rose to power, ending the French Revolution's radical phase. Napoleon was the revolution now. He wanted to resurrect the glory of the French Empire, which meant bringing the Caribbean colonies back into the fold and expanding plantations. Toussaint was in sole control of Saint-Domingue and had good reason to suspect Napoleon's intentions. Even though Napoleon promised not to reinstate slavery, Toussaint did not believe him. His suspicions seemed justified when Napoleon forbade Toussaint from invading Spanish Santo Domingo to emancipate enslaved peoples there. Defying Napoleon, Toussaint invaded eastern Hispaniola in 1801, abolished slavery, and gained control of the whole island.

While Toussaint fervently opposed slavery, he did not oppose all coercive labor systems. He insisted on bringing back whites to resurrect the plantations and jump-start a war-ravaged economy. With growing fear of a Napoleonic invasion, Toussaint believed he needed plantations to generate money and bolster the colony's defense against Napoleon. However, the masses resented the idea of returning to plantations, even if paid for their labor. As a result, Toussaint implemented measures to force people back to the plantations for pay, what has been called "militarized agriculture." Toussaint announced, "Work is necessary, it is a virtue. All lazy and errant men will be punished by the law" (quoted in Dubois 2005, p. 188). Toussaint's thinking went something like this: "plantations were part of the war to preserve liberty, and their residents must accept their roles as soldiers in that war and the discipline it made necessary" (Dubois 2005, p. 239).

Was Toussaint a realist, a revolutionary, a conservative? Certainly, a bit of all. From a "realist, state" perspective, he had good reason to be concerned about Napoleon's intentions. For someone like Toussaint, the main goal of the revolution had been abolishing slavery. The government had to do everything in its power to ensure that continued. To resist slavery's reimposition, he needed to take drastic measures to make money and shore up the colony. Did this make him conservative too? Frankly, yes. After all, enslaved peoples had fought not only to abolish slavery but also to enjoy the freedom to live on their own parcels of land and shape their own destinies. In this sense, the goals of the state (Toussaint) opposed the goals of the nation (the former slave masses).

In February 1801, on the seventh anniversary of slavery's official abolition, Toussaint created a new constitution further increasing state control and lessening freedom in Saint-Domingue. The constitution made slavery unconstitutional (not just illegal), but it also limited the nation's freedom. For instance, the constitution restricted one's movement, banned divorce, forbade the practice of any religion except Catholicism, and prohibited free assembly. It named "Citizen Toussaint" as Governor for Life and gave him authority to choose his successor.

Resisting Toussaint's State

Freed peoples resisted this new coercion from their revolutionary leadership. Perhaps the two most hated dimensions of the new constitution—and thus of Toussaint's rule—rested on principles regarding religion and movement. The former effectively made it unconstitutional to practice the most common religion on the island—Vodou. The constitutional article attacked the spiritual heart of formerly enslaved men and women and acted as an almost counter-revolutionary initiative against a religion whose ceremony in Bois Caïman had launched the revolution in 1791. Meanwhile, mobility restrictions barred people from leaving plantations, but, of course, leaving was what people mostly wanted: gain a plot of land to be self-sufficient and "masterless," not tied to plantations from which they had freed themselves. Plus, since these were now plantations mostly run by French whites invited back by Toussaint—and whose owners grew increasingly outlandish in threatening their employees with a return to slavery—people were not happy.

In October 1801, Toussaint's nephew Moïse rebelled. Moïse, general of the Northern Plain, saw the new militarized agriculture, constitution, dependence on whites, and Toussaint's centralization of power as an affront to the masses' revolution. His hatred for whites resounded when he noted that he would love white people "only when they have given me back the eye they took from me in battle" (quoted in Forsdick and Høgsbjerg 2017, p. 97). That month, some 6000 workers in the north rose in rebellion, killing several hundred whites, including Toussaint's friend and former master. Moïse's peasant rebels sought a declaration of independence from France, redistribution of plantation lands to individuals, and exiling whites from the island. A furious Toussaint accused Moïse of inspiring the violence. Toussaint's key generals, Henri Christophe and Jean-Jacques Dessalines—though sympathetic to the goals of the masses—remained loyal to Toussaint. Toussaint arrested Moïse and ordered his execution by firing squad without trial. The rebellion drove Toussaint to more repressive measures, including killing 1000 rebels, mass surveillance, and creation of a pass system designed to restrict mobility even further. All was done in the name of the revolution—or at least in the name of the revolutionary state.

The French Invasion and the Declaration of Independence

A year later, in 1802, Toussaint's international fears were realized. Napoleon's 7000-man invasion force led by his brother-in-law General Leclerc arrived in Saint-Domingue. Initially, the United States supported Napoleon. Like European powers, the Jefferson administration in Washington hoped slavery would be reinstated, and the image of a successful slave revolt reversed. Jefferson attempted to embargo Toussaint's government and promised to send aid to Leclerc. However, others in the United States opposed Jefferson's position. Some believed it was politically wrong to aid French imperialism in the

Western Hemisphere. Others believed Jefferson's policy would strengthen Napoleon's hold on Louisiana and restrict shipping through the French port of New Orleans.

Toussaint's generals, the island's masses, and swarms of disease-spreading mosquitoes solved Jefferson's political dilemma and ushered in a new era in Caribbean history. Initially, Leclerc's French forces overwhelmed General Christophe's poorly manned troops, forcing him to retreat in the north. Then, Leclerc's soldiers confronted General Dessalines, who, as he retreated to the mountains, ordered fires set to destroy everything, including his own mansion filled with the remains of several hundred white French residents. By mid-1802, both Christophe and Dessalines surrendered, possibly not believing their loyalty to Toussaint would pay off, possibly just tired of war, possibly believing the French would respect the rights of the colony's residents. Upon surrendering, they joined Leclerc's forces to fight their former comrades. Believing that Toussaint's continued presence undermined his ability to control the island, Leclerc then arrested Citizen Toussaint and deported him to France, where he was imprisoned and died in a cold, damp jail cell.

It was a short, hollow victory for Leclerc. Yellow fever killed hundreds of French and Polish soldiers. The fever killed Leclerc too. Increasingly disease-ridden and overburdened European soldiers fought men and women who refused to bow as their leaders had. French brutality, indiscriminate killing of islanders, and announcements that the slave trade would be reinstated propelled men and women of African descent to stiffen their resistance to the French—resistance that ultimately finished off Napoleon's Caribbean adventure. As Laurent Dubois writes, "Too many now understood that this was a war between slavery and freedom" (Dubois 2005 , p. 286). New resistance leaders like San Souci and Macaya refused to follow Christophe and Dessalines to the French side. In addition, soldiers of African descent defected from French units and joined the resistance. Then in late 1802, following the lead of their poor, rebellious brethren, the main generals shifted sides again as Alexandre Pétion, Christophe, and Dessalines rejoined the masses to battle French troops anew. By early 1803, Dessalines controlled most of the militarized opposition to the French. Over the coming year under his leadership, the revolutionary masses won victory after victory, driving out the French once and for all in November.

On 1 January 1804, Dessalines did what Toussaint would not. He proclaimed the independent Republic of Haiti—a name taken from one of the original Taíno names for the island: Ayiti (land of mountains). Yet, independence became just one more mountain the masses would have to climb. Dessalines set out to eliminate all French presence, the masses still fought for their own land, peoples of African descent fought each other, and the international community isolated the new regime.

THE NEW COUNTRY OF AYITI

In the waning days of fighting in 1803, French forces had massacred hundreds of prisoners, prompting Dessalines to answer in kind. Declaring "*Koupe tet, boule kay*" (Cut off heads, burn houses), he ordered the mass execution of some 500 French prisoners of war. After declaring independence, officials discovered a plot by French residents to topple Dessalines' government. Dessalines showed little mercy and ordered public executions of thousands of French landowners, merchants, and poor people. Remaining whites fled the island for good.

The war he waged on whites after 1804 led detractors to portray Dessalines as a savage. For most of the 200+ years since declaring independence, much of the outside world agreed with his opponents. However, Dessalines had supporters—those who emphasize that he was a man who led his people out of colonial rule and should be seen in the same light as Thomas Jefferson. Both were Enlightenment-era freedom fighters. However, unlike the touted Jefferson, Dessalines picked up arms for his people's freedom, never owned people, and ensured slavery would never rise again under his watch.

Over the next two years, Dessalines pursued policies both popular and opposed. Dessalines' new constitution reversed Toussaint's in terms of religion. While Toussaint gave state sanction only to Catholicism, the new constitution granted freedom of religion while acknowledging the role of Vodou in the revolution's beginnings and the lives of Haiti's masses. However, Dessalines did not pursue massive land redistribution. In fact, under his rule, all able-bodied men had to work on plantations or serve in the military—both portrayed as key to defending the island's independence.

Once again, formerly enslaved peoples resisted the export-based, plantation system implemented by elites. For generations, they had created a counterplantation culture in the heart of the plantation system by working their own provision grounds. As one scholar speculates, these provision grounds had a large "ideological significance" in shaping the masses' politics (Trouillot 2000, p. 39). That is, people realized that within the highly coerced plantation system, they still had elements of self-determination. They were more than "slaves," and through work on their grounds and selling in the market, they developed an identity separate from that of being an enslaved person. In short, they controlled aspects of their lives while being owned.

As Haiti's black and mixed-race elite pursued large-scale plantation production, newly liberated peoples resisted and fled plantation life to work their own lands—if they could acquire them. Just as people fled plantations under slavery as maroons, so now the masses continued to flee the demands of the Haitian state, becoming what Johnhenry González calls a "maroon nation." The constant flight from plantations and toward freedom devastated the government's efforts to revive export agriculture. While Saint-Domingue produced 14 million tons of sugar per year on the eve of revolution in 1789, by 1821 Haiti produced just 600,000 tons of sugar. In this climate, not only did average people work for themselves, but also they freely and legally worshipped their own gods, spoke their own language, lived remotely, evaded taxation, and created counterinstitutions to pursue freedom in "extra legal means." They undermined the elites' plantation economy, making it "one of history's most successful acts of industrial sabotage" (González 2019, p. 35).

Now, history is never so cut-and-dry, rarely so neat as to pit one group versus another in terms of black and white, good and bad. A deeper analysis reflects this in a couple of ways. First, not all of Haiti's working masses benefited equally from their new freedoms. Women might be free from the shackles of enslavers' chains; however, the new republic did not recognize women as citizens. Article 22 of the 1816 revised Haitian Constitution stated: "No one is a good citizen if he is not a good son, good father, good brother, good friend, good husband." If you were not a good man in multiple capacities, then you were not a citizen. Article 52 provided government protection for married spouses, but protection and citizenship are not the same. And, what about unmarried women? Certainly, this was not unique to governments—republican or otherwise—in the nineteenth century. Yet, it should temper any celebratory feeling one might have for the new country if half of the population lacked basic citizenship rights. Plus, in a society where the government emphasized that all able-bodied men were to work on plantations or serve in the military, Haiti took on a strong, masculine dimension—a dimension that translated a "second-class" status to women.

A second way to understand the complexities of postindependence Haiti is to think deeper about race and color. During French colonial rule, some non-whites also owned men and women. Other free people of African descent controlled enslaved peoples for their enslavers: one remembers that Toussaint was a plantation driver after his emancipation, working for wages to ensure that slave gang overseers did their jobs to get enslaved people to produce their quotas. So, race, color, and class were complicated on the island, as they were across the region. After independence, mixed-race Haitians gained control of most white-owned property. This created multiple tensions between the masses, the mixed-race economic elite, and the Dessalines-run state. Dessalines soon nationalized all plantations, especially targeting mulatto-controlled lands. He sought to end the island's caste system of light-skinned privilege. Driving out the white French was the first step; forbidding mulattoes to own land was his second. Incensed mixed-race Haitians plotted revenge.

On 17 October 1806, the revolution continued to eat its own when mulattoes ambushed Dessalines and bayonetted him to death. The island then split into two, with General Henri Christophe ruling the Kingdom of Haiti in the north and mulatto general Alexandre Pétion ruling the Republic of Haiti in the south: two states but still one nation of masses wanting their own lands. Christophe wanted to create a free public education system for the northern masses, proclaiming that his "subjects inherit the ignorance and prejudice that belong to slavery. At this moment they have made but very little progress in knowledge. Where could they acquire it, for, in gaining their liberty, they have seen nothing but camps and war?" (Christophe 1952, p.64). More controversially, though, Christophe embarked on a land nationalization policy that favored creating sugar plantations for an export-based economy—in essence, continuing Dessalines' and Toussaint's policies. Meanwhile, Pétion launched a land redistribution effort, breaking up plantations and giving land to peasants—a policy he continued until his death in 1818. Ironically, it was the mixed-race leader (and his successor Jean-Pierre Boyer) who did more to fulfill the masses' revolutionary economic goals than the masses' own black leaders.

The Transnational Impact of the Haitian Revolution

The Haitian Revolution spawned fear among enslavers around the region that Haiti's successful slave revolt might encourage their own enslaved peoples to rebel, which happened. Enslaved men and women from South Carolina in the United States to Brazil and around the waters of the Caribbean Sea heard about the revolution and conspired on their own. One thing is important to keep in mind: Haiti did not intentionally export revolution. From the 1790s to 1820s, Haitians were too focused on their own drama to think about manning liberation armies to attack other slave-holding colonies—with one exception: Spanish Santo Domingo. As noted earlier, Toussaint invaded the Spanish colony in 1801, temporarily freeing enslaved peoples. Then in 1822, Haitian president Boyer invaded the eastern two-thirds of the island, kicked out Spanish colonial administrators, and abolished slavery again. Known as the "Occupation" by detractors and the "Unification" by sympathizers, Boyer's troops stayed until 1844. However, no Haitian leader set their sights beyond Hispaniola's shores. In fact, Dessalines' 1804 Constitution explicitly stated that a "missionary spirit" to liberate other enslaved peoples should not interfere with Haiti's work: "Let us allow our neighbors to breathe in peace; may they live quietly under the laws that they have made for themselves, and let us not, as revolutionary firebrands, declare ourselves the lawgivers of the Caribbean, nor let our glory consist in troubling the peace of the neighboring islands."

Inspiring Revolts around the Caribbean

Still, regional enslavers feared their own enslaved workers would revolt. Sailors, dockworkers, traders, maroons, deserters, and refugees personally spread news and rumors of the Haitian Revolution along vast nineteenth-century communication networks linking slaveholding lands. In the process, people "resisted authority while modeling their own thinking on revolutionary values such as freedom, mobility, equality, and citizenship" (Soriano 2020, p. 932). Local slave conspiracies emerged in New Orleans and Caracas in 1793 and 1794. In May 1795, 400 enslaved, free, and indigenous peoples heard about the Saint-Domingue rebellion and revolted on the Caribbean coast of Coro in modern-day Venezuela. Due to trade connections between Venezuela, Saint-Domingue, and the neutral maritime port of Dutch Curaçao, enslaved peoples on Curaçao heard about the uprisings and rebelled in 1795. A rebel leader in Curaçao named his son Toussaint while another leader called himself Toussaint. In 1805, Afro-Brazilian soldiers in Rio de Janeiro wore medallions with Dessalines' portrait.

British officials believed that the Saint-Domingue uprising inspired the 1795 maroon war in Jamaica. They further feared that Saint-Domingue planters fleeing to Jamaica carried the seeds of rebellion with them when they brought their enslaved men and women to the British colony. Meanwhile, some free Jamaicans of African descent went to revolutionary Saint-Domingue, causing British officials to fear what would happen in Jamaica if they returned.

When British troops arrived in the Caribbean to repress uprisings and hopefully gain French territories, they confronted rebellious formerly enslaved peoples as well as angry French residents and native peoples. Enslaved men often comprised these British West Indian Regiments. In fact, the British government bought some 13,000 Africans from 1795 to 1807 to help suppress slave revolts or take French islands. Yet, when the BWIR slave-soldiers arrived to attack French islands, many mutinied and joined the recently freed men and women on those islands.

In 1816, enslaved peoples in British Barbados rose in rebellion. Though led by a man named Bussa, it was the enslaved woman Nanny Grigg who was the "conceptualiser and ideologue of the 1816 slave rebellion" (Beckles 2011, p. 373). Grigg listened to the Caribbean rebel communication network. She learned about the Haitian Revolution and the 1816 Haitian Constitution promising freedom to all who reached Haiti. She told her followers to fight for their freedom and urged people to set fire to the island.

On British-occupied St. Vincent, native Kalinago populations joined this spirit of revolt that punctuated the Age of Revolutions. In March 1795, they launched their own anti-colonial war in alliance with enslaved peoples and French residents who resented British control. As part of his regional efforts to drive out the British, Victor Hugues based in Guadeloupe encouraged French residents in St. Vincent to rebel. Kalinago, slave rebels, and French residents burned British plantations, killed white enslavers, and attacked enslaved men and women who did not join the rebellion. While the island's French soon surrendered, the former slaves and the Kalinago continued guerrilla warfare against the British. Eventually, between 4000 and 5000 "Black Caribs" (as these resistance fighters were called) surrendered or were captured in 1796. To remove the threat once and for all, the British forcibly exiled thousands to the Caribbean coast of Central America. Yet, defiance persisted. A Kalinago leader asserted his masterlessness: "I do not command in the name of anyone. I am not English, nor French, nor Spanish, nor do I care to be any of these. I am Carib, a Carib subordinate to no one." As Julie Chun Kim concludes, this leader refused to acknowledge his defeat and forced submission upon being relocated to Central America. Rather, one should "take it as a final, defiant statement of independence and self-sufficiency" (Kim 2013, p. 132).

In the United States, the Haitian Revolution frightened enslavers. When thousands of French colonists with their enslaved men and women arrived in New Orleans and Charleston, whites feared that stories of the island revolt could inspire locally enslaved people. Yet, US president John Adams aligned with Toussaint for a brief time. When the United States broke relations with France during the 1798–1800 Quasi War, Adams maintained relations with Toussaint. However, Adams' successor Thomas Jefferson reversed these policies. Seeing Saint-Domingue as a threat to southern slavery, Jefferson broke relations and imposed a boycott of Haiti after 1804. This did not end Haiti's influence though. In 1822, Denmark Vesey—an enslaved man in the US state of South Carolina and who had lived as a youth in Saint-Domingue—led an ill-fated slave rebellion, telling his followers that Haiti would come to their aid.

Both the 1789 French Revolution and the 1791 Saint-Domingue revolt shaped events in the French islands of Guadeloupe and Martinique. Rumors in 1789 that Paris had abolished slavery, inspired some enslaved peoples to launch a failed revolt in Martinique. As in Saint-Domingue, news of the French Revolution divided free peoples, who frequently turned on each other. In 1792, white colonial governments rebelled against revolutionary Paris. A small French force suppressed the rebellion, partly by promising equality to free peoples of African descent, though not promising abolition of slavery. In Martinique, white planters allied with Great Britain, helping the British take over by 1794 and ensuring slavery was never abolished. In 1793, Guadeloupe's enslaved peoples revolted and massacred white planters who opposed the French Revolution. Then, the British invaded Guadeloupe. A French force under Victor Hugues arrived. Hugues abolished slavery and armed former slaves to fight the British. After driving out the British, though, Hugues—as Toussaint would do in Saint-Domingue—ordered forced labor of free workers, suppressing those who resisted this new labor regime.

In 1800, as tensions mounted between Napoleon and Toussaint on Saint-Domingue, Napoleon's agents arrived in Guadeloupe. In 1801, workers and soldiers of African descent rebelled. Napoleon's troops attempted to arrest a mixed-race officer, Magloire Pélage. More troops arrived to support the new government, but black soldiers deserted and joined the insurrection. In response, Napoleon sent 3500 troops to Guadeloupe. French troops under General Antoine Richepance arrived in May 1802 and began disarming Guadeloupe's black army—a move he believed essential to establish order and end opposition to Napoleon's rule. Meanwhile, residents in Guadeloupe grew weary because they had heard news of fighting between Toussaint and Leclerc in Saint-Domingue.

Then, Louis Delgrès rebelled. Delgrès—a mixed-race military officer opposed to Napoleon's authoritarianism—reflected the fears of many people of African descent that Napoleon would reinstate slavery and deprive all people of color of their rights. Delgrès invoked the spirit of the revolutionary age: "Citizens of Guadeloupe...Resistance to oppression is a natural right. Divinity itself cannot be offended that we are defending our cause, which is that of humanity and justice" (quoted in Dubois and Garrigus 2006, p. 174). Pursued by Richepance's forces, Delgrès and his followers fled to the Soufrière volcano flying the flag that Dessalines would fly two years later (the red and the blue; no white). Women joined this resistance. They carried ammunition and sang the "La Marseillaise" alongside men as they fought French efforts to reimpose slavery. One woman, Solitude, joined Delgrès's rebellion even though she was eight months pregnant. However, Solitude was soon captured and then gave birth. Authorities hung her and gave the baby to Solitude's owner. Ultimately, Delgrès's rebels were trapped. In an ultimate act of defiance, they mined the volcano, and on 28 May 1802 ignited the charges in a mass suicide as French troops arrived. Two months later, Richepance reinstated slavery in Guadeloupe.

Haiti's impact also penetrated the Spanish Caribbean. With the world's former number one sugar producer now exporting a fraction of its former quantities, the Spanish colony of Cuba brought record amounts of sugar lands under production. Between 1790 and 1806, sugar exports rose from 15,000 metric tons to 40,000 metric tons. By the 1820s, Cuba exported 105 million metric tons of sugar annually. Of course, planters needed slave labor to pull this off. Spain imported over 325,000 Africans to Cuba between 1795 and 1820. In addition, in the last half of 1803, some 18,000 French fled Dessalines's anti-white violence in Saint-Domingue and settled in eastern Cuba—many with their enslaved workers. As Ada Ferrer notes, these exiles in eastern Cuba fled Haiti to create "a reactionary order" where they "could start anew and thus partially undo the revolution that had almost destroyed them" (Ferrer 2014, p. 182).

Spanish officials feared that these arrivals from Haiti would spread information about the revolution to newly arrived enslaved Africans, which happened. Enslaved Haitians arrived in Cuba singing songs praising Haiti's rebels, and rebellious enslaved workers on Cuban estates invoked the Haitian rebellion. While historians suggest some of these rebels might have tried communicating with Dessalines, most insurgent conspiracies were led by what Ferrer calls "self-appointed agents, men and perhaps women who acted, or thought they acted, in the spirit represented by the independent state of Haiti—whether or not they were charged to do so by Dessalines or anyone else" (Ferrer 2014, p. 213).

As Cuban sugar, coffee, and slavery rose, so too did marronage. Enslaved peoples from French- and Spanish-owned plantations fled to Cuba's mountains where they met other runaways fresh from slave ships or who had escaped French masters who had relocated to Cuba. Several slave conspiracies linked to Haiti emerged from these marronage connections between Cuban, African, Jamaican, and Haitian enslaved peoples—along with free Cubans of color. In 1805, near the eastern Cuban city of Bayamo, a Jamaican led a rebellious slave conspiracy. A year later in the western city of Güines, an enslaved man born in Saint-Domingue led another.

In 1812, the Aponte Conspiracy seeking to end slavery erupted across Cuba. Men in free black militias, maroons in mountains and forests, and both urban and rural enslaved peoples rose in loosely coordinated acts of armed militancy.

As they moved around the island, they transmitted news and rumors such as reports that kings in Europe had abolished slavery, but colonial officials refused to implement such decrees. Whether or not the uprisings were centrally coordinated by a revolutionary leadership is still unknown, but Spanish officials arrested, tried, and decapitated José Antonio Aponte (a captain in Cuba's free black militia) for his supposed leadership role.

The Haitian Revolution inspired some Aponte conspirators. During investigations, Spanish officials found portraits of Christophe, Toussaint, and Dessalines in Aponte's home, along with a fake emancipation proclamation supposedly signed by Christophe. The very idea of forging a document "signed" by a Haitian leader attests to the symbolic power of Haiti's image to these Cuban rebels, even if Christophe denied any intentions of an aggressive foreign policy against Haiti's neighbors. The Haitian image proved important in other islands too because Saint-Domingue whites took their enslaved workers to Trinidad and Jamaica. There, enslaved peoples sang pro-revolution tunes like this in Trinidad in 1805: "The bread is the flesh of the white man, San Domingo! / The wine is the blood of the white man. / We will drink the white man's blood, San Domingo! / The bread we eat is the white man's flesh. / The wine we drink is the white man's blood" (quoted in Gott 2011, p. 152).

HAITI AND CARIBBEAN POLITICAL RADICALISM

The Haitian Revolution's transnational dimensions affected more than Caribbean slavery. It became a symbol of anti-colonialism and republicanism in the region too. After Dessalines' assassination in 1806 and the country splitting in two, Pétion's southern republic inspired many in the region for its commitment to independence and democratic principles—at least until 1816 when, having grown frustrated by the republic's legislature, Pétion proclaimed himself President for Life and then two years later suspended the legislature. However, in that decade, Pétion's regime was the closest thing to political democracy the Caribbean had known. Just as the 1791 revolution inspired enslaved Caribbean peoples, so too did the Republic of Haiti become a symbol of popular republican ideals and a haven for those launching anticolonial struggles.

While the 1816 constitutional revisions declared Pétion as President for Life, it also extended the concept of freedom beyond the republic's borders. Article 44 declared that "Every African, Indian and those issued from their blood, born of colonies or foreign countries, who might come to reside in the Republic, will be recognized as Haitians, but shall not enjoy the rights of citizenship except after one year of residence." In short, Pétion sent notice to all males born enslaved or under coercion that if they made it to Haiti, they could become free Haitian citizens. And if they were enslaved women? While women would not be citizens, they nevertheless would be free from slavery. Over the coming years, thousands of people from the United States and the Caribbean Basin arrived to become Haitians—some on their own initiative, others at

Pétion's invitation. President Boyer continued this policy into the 1820s. The 1816 revisions had other transnational effects. Inspired by their Saint-Domingue equals, free people of African descent in the region defied whites. For instance, in 1823, free men of color in Jamaica sought more political rights under the British system. Such ideas in part emerged from people reading Haitian newspapers and from Haitian migrants who demanded political rights in Jamaica.

In Venezuela, while anti-colonial leaders developed relationships with Haiti's new governments, average people also heard about the revolution. From the 1790s to the 1810s, they spread revolutionary ideas of independence and political democracy, scaring Spanish colonial elites. Meanwhile, the liberalizing traits of the Enlightenment and the French and Haitian Revolutions found growing acceptance among many in early-1800s Cartagena in modern-day Colombia. *Pardos* (mixed-race peoples) dominated Cartagena. By 1810, the pardo population largely supported independence, and pushed for equal rights for all free people regardless of color. In 1811, the short-lived Republic of Cartagena gained political independence from Spain. Its 1812 constitution legislated racial equality between all free peoples. For some sectors of the pardo population, ideas of racial equality grew less from Enlightenment theory and more from the "image of popular republicanism" associated with the Haitian Revolution (Lasso 2001, p. 186). News of the revolution and Pétion's republic inspired pardo support for a republic of equals in Cartagena. However, these republican virtues did not extend to slavery. In fact, Cartagena's pardo population did not generate a racial consciousness or identity with Cartagena's enslaved peoples. Instead, they largely pursued a class identity with free whites. While the 1812 constitution banned new imports of enslaved Africans into Cartagena, it did not outlaw slavery.

The relationship between Haiti and emerging Latin American independence movements continued after the Republic of Cartagena collapsed. Beginning in late 1815, Pétion protected, armed, and manned independence leader Simón Bolívar. Bolívar and around 2000 residents from Colombia and Venezuela resided in Haiti in exile. From Haiti, Bolívar plotted the liberation of Spain's mainland Caribbean colonies. In return, Bolívar promised Pétion that he would free people he found on captured vessels and send them to freedom in Haiti as well as abolish slavery in lands he liberated from Spanish rule.

Revolutionary Privateering

If the Haitian Revolution politically inspired Cartagena's pardos, the two republics shared another characteristic: striking against British and Spanish colonialism in the region. Again, while Haitian governments did not export revolution nor force slaveholding colonies to abolish slavery, Haiti did provide aid and comfort to those who shared republican ideals. Cartagena went on the offensive to maintain its independence from Spain. Part of that offensive included "revolutionary privateering" (Pérez Morales 2018, p. 1). Privateers and pirates marauded across the region. The latter tended to operate on their own, while the former operated with government license. In the early decades of the 1800s, privateers came from North America, Europe, and the Caribbean. Some represented Haiti, while others acquired commissions from Latin American revolutionaries seeking independence from Spain and used these commissions "as tools of revolutionary politics" to support Caribbean liberation movements (Mongey 2020, p. 6). Across the region, they used mobile presses to print revolutionary declarations against European colonial powers and in support of newly liberated revolutionary communities like the island of Providencia in the Western Caribbean in the late 1810s. These declarations took inspiration from the Republic of Haiti as well as language from the French *Declaration of the Rights of Man and Citizen* and the US *Declaration of Independence*. Privateers then distributed these self-published manifestoes throughout the Caribbean.

In revolutionary Guadeloupe, Victor Hugues used his rule to incite slave rebellions in the British-occupied islands of Sainte-Lucie, Grenada, and St. Vincent through revolutionary privateering. Hugues's navy spread revolutionary messages and troops to these islands while helping to arm French citizens and enslaved peoples alike. Meanwhile, Hugues' privateers waged war against British commerce in the Caribbean. At least 40 government-sponsored privateers were based in Guadeloupe in 1796. These—combined with private outfits—captured or sank hundreds of British vessels. Like privateers across the region, the crews were multiracial.

Between 1811 and 1820, Haitian privateers caught at least four slave ships and freed hundreds of people. Meanwhile, Cartagenan privateers targeted Spanish shipping in and out of Cuba during its post-Haitian Revolution sugar boom. Cartagenan captains largely hired Afro-Caribbean seafarers, especially Haitians, to man the vessels. When Spanish ships pursued Cartagenan ships, privateers found safe haven in Haitian ports. After the Cartagenan republic fell in 1815, many privateers found refuge in Haiti.

Several privateers proclaimed universal rights, freed enslaved Africans from slave ships, and encouraged slave uprisings against the British and Spanish. However, not all did. Some privateers profited from slave trading. For instance, the freeborn, mixed-race Haitians Joseph Savary and Marcelin Guillot joined various privateering enterprises throughout the Caribbean and advocated freedom—but not for enslaved peoples. In fact, Guillot made thousands of dollars from selling enslaved workers and slave-produced goods captured from Spanish ships. These men wanted the same rights as whites, which in most of the region still meant the right to own people.

Conclusion

While Haitian foreign policy was officially neutral, the revolution and the governments that followed inspired antislavery and anti-colonial resistance movements across the Caribbean. As Ferrer concludes, such inspiration and action were tantamount to "extending the physical reach of Haitian free soil into Caribbean and Atlantic waters" (Ferrer 2012, p. 61). Enslavers and colonial governments feared the image and impact of the Haitian Revolution, but Spain saw the revolution as a means to increase Cuba's market share in the global sugar trade and generate new wealth. For free people of color across the Caribbean, the Haitian Revolution symbolized people standing up to claim their rights as citizens. For thousands of people, the Haitian Revolution not only inspired but also allowed enslaved peoples "to assert their worthiness, to manipulate the fears of white overlords, to express immediate and urgent grievances, or, maybe, to help imagine a place without whites or a place without slavery" (Ferrer 2014, p. 223). As Robin Blackburn suggests, the Haitian Revolution was "a symbol of black power and authority, not of desperate rebellion, and this is why it could inspire or terrify" (Blackburn 2001, p. 17).

Was the Haitian Revolution a success or failure? This question has guided discussions of the revolution for two centuries with supporters glorifying it and critics demonizing it. It is difficult to determine how much we can credit the revolution with the ultimate collapse of Caribbean slavery. Certainly, Bolívar's liberated territories (at least initially) and Boyer's occupied Spanish Santo Domingo benefited on this score, but Cuba saw slavery increase in the aftermath of the revolution. Free peoples of African descent gained an important symbol, if not necessarily a lot of material benefit, from the Haitian example. And, until Pétion began redistributing land to Haitians, it is reasonable to ask how much the revolution materially benefited the island's masses—beyond the actual elimination of chattel slavery of course.

It is also worth remembering that the Haitian Revolution was by no means monolithic. Most enslaved men and women fought for freedom, but some fought for their owners. Toussaint showed his willingness to return people to their enslavers in late 1791 before becoming a dedicated abolitionist. Free peoples of African descent often fought for rights for their class, not for slave abolition, though sometimes they fought with enslaved peoples in campaigns that ended slavery. Some rebels wanted independence from France; others were happy to remain a loyal French colony.

We should also consider Haitian historian Jean Casimir's interpretations: "On the one hand was the trajectory of a nation seeking a better life, defined on its own terms; on the other were public authorities seeking to prevent the population from gaining access to the resources necessary to fulfill their aspirations for well-being. The authorities considered the aspiration of the population irrelevant." While leaders might have opposed slavery and eventually colonialism, they nevertheless adopted many of French colonialism's core ideas of a Eurocentric state, the need for plantation labor as part of a capitalist exporting economy, and the goal of preventing the masses from gaining their own lands. The revolution's leaders ("oligarchs" as Casimir calls them) "set themselves up in opposition to the laboring classes" (Casimir 2020, pp. 3, 47). Oligarchs' goals flew in the face of the masses' desires. The interests of black and mixed-race elites who controlled state powers and wanted plantation-based export agriculture battled the masses who believed owning their own land was key to their freedom. Many conflicts, many competing goals: *Dèye mòn, gen mòn.*

WORKS CITED AND FURTHER REFERENCES

M. Barcia (2020) "From Revolution to Recognition: Haiti's Place in the Post-1804 Atlantic World," *American Historical Review*, 125/3, 899–905.

H. McD. Beckles (2011) "Taking Liberties: Enslaved Women and Anti-Slavery Politics" in Engendering Caribbean History: CrossCultural Perspectives, a Reader (Ian Randle), 369–80.

R. Blackburn (2001) "The Force of Example" in David Geggus (ed.) *The Impact of the Haitian Revolution in the Atlantic World* (University of South Carolina Press), 15–22.

O.M. Blouet (2001) "Bryan Edwards and the Haitian Revolution" in David Geggus (ed.) *The Impact of the Haitian Revolution in the Atlantic World* (University of South Carolina Press), 44–57.

A. Carpentier (2017) *The Kingdom of This World* (Ferrar, Straus and Giroux).

J. Casimir (2020) *The Haitians: A Decolonial History* (University of North Carolina Press).

H. Christophe (1952) *Henri Christophe & Thomas Clarkson: A Correspondence* in E.L. Griggs and C.H. Prator (eds.) (University of California Press).

W.S. Cormack (2019) *Patriots, Royalists, and Terrorists in the West Indies: The French Revolution in Martinique and Guadeloupe, 1789–1802* (University of Toronto Press).

L. Dubois (2005) *Avengers of the New World: The Story of the Haitian Revolution* (Harvard University Press).

——— (2020) "Going to the Territory," *American Historical Review*, 125/3, 917–20.

——— (2011) "The Haitian Revolution" in Stephan Palmié and Francisco Scarano (eds.) *The Caribbean: A History of the Region and Its Peoples* (University of Chicago Press), 273–87.

——— (2001) "The Promise of Revolution: Saint-Domingue and the Struggle for Autonomy in Guadeloupe, 1797–1802" in David Geggus (ed.) *The Impact of the Haitian Revolution in the Atlantic World* (University of South Carolina Press), 112–34.

L. Dubois and J.D. Garrigus (2006) *Slave Revolution in the Caribbean: A Brief History with Documents* (Bedford/St. Martin's).

L. Dubois and R.L. Turitis (2019) *Freedom Roots: Histories from the Caribbean* (University of North Carolina Press).

P. Eser (2008) "Cultures of Resistance: Dialectical Images of the Haitian Revolution in Haitian Culture and Literature" in Wiebke Beushausen, et al (eds.) *Practices of Resistance in the Caribbean: Narratives, Aesthetics, and Politics* (Routledge), 104–21.

A. Ferrer (2014) *Freedom's Mirror: Cuba and Haiti in the Age of Revolutions* (Cambridge University Press).

——— (2012) "Haiti, Free Soil, and Antislavery in the Revolutionary Atlantic," *American Historical Review*, 117/1, 40–66.

C. Forsdick and C. Høgsbjerg (2017) *Toussaint Louverture: A Black Jacobin in the Age of Revolutions* (Pluto).

J. González (2019) *Maroon Nation: A History of Revolutionary Haiti* (Yale University Press).

J.R. González Mendoza (2001) "Puerto Rico's Creole Patriots and the Slave Trade after the Haitian Revolution" in David Geggus (ed.) *The Impact of the Haitian Revolution in the Atlantic World* (University of South Carolina Press), 58–71.

R. Gott (2011) *Britain's Empire: Resistance, Repression and Revolt* (Verso).

G. Heuman (2014) *The Caribbean: A Brief History*. 2nd edition (Bloomsbury).

C.L.R. James (1989) *The Black Jacobins: Toussaint Louverture and the San Domingo Revolution*. 2nd edition (Vintage).

J.C. Kim (2013) "The Caribs of St. Vincent and Indigenous Resistance during the Age of Revolutions," *Early American Studies* 11/1, 117–132.

M. Lasso (2001) "Haiti as an Image of Popular Republicanism in Caribbean Colombia: Cartagena Province (1811–1828)" in David Geggus (ed.) *The Impact of the Haitian Revolution in the Atlantic World* (University of South Carolina Press), 176–90.

N. Lightfoot (2020) "*The Common Wind*: A Masterful Study of the Masterless Revolutionary Atlantic," *American Historical Review*, 125/3, 926–30.

B. Moitt (2011) "Women, Work and Resistance in the French Caribbean during Slavery" in Engendering Caribbean History: Cross-Cultural Perspectives, a Reader (Ian Randle), 381–94.

V. Mongey (2020) *Rogue Revolutionaries: The Fight for Legitimacy in the Greater Caribbean* (University of Pennsylvania Press).

P. Morgan (2011) "Slave Cultures: Systems of Domination and Forms of Resistance" in Stephan Palmié and Francisco Scarano (eds.) *The Caribbean: A History of the Region and Its Peoples* (University of Chicago Press), 245–60.

D. Paton (2011) "The Abolition of Slavery in the Non-Hispanic Caribbean" in Stephan Palmié and Francisco Scarano (eds.) *The Caribbean: A History of the Region and Its Peoples* (University of Chicago Press), 289–301.

E. Pérez Morales (2018) *No Limits to Their Sway: Cartagena's Privateers and the Masterless Caribbean in the Age of Revolutions* (Vanderbilt University Press).

Revision of the Haitian Constitution of 1806 (1816) https://en.wikisource.org/wiki/Translation:Revision_of_the_Haitian_Constitution_of_1806

J.S. Scott (2019) *The Common Wind: Afro-American Currents in the Age of the Haitian Revolution* (Verso).

M. Sheller (2000) *Democracy after Slavery: Black Publics and Peasant Radicalism in Haiti and Jamaica* (University Press of Florida).

C. Soriano (2020) "Julius Scott's Masterless Caribbean and the Force of Its Common Wind," *American Historical Review*, 125/3, 931–35.

——— (2018) *Tides of Revolution: Information, Insurgencies, and the Crisis of Colonial Rule in Venezuela* (University of New Mexico Press).

The 1805 Constitution of Haiti. http://faculty.webster.edu/corbetre/haiti/history/earlyhaiti/1805const.htm

M.-R. Trouillot (2000) *Haiti: State against Nation* (Monthly Review).

W. Zips (1999) *Black Rebels: African Caribbean Freedom Fighters in Jamaica* (Marcus Wiener).

CHAPTER 3

Liberating Ourselves: Slave Resistance and Emancipation

In the early 1800s, with European demand for sugar growing, Caribbean supplies falling and thus prices rising, smart investors saw the possibility of reaping immense wealth by growing sugar in Cuba. Cuba quickly became a leading global sugar supplier, but this required more enslaved workers from Africa—and with them the ever-real threat from people who had known freedom, acquired military skills in Africa, and were willing to flee plantations once they arrived. As new Africans disembarked on the island, they engaged with enslaved peoples either born in Cuba or newly brought from Haiti. The necessity of labor to fuel profits had sewn in its capitalist logic the seeds of slave resistance.

The 1812 Aponte Conspiracy outlined in the previous chapter represents one of dozens of Caribbean slave revolts and conspiracies in the early 1800s: Tobago 1801, Trinidad 1805, Dominica 1813, Barbados 1816, British Honduras 1820, Puerto Rico 1821, Demerara 1823, Jamaica 1831, Cuba 1840s, and many more. In this chapter, we explore how enslaved people fought to end slavery on their own terms. Often transnational forces like religion, the Haitian Revolution, and rumors of monarchs abolishing slavery influenced them. Rumors attest to peoples' engagement with the world beyond their colony—a transnational communication system in action. Women joined this resistance in numerous ways: practicing abortion or infanticide, fighting as mothers to solidify their families as best they could in oppressive conditions, laboring to love whomever they desired, using legal systems to protect themselves and their children or even to gain freedom for their families, struggling to remain in or go to cities to avoid the harsh realities of rural fieldwork, maintaining traditional cultures, providing support and leadership in slave rebellions, and selling items in Sunday markets where they made money to better their lives and improve their chances to purchase freedom.

Historians have explained slavery's abolition in numerous ways. First, it was due to increasing moralistic, Christian rationales in Europe which served as the

K. Shaffer, *A Transnational History of the Modern Caribbean*, https://doi.org/10.1007/978-3-030-93012-7_3

backbone of Christian abolitionists who were mostly white or free peoples of African descent. Second, following an economic argument most famously described by historian Eric Williams (future prime minister of Trinidad and Tobago), slavery became an outdated form of labor by the mid-nineteenth century and needed to be replaced by wage-earning workers in a modernizing capitalist system. Today, while historians agree that both the Christian abolitionist and economic arguments played roles to end slavery, most historians argue that it was the continued and intensified resistance of enslaved peoples themselves that forced imperial governments to outlaw slavery. Laurent Dubois and Richard Lee Turits argue that we should think of rebellious enslaved peoples as "abolitionists" themselves and reframe slave resistance, slave revolts, and even the Haitian Revolution as radical abolitionist acts (Dubois and Turits 2019, p. 105). As Hilary Beckles famously noted, there was a protracted slave struggle for freedom from the 1630s to 1830s—a "200 Years War" (Beckles 1982, p. 1). Diana Paton concludes, "In practice, emancipation was everywhere a response to the actions of enslaved peoples—whether directly, as in Martinique and St. Croix, or less directly, as in the British Caribbean and Suriname. Without this continual pressure, punctuated by slave rebellions, slavery surely would have lasted much longer than it did" (Paton 2011, p. 300).

MOTHERHOOD AND RESISTANCE

Across the Caribbean, as many as half of enslaved women's infant children died in their first two weeks of life and another 25% died before age two. Numerous reasons explain this: poor healthcare for pregnant women, disease like neonatal tetany (twitching and convulsions due to low calcium) and tetanus, overwork of pregnant women, malnutrition, poor hygiene, and even infanticide. Though white doctors recognized that nutrition and disease caused infant deaths, other whites believed stereotypes that black women were depraved, malicious, and killed kids to hurt enslavers' wallets. Thus, here at least, the notion of the "murdering mother" was partly a white, pro-slavery fiction.

Before the 1800s, not all enslavers wanted women to have children. For instance, until the early 1800s, enslaved men and women worked side by side in Jamaica's sugarfields. If a woman became pregnant and could not work, enslavers lost that woman's labor power. So, if women had abortions or killed their children in these years, then, as Trevor Burnhard notes, they "were unrelated to what their owners thought of such actions" (Burnhard 2018, p. 41). In other words, from an enslaver's point of view, it would have been beneficial if his pregnant worker aborted the fetus and continued to work.

Sasha Turner argues, though, that after the abolition of the British slave trade in 1807, planters knew that it would be difficult to replace enslaved workers with new imports from Africa. They created "neonatalist" policies to encourage enslaved women to give birth. In response to these new policies, "enslaved mothers understood the importance of their children to planters, and took extreme measures, including infanticide, to prevent separation and premature weaning" (Turner 2017a, p. 253). Jessica Marie Johnson adds that it is "impossible to quantify…black women's determination not to bring their children to term or to raise children in a world of slaves" (Johnson 2020, p. 117). Turner argues that we cannot rule out that many mothers killed their children, suggesting women sought to control fertility in part "as an act of defiance against sexual exploitation and the capital claims slaveholders made on women's reproductive ability" (Turner 2017b, p. 233). In Jamaica, "infanticide was a political statement against slavery and motherhood, and along with the less morally judged practices of abortion and contraceptive use, enslaved women used it to control their bodies" (Turner 2017a, p. 254).

On the flip side, pregnant enslaved women sometimes benefited from neonatalist policies. Pregnant women left fieldwork, received better treatment, more food, and better conditions. In mid-nineteenth-century Cuba, young women noticed this. It was not uncommon for some enslaved women to fake a pregnancy "in order to obtain such tangible benefits as additional food and freedom from forced labor" (Franklin 2012, p. 36).

Motherhood also could be a source of joy rooted both in the human condition and in African cultures. As Deirdre Cooper Owens notes, women becoming mothers "could often serve as a powerful antidote to their suffering." In this spirit, a mother could assert her humanity as more than just a piece of capital. Motherhood "cemented notions of family and self even on a shaky foundation," and reflected what one might call "a liberation doctrine, one that asserted their [mothers'/women's] humanity, strength, resiliency, and intelligence"— even if the child was the offspring of white enslavers' rape or a forced sexual encounter with an enslaved man. A woman could choose to love, and in that choice she proclaimed her humanity—and defied her enslaver (Cooper Owens 2017, pp. 81–85). Besides one's humanity, African societies placed a premium importance on motherhood. As Burnhard concludes, an enslaved woman might have killed her fetus or infant "as a form of self-defiance" but such an act "flies in the face of the high value placed on motherhood within African societies as a mark of defining what becoming a woman meant" (Burnhard 2018, p. 41).

Obviously, then, enslaved women in the Caribbean held different ideas about motherhood. Undoubtedly, some women purposefully (and, yes, even politically) sought to deny enslavers control over their children by engaging in birth control, abortion, and infanticide as acts of resistance, but women also embraced motherhood. Such a choice might result ultimately in their children dying from the hideous conditions on plantations; however, those who lived might become the basis for a woman to start or expand a family. As a group of historians concludes, "motherhood was a particular site of conflict in slave societies because it compounded exploitation of women's labour with oppression through the most intimate aspects of their lives, while also providing space for the building of relationships that could enable survival" (Cowling et al. 2017, p. 224).

Slavery lasted deep into the nineteenth century in the Spanish colonies of Puerto Rico and Cuba. During that time, enslaved mothers learned how to exploit Spanish law to their benefit. Cuba offers two illuminating examples. First, in 1817, as slavery expanded on the island, the Spanish king freed over 200 enslaved peoples originally sold in 1795. The free women then launched a search to find children they had birthed on Cuban plantations. Throughout the Caribbean, a child's status reflected their mother's status, and in Spain's colonies, Spanish law granted free parents custody of their progeny. These newly freed mothers sought to free their enslaved children. Enslavers tried to prevent the children's emancipation since most were in their prime working years by 1817 and because Madrid refused to compensate enslavers. The mothers persisted, demanding the law be applied as written. Eventually, most children reunited with their mothers. This act of resistance against slavery—by invoking Spanish law—"was one significant way in which [these women] might practice motherhood" (Perera Díaz and de los Ángeles Meriño Fuentes 2018, p. 902).

Second, the 1842 *Código Negro* (Black Code) banned mother-child separation before age 3. The 1870 Moret Law expanded this ban to age 14. Throughout these years, mothers sued when enslavers took their young children. As Spain phased out slavery in the 1870s and 1880s, enslaved mothers in Cuba sued to expedite their freedom and that of their children. Key to this was the *coartación* in which enslaved people made a down payment to purchase their freedom. For enslaved peoples in cities, this down payment gave them three days to find a new owner to prevent being sold and transferred to rural plantations. While few purchased their freedom, the coartación gave enslaved people greater control over who bought them and whether they would be sent to the countryside or stay in the city. Staying in cities was important, especially for enslaved mothers, because it provided a more secure environment for having their legal cases heard to prevent mother-child separation when a child might be sold to a plantation. Take the case of the enslaved young man Francisco, who traveled to Havana from the countryside to make a down payment for his coartación. Soon, Francisco's mother arrived and deposited more money and, more importantly, kept her son in Havana. As Camillia Cowling concludes, "Keeping him in Havana had a practical purpose, since it might ensure a lower manumission price" because it was away from the rural enslaver's ability to influence "an artificially higher price being set" (Cowling 2018, p. 945). Motherhood and resistance went hand in hand.

Enslaved mothers also played key roles in cultural survival—and thus resistance. Enslavers and colonial authorities portrayed European culture as superior to anything African or Afro-Caribbean. They taught enough of the Bible and Christianity to allegedly make enslaved peoples see how much better the white world was. Performing European chamber and baroque music demonstrated the sounds of a supposedly higher civilization. However, enslaved peoples had other ideas. Often, they retained their languages or created new creole hybrids. They might practice Christianity but often maintained allegiance to

African deities and belief systems. They might hear chamber music echoing from plantation houses but still dance and sing to traditional drumming. They also told stories that served as cautionary tales on how to navigate the worlds of race and slavery. Some stories rooted in African oral traditions told tales of ancestors, ancient morality, and resistance like Anancy stories about a small spider who turns the tables on powerful enemies. Enslaved mothers and grand-mothers taught children these lessons and in the process gave the next genera-tion tools to interact with and resist European culture on their own terms.

TRANSNATIONAL RELIGION AND RESISTANCE

African and European religions contributed to Caribbean slave resistance. Rebel leaders in Saint-Domingue initiated the 1791 slave revolt with a Vodou ceremony in Bois Caïman, though some speculate "Boukman" might have been a French phonetic spelling of the English "Bookman," that is, man of the book, suggesting that he and other rebel leaders had Muslim origins (Diouf 1998, pp. 152–153). Both Vodou in the French islands and Santería in the Spanish islands were African-based religions with a Catholic guise over them. That is, while whites believed enslaved men and women prayed to Catholic saints, worshippers saw this differently. They associated Santería orishas or Vodou loas with these saints. For instance, when enslaved peoples in Cuba appeared to be worshipping the Catholic Saint Barbara, they were worshipping Shangó, an orisha embodying force, power, and justice. When enslaved peoples in Saint-Domingue appeared to worship the Catholic St. James, they were honoring Ogoun, the Vodou warrior loa. Enslaved peoples, thus, continued to worship spiritual figures linked to ancestral African homelands. These religions helped maintain a sense of cultural identity—cultural survival as cultural resis-tance. Geoffroy de Laforcade and Devyn Springer lay it out beautifully: "Instead of finding the Baobab they found the Ceiba, still massive in grandeur but a more vertical, thicker limbed tree. They made do. They maintained. They translated the Earth they'd grown acquainted with into a world in which they had to redefine their spiritualities, unmoored but marooned, not dead but now 'diasporic'" (de Laforcade and Springer 2019, p. 340).

In the British West Indies, something else was at work behind Christian scenes. Obeah beliefs originated from Ashanti-Akan peoples of West Africa. Believers used Obeah for protection, revenge, punishment, and spellcasting. In eighteenth-century Jamaica, Myal emerged as a form of spirit worship. Myal might have originated in Central Africa, but some believe it was based on secret societies rooted in West Africa. If one's spirit could be caught by an Obeah Man or Obeah Woman, then a Myal Man could free and restore the spirit.

White British religious authorities from different Christian sects viewed slav-ery differently. The Anglican Church—the official church of England and thus of the colonies' elite—saw no contradiction between Christianity and slavery. There was little Christian outreach to or conversion of enslaved workers until the late 1700s when nonconformist Protestant sects like Congregationalists,

Moravians, Methodists, and Baptists sent missionaries. Missionaries worked in slave communities, converting ever-larger numbers of people to Christianity while creating missionary towns that functioned as abolitionist spaces beyond the plantations. Nonconformist missionaries opposed slavery, arguing that it was wrong to enslave one's "brother in Christ." As a result, numerous enslaved peoples became leaders in nonconformist churches—and sometimes leaders of revolts. These transnational religious dimensions shaped two large-scale uprisings in Demerara and Jamaica.

In 1815, the Netherlands ceded the Demerara coast of South America to Great Britain. Missionaries seeking to "civilize" enslaved peoples arrived but soon "discovered 'humanity' in the slaves and 'savagery' in the people of their 'own kind'" (da Costa 1994, p. xvii). White Congregationalist missionaries and enslaved deacons preached the symbolism of Jesus as liberator, the poor versus the rich, the powerless versus the powerful, and universal brotherhood. The British had abolished the slave trade in 1807, but as a result, prices for enslaved peoples rose just when prices for sugar began declining as global sugar supplies grew due to Cuban production. The economic downturn led to an intensification of forced labor and less time for enslaved workers to spend on their provision grounds. In response, people grew more rebellious. When enslavers forced pregnant women to work, the latter complained to the courts, believing they had rights that owners infringed upon. Missionaries supported these claims, angering authorities who feared alliances between enslaved peoples and missionaries. In 1822 and 1823, tensions rose following a wave of arson in Georgetown and increased marronage. Plantation rumors spread that London had abolished slavery, but colonial authorities refused to free people. In response, enslaved people organized along the coast and reached out to maroons. On each plantation, enslaved catechism teachers used Bible study meetings to organize and spread the date of an uprising. On 17 August 1823, 12,000 men and women on 60 plantations revolted. Their goals: force the government to implement abolition and grant workers more free time. Tipped off by an informant, authorities quickly suppressed the rebellion, killing more than 200 people and convicting missionaries for their supposed roles in the plot. When rebels later discovered the source of their betrayal, they poisoned to death the traitor's wife.

A similar religiously inspired slave uprising emerged in Jamaica in 1831. Samuel Sharpe was born into slavery in 1805, received a Baptist-led education in missionary towns, and became a Baptist deacon. He taught enslaved peoples they had rights and should be free to work for wages. He called for a peaceful strike just after Christmas as the cane harvest season began. However, planters brutally repressed the strike. Enslaved peoples responded by rebelling in what is known by many names: the Christmas Rebellion, the Baptist War, and the Sam Sharpe Rebellion. At least 60,000 people (around one-fifth of the island's enslaved population) torched estates. In early January 1832, colonial militiamen and maroons suppressed the revolt, killing 300 rebels (Fig. 3.1).

Fig. 3.1 Mural of Sam Sharpe and Nanny of the Maroons (Creative Commons/ David Drissel)

In interviews with rebels, colonial authorities discovered transnational influences leading to the rebellion. First, participants recounted how they heard the king had abolished slavery but (as in Demerara earlier) whites refused to implement the decree. From their point of view, they rebelled to assert their legal rights as freed peoples who were being illegally kept in bondage. As one rebel put it: "Samuel Sharpe told the negroes that their freedom was given them since last March, that he (Sharpe) had read it so in the newspapers; but that unless they fought for it they would not get it" (quoted in *The Caribbean Reader* 2013, p. 148). Second, most of the rebellion's leaders—like Sharpe— were Baptist deacons preaching the Gospel's messages of equality and brotherhood to contrast how whites continued to abuse enslaved workers. Third, Obeahmen and Myalmen joined in acts of revenge. As historian Jean Besson suggests, some enslaved persons interpreted Baptism through the lens of their Obeah and Myal spiritual beliefs. Enslaved Jamaicans hid these practices behind Baptism. Thus, when people rebelled, they used their Obeah-Myal beliefs— channeled through Baptism—"to resist the masters' domination by protecting themselves from the owners' 'sorcery' of slavery" (Besson 2011, p. 321). In short, enslavers were not just anti-Christian but also sorcerers whose powers had to be attacked by both Baptism and Obeah-Mayalism. In the end, authorities executed Sam Sharpe in May 1832, but London knew slavery's days were numbered. On 28 August 1833, in response to new economic arguments that slavery was no longer a viable form of labor, religious arguments that slavery was immoral and the ever-present slave rebellions that had to be violently crushed, London passed the Slavery Abolition Act that formally abolished slavery in the British Caribbean the following August.

CARIBBEAN RESISTANCE AND ITS TRANSNATIONAL IMPACT ON THE UNITED STATES

Resistance and abolitionist initiatives in the British West Indies also impacted the United States. Edward Rugemer argues that "Britain's abolition of slavery should be understood as a seminal event in the history of the United States, a critical moment in the drift toward the Civil War thirty years later" (Rugemer 2008, p. 6). The US press covered British debates about abolition and the multiple acts of Caribbean armed slave resistance. Accounts generally blamed abolitionists for rebellions. Similarly, the US press blamed abolitionists when Denmark Vesey and Nat Turner led rebellions in the United States in 1822 and 1831, respectively. Meanwhile, US enslavers and abolitionists debated slave rebellion and abolition in terms of how they viewed Caribbean slavery. Enslavers believed that abolitionist agitation led to rebellion, while abolitionists thought that abolition was the only way to prevent slave uprisings. Following British emancipation, US abolitionists painted a portrait of Caribbean tranquility where formerly enslaved peoples worked their own land, whites had security, violence had been eliminated, Christianity spread, and literacy rose. US enslavers interpreted British emancipation differently. They thought Caribbean abolitionists were plotting to topple the US southern plantocracy from Jamaican bases of operation.

TRANSNATIONALISM, RESISTANCE, AND ABOLITION IN THE FRENCH WEST INDIES

Napoleon reimposed slavery in 1802, touching off decades of slave rebellions and conspiracies across the French Caribbean. Repression began easing by the 1830s partly due to efforts of Cyrille Bissette—a free man of African descent from Martinique. In 1824, he published a pamphlet on conditions of free black and mixed-race peoples on the island. Authorities quickly sent him and hundreds of other free people of African descent into exile. In France, Bissette spearheaded a new abolitionist movement. Through his efforts, French public opinion turned against slavery. In 1830, the Liberal government issued reforms increasing the rights of free peoples of African descent and forbade planters from whipping enslaved women. Meanwhile, between 1834 and 1838, maritime marronage spiked as enslaved peoples in the French Caribbean increasingly fled by sea. Since the 1810s, people had sought freedom and citizenship in Haiti as that government welcomed all enslaved and coerced people who made it to Haitian shores. Following abolition in 1834, the British Caribbean became a new potential slavery-free refuge.

Enslaved Martinicans also resorted to violence. On 20 May 1848, they rebelled after authorities jailed a fellow worker. As violence quickly engulfed the island, Martinique's governor discovered he had few options. He hastily abolished slavery two days into the revolt to stop the uprising. A few days later, Guadeloupean authorities abolished slavery. Unbeknownst to colonial officials, a decree from Paris to abolish slavery throughout the French Empire was at that very moment in transit to the islands.

These events were felt beyond the French colonies. Less than 200 miles from Guadeloupe lay the Danish island of St. Croix. Denmark had been the first European country to abolish the slave trade in 1803—four years before the British—but slavery continued. The revolts engulfing Martinique and Guadeloupe in mid-1848 spread north, reaching St. Croix by early July when John Gottlieb led followers to burn plantations and lay siege to the town of Frederiksted. When Governor-General Peter von Scholten arrived on the scene, he had no option. Though lacking legal authority to do so, von Scholten abolished slavery. As the 1848 violence spread to St. Croix, Spanish officials in next-door Puerto Rico looked on with alarm. Enslaved peoples in Vega Baja heard about the St. Croix uprising and rebelled too. Puerto Rican governor Prim not only suppressed his own rebellion but also sent 500 infantrymen to help restore peace in St. Croix. Then, Prim issued a decree granting whites the right to kill any person of African descent who challenged whites. The decree's effectiveness is questionable. After 1848, enslaved Puerto Ricans continued rebelling, but rather than revolt to end slavery, they generally rose to murder overseers.

RESISTANCE IN THE SPANISH CARIBBEAN, 1790s–1840s

Between 1795 and 1848, at least 22 antislavery conspiracies rocked Puerto Rico. In the early 1820s alone, enslaved people launched five well-organized revolts, including one in 1821 by Marcos Xiorro, who led 1500 people in rebellion. Spanish officials believed Haiti directed many of the conspiracies and revolts. For instance, in 1822, the colonial government grew concerned following Haitian president Boyer's occupation of Spanish Santo Domingo and his order to abolish slavery there. Officials believed the growing number of conspiracies in Puerto Rico were precursors of Boyer's larger plans to attack Puerto Rico and free its enslaved population. Though enslaved peoples revolted mostly due to poor conditions and treatment, they also heard whites talking about Boyer, his liberation of Santo Domingo, and his freeing of people. They hoped someone abroad would come to their aid.

Meanwhile, the rapid import of enslaved Africans transformed rural Cuba. As numbers grew, so too did slave resistance. Enslaved peoples in rural Cuba rebelled regularly beginning in the 1790s, with at least 27 revolts between the 1820s and 1840s alone. Of course, this does not count their daily acts of passive resistance. African-born enslaved men and women tended to use violent resistance, while those born in Cuba who knew Spanish often used courts and institutions to appeal their grievances—though both groups utilized both strategies. The murder of enslaved workers often sparked armed revolt and targeted killings of whites. For instance, in 1827, whites killed several enslaved people, prompting their friends to rebel. Meanwhile, when Cuban plantation managers or overseers used whippings, insults, and more against workers, enslaved peoples responded with poisons and machete attacks in targeted killings of whites. "Homicides were often acts of retaliation," writes Manuel Barcia (Barcia 2008, p. 33). Besides murdering whites, revolting, and using the legal system, sometimes enslaved Cubans perpetrated mass suicide as resistance like a group of Lucumí did in 1827 in response to excessively harsh treatments.

Between the 1820s and 1840s, enslaved peoples carved out spaces of freedom on plantations, between plantations, and between plantations and towns. Many traveled due to their jobs. Others paid Sunday visits to neighboring estates or villages. Through this mobility, they developed networks while creating, as Aisha Finch puts it, "small spaces of freedom within their enslavement" (Finch 2005, p. 65). Through mobility and autonomous spaces, enslaved peoples interacted with maroons, engaged in petit marronage, and coordinated between these free spaces.

Armed violence occurred concurrently with the growth of marronage. Throughout eastern Cuba—that part of the island closest to Haiti—people increasingly formed maroon towns (*palenques* in Spanish). In June 1820, fearing possible maroon-Haitian contacts, the king ordered Cuban militias to attack palenques. By the 1840s, armed bans of runaways in the west and palenques in the east continued to alarm colonial authorities. However, constant repression forced maroons into ever-more isolated areas of the island. Palenque residents generally did not fight back but instead fled to survive another day. Officials hoped that by pushing the palenques further from the plantations, maroons would become more isolated and thus less attractive to enslaved peoples. They were mistaken.

In Madrid, San Juan, and Havana, both Cuban nationalists and abolitionists challenged Spain's colonial economic policy. In 1830s Cuba, José Antonio Saco demanded Spain reform its economic policy for the colony and prohibit importing new enslaved workers. Saco's argument was not about the inherent humanity of people of African descent or that they were "brothers in Christ" or that even slavery should be abolished. Rather, Saco argued that if Madrid continued to increase the slave population on the island, then that would lead to more slave rebellions, which in turn would require Spain to expand its military presence. For nationalists like Saco, increased Spanish military presence would undermine Cuban desires for autonomy or independence. Meanwhile, one of Britain's leading abolitionists, David Turnbull, spent the last months of 1838 and early 1839 touring Cuba. In 1840, he published a book condemning slavery and the slave trade. That same year, as though to insult Spain, London appointed Turnbull as British consul to Cuba. Convinced that Turnbull spread abolitionist sentiment on the island, Cuban authorities expelled him in 1842.

Meanwhile in the early 1840s, enslaved peoples heard rumors that Madrid had abolished slavery. They also heard stories about the actual end of slavery in the British Caribbean. In November 1843, fed by rumors and stories of abolition, a surge in African arrivals who had warfare experience in Africa and creation of their own alternative geographies, enslaved workers in Cuba rebelled in the largest uprising to that point known as *La Escalera*—"the ladder" because leaders were punished by being tied to a ladder and brutalized. Enslaved women like Fermina and Carlota Lucumí organized some of the revolts. Carlota—a Yoruba-born woman from West Africa—today is honored by a statue in western Cuba, and her name emblazoned Cuba's Cold War-era military intervention in Angola: Operation Carlota. Interestingly, colonial officials did not blame enslaved peoples for the violence. Rather, they blamed Turnbull, claiming he incited abolitionism in Cuba and thus inspired people to revolt. While abolitionist sentiment existed in Cuba, it was enslaved workers and maroons organizing at local levels who launched uprisings across the island. In 1844, colonial officials suppressed the revolts, convicted Turnbull *in absentia* of plotting the uprising, punished rebel leaders, jailed or tortured or executed thousands of free and enslaved people of African descent, and ended a two-decade stretch of armed slave resistance that did not surge again for another 20 years—a topic explored in coming chapters.

On the Caribbean mainland, things were different. In the last decades of Spanish rule in New Granada, enslaved peoples resorted less to violence and more to lawsuits against abusive masters, utilizing the Spanish government's Black Code that declared certain rights and duties that both enslaved peoples and enslavers had to respect. Aline Helg refers to it a "slave bill of rights" (Helg 2004, p. 114). As noted in the previous chapter, important relations developed between the short-lived Republic of Cartagena and Haiti. However, the Haitian Revolution had little impact on slavery in the post-Cartagena country of Gran Colombia. Only a few plantations on the Caribbean coast had many enslaved workers. In addition, palenques serving as refuges might have diffused potential slave revolts. Plus, free peoples of African descent lived thinly dispersed across the region, making it difficult for them to lead or shape any potential rebellion. Enslaved peoples in cities likewise did not revolt. When Gran Colombia gained independence in 1821, authorities did not free enslaved peoples, prompting some to fear Haiti would step in to incite rebellion on the coasts. The fear was rich enough that in 1826 as he planned the Congress of Panama (the first Pan American meeting, which partly sought to free Cuba and Puerto Rico from Spanish rule), Gran Colombia's first president, Simón Bolívar, refused to invite his old protector—Haiti—to the congress.

Rebellious Market Women of the Caribbean

Sunday was market day across the Caribbean when people did not work for enslavers; they worked for themselves. Or more accurately, they sold goods often produced in their households or foodstuffs grown on provision grounds.

Women dominated Caribbean markets, placing them centrally in that middle space between plantations and free society. Sometimes women took their market earnings and ran off, becoming maroons with money. More often, women pocketed earnings and returned week after week, using earnings to buy items to make life a bit better or gradually saving to purchase their freedom or that of a loved one. As Natasha Lightfoot concludes, enslaved women wandered between plantations and markets, gaining the prospect for freedom with each new sale of an item. Due to this mobility and autonomy to earn money, slave women "tast[ed] freedom before formal abolition" (Lightfoot 2015, p. 48).

In Antigua, these dynamics shaped the 1831 Sunday Market Rebellion. Markets were about more than just material benefits. On market day, people from different plantations met, talked, shared, and generated a sense of community beyond plantations and thus beyond their roles as workers. So, when colonial officials sought to restrict or end market days, enslaved women saw this as an attack on their futures, their communities, and even their rights because they had come to see Sunday market days as an entitlement. Enslaved peoples believed that British laws protected them as well as their enslavers, an idea encapsulated by the phrase "so them make law for Negro, so them make law for Master" (quoted in Lightfoot 2015, p. 66).

However, in May 1831, Antiguan officials banned Sunday markets, calling them an affront to the Christian sabbath. Enslaved women publicly objected. Their protests quickly spread as rebels torched one-seventh of the island's plantations over four nights. Ultimately, rebel actions forced government concessions. Officials kept market day but moved it to Saturday. As Lightfoot reminds us, these market day slave protests were not about ending slavery or capitalism. They were efforts by enslaved peoples to retain the community and material benefits of the markets while pursuing "larger-term expectations as imperial subjects"—essentially demanding the government protect enslaved peoples' rights (Lightfoot 2015, p. 81). While the protests might not have had the goal of abolition, they were one more example of enslaved peoples' resistance that prompted London to end chattel slavery.

CONCLUSION

The Haitian Revolution symbolized that enslaved people could gain their own freedom. They did not need to wait for Madrid, Paris, Copenhagen, or London to issue decrees on paper. They did not need to hear arguments that slave labor was antiquated and should be replaced by a wage labor system. They did not need Christian missionaries explaining why slavery was an affront to the teachings of Jesus. Sure, they likely appreciated these, but in the post-Haiti world, people continued a long practice of resisting slavery on their own terms.

Sometimes resisters aimed to destroy colonial slave systems. Other times, they had less grandiose goals: gaining greater autonomy, earning money, engaging fellow enslaved men and women in community building, and more. People replicated these local acts of everyday resistance across the Caribbean. Frequently, acts of resistance were grounded in transnational inspiration—like African and Christian influences, rumors, and the regional influence of Haiti. Acts of resistance inspired others in the region to rebel like the 1848 slave revolts in Martinique and Guadeloupe with their impacts on St. Croix and Puerto Rico. Everywhere, enslaved peoples contested slavery.

In 1822, President Boyer of Haiti invaded Spanish Santo Domingo and liberated people from slavery while European empires outlawed slavery at different times: 1834 in the British Caribbean, 1848 in the French Caribbean, 1863 in the Dutch empire, 1873 in Spanish Puerto Rico, and 1886 in Spanish Cuba. Independent countries on the Caribbean mainland abolished slavery between 1821, when Mexico freed Mexican-born enslaved peoples, and 1851, in New Granada. In the next chapter, we explore the ramifications of emancipation in the Caribbean, what replaced it, and how workers resisted new forms of coercion.

WORKS CITED AND FURTHER REFERENCES

G.A. Baralt (2007) *Slave Revolts in Puerto Rico* (Markus Wiener).

M. Barcia (2008) *Seeds of Insurrection: Domination and Slave Resistance on Western Cuban Plantations, 1808–1848* (Louisiana State University Press).

H. McD. Beckles (2011) "Taking Liberties: Enslaved Women and Anti-Slavery Politics" in Verene A. Shepherd (ed.) *Engendering Caribbean History: Cross-Cultural Perspectives* (Ian Randle), 369–80.

——— (1982) "The 200 Years War: Slave Resistance in the British West Indies: An Overview of the Historiography," *Jamaica Historical Review*, 13, 1–12.

J. Besson (2011) "Missionaries, Planters, and Slaves in the Age of Abolition" in Stephan Palmié and Francisco Scarano (eds.) *The Caribbean: A History of the Region and Its Peoples* (University of Chicago Press), 317–29.

——— (1998) "Religion as Resistance in Jamaican Peasant Life: The Baptist Church, Revival Worldview and Rastafari Movement" in Barry Chevannes (ed.) *Rastafari and Other African-Caribbean Worldviews* (Rutgers University Press), 43–76.

T. Burnhard (2018) "Toiling in the Fields: Valuing Female Slaves in Jamaica, 1674–1785" in D. R. Berry and L.M. Harris (eds.) *Sexuality and Slavery: Reclaiming Intimate Histories in the Americas* (University of Georgia Press).

J. Casimir (2020) *The Haitians: A Decolonial History* (University of North Carolina Press).

B. Chevannes (1998) "Introducing the Native Religions of Jamaica" in Barry Chevannes (ed.) *Rastafari and Other African Caribbean Worldviews* (Rutgers University Press), 1–19.

M. Childs (2006) *The 1812 Aponte Rebellion in Cuba and the Struggle against Atlantic Slavery* (University of North Carolina Press).

E.V. da Costa (1994) *Crowns of Glory, Tears of Blood: The Demerara Slave Rebellion of 1823* (Oxford University Press).

C. Cowling (2013) *Conceiving Freedom: Women of Color, Gender, and the Abolition of Slavery in Havana and Rio de Janeiro*. (University of North Carolina Press).

——— (2018) "Gendered Geographies: Motherhood, Slavery, Law, and Space in Mid-Nineteenth-Century Cuba," *Women's History Review* 27/6, 939–53.

C. Cowling, M.H.P. Toledo Machado, D. Paton, and E. West (2017) "Mothering Slaves: Comparative Perspectives on Motherhood, Childlessness, and the Care of Children in Atlantic Slave Societies," *Slavery & Abolition* 38/2, 223–31.

G. de Laforcade and D. Springer (2019) "The *Red Barrial Afrodescendiente*: A Cuban Experiment in Black Community Empowerment," *Souls*, 21/4, 339–46.

S.A. Diouf (1998) *Servants of Allah: African Muslims Enslaved in the Americas* (New York University Press).

L. Dubois and R.L. Turits (2019) *Freedom Roots: Histories from the Caribbean* (University of North Carolina Press).

A.K. Finch (2005) *Rethinking Slave Rebellion in Cuba: La Escalera and the Insurgencies of 1841–44* (University of North Carolina Press).

S.L. Franklin (2012) *Women and Slavery in Nineteenth-Century Cuba* (University of Rochester Press).

R. Gott (2011) *Britain's Empire: Resistance, Repression and Revolt* (Verso).

A. Helg (2004) *Liberty and Equality in Caribbean Colombia, 1775–1830* (University of North Carolina Press).

G. Heuman (1994) *The Killing Time: The Morant Bay Rebellion in Jamaica* (The University of Tennessee Press).

J.M. Johnson (2020) *Wicked Flesh: Black Women, Intimacy, and Freedom in the Atlantic World* (University of Pennsylvania Press).

G. La Rosa Corzo (2003) *Runaway Slave Settlements in Cuba: Resistance and Repression* (University of North Carolina Press).

N. Lightfoot (2015) *Troubling Freedom: Antigua and the Aftermath of British Emancipation* (Duke University Press).

B. Moitt (2011) "Women, Work and Resistance in the French Caribbean during Slavery, 1700–1848" in Verene A. Shepherd (ed.) *Engendering Caribbean History: Cross-Cultural Perspectives* (Ian Randle), 381–94.

D.C. Owens (2017) *Medical Bondage: Race, Gender, and the Origins of American Gynecology* (University of Georgia Press).

D. Paton (2011) "The Abolition of Slavery in the Non-Hispanic Caribbean" in Stephan Palmié and Francisco Scarano (eds.) *The Caribbean: A History of the Region and Its Peoples* (University of Chicago Press), 289–301.

——— (2017) "Maternal Struggles and the Politics of Childlessness under Pronatalist Caribbean Slavery," *Slavery & Abolition* 38/2, 251–68.

A. Perera Díaz and M. de los Ángeles Meriño Fuentes (2018) "The African Women of the *Dos Hermanos* Slave Ship in Cuba: Slaves First, Mothers Second," *Women's History Review* 27/6, 892–909.

E. Rugemer (2008) *The Problem of Emancipation: The Caribbean Roots of the American Civil War* (Louisiana State University Press).

C. Schmidt-Nowara (1999) *Empire and Anti-slavery: Spain, Cuba, and Puerto Rico, 1833–1874* (University of Pittsburgh Press).

R. Scott (2008) *Degrees of Freedom: Louisiana and Cuba after Slavery* (Belknap).

———— (2000) *Slave Emancipation in Cuba: The Transition to Free Labor, 1860–1899* (University of Pittsburgh Press).

V.A. Shepherd (1999) *Women in Caribbean History: The British Colonised Territories* (Markus Wiener).

The Caribbean History Reader (2013) Nicola Foote (ed.) (Routledge).

S. Turner (2017a) *Contested Bodies: Pregnancy, Childrearing, and Slavery in Jamaica* (University of Pennsylvania Press).

———— (2017b) "The Nameless and the Forgotten: Maternal Grief, Sacred Protection, and the Archive of Slavery," *Slavery and Abolition* 38/2 (2017), 232–50.

K.K. Weaver (2004) "'She Crushed the Child's Fragile Skull': Disease, Infanticide, and Enslaved Women in Eighteenth-Century Saint-Domingue," *French Colonial History* 5/1, 93–109.

E. Williams (1994) *Capitalism and Slavery* (University of North Carolina Press).

CHAPTER 4

Liberating Ourselves: Freedom Fighting after Slavery

Emancipation did not bring equality—or necessarily freedom. Whites and many people of mixed race used voting restrictions, biases in courtrooms, coerced labor systems, and symbolic acts like refusing to use titles when addressing peoples of African descent to deny equality and freedom to former enslaved peoples. Meanwhile, some British Caribbean people of African descent freed before emancipation in 1834 tried to increase their power by appealing to newly liberated peoples for racial support. For instance, in Jamaica, previously freed people formed a political party that gained seats in Jamaica's House of Assembly. However, these politicians soon abandoned racial alliances with newly freed men because they found their economic and class interests with white and mixed-race Jamaicans more important than their racial interests. In Dominica in 1838, men of African descent gained control of the legislative assembly. However, after white complaints, London reorganized the legislature, allowing for white control again. Political power was hard to come by for newly freed Afro-Caribbean peoples.

Economically, planters knew—and Haiti had borne this out—that freed people would flee plantation labor to be masterless and live on their own. As a result, colonial legislatures enacted new laws restricting people's movements. Pass laws prevented wage laborers from leaving plantations to seek better wages until workers proved they had fulfilled their contract terms and paid off all debts incurred from renting shacks, buying food, purchasing tools, and the myriad of ways owners devised to ensure workers always owed more than they earned. In Martinique, if someone were caught on the road without an approved passbook, they could be charged with loitering, taken to jail, and pressed into a work gang to provide free labor for municipalities or planters like digging irrigation ditches. A head tax required each Martinican resident to pay a tax for the simple fact that they were a living, breathing human being. The tax was higher in towns to discourage workers from leaving plantations. To

© The Author(s), under exclusive license to Springer Nature Switzerland AG 2022
K. Shaffer, *A Transnational History of the Modern Caribbean*,
https://doi.org/10.1007/978-3-030-93012-7_4

dissuade people from growing their own crops, the government levied a tax on crops other than sugar. Enforcing these made life particularly difficult for newly freed peoples and their freeborn descendants, prompting many Martinicans by the 1880s to migrate to the Colombian province of Panama to work on the French canal project. While new laws might have prevented overseers from whipping workers, no law required owners to pay a living wage. In the movie "La Rue Cases-Nègres" (Sugar Cane Alley) set in 1930s Martinique—80-plus years after emancipation—the old man Medouze tells his young protégé Jose how little changed after official abolition. To paraphrase Medouze, the "master" simply became the "boss."

In the British Caribbean, planters fared better than former enslavers in other imperial colonies. London set aside £20 million—roughly £2.4 billion/$3.125 billion in 2020 terms—to compensate enslavers for their "lost property." London also created a system of apprenticeship (except in Antigua) from 1834 to 1838 whereby newly freed people had to work on plantations for barely subsistence wages. Later in Puerto Rico (1873–1876) and Cuba (1880–1886), the Spanish government created an apprenticeship system known as the *patronato*—what Rebecca Scott calls "an intermediate relationship between master and former slave that would provide the master with indemnification in the form of labor and provide the slave with 'tutelage'" (Scott 2008, p. 123).

Meanwhile, colonial governments shipped a new wave of coerced workers into the Caribbean. The British imported indentured workers mainly from colonial India. The Dutch initially brought workers from India too but switched to importing workers from their Southeast Asian possessions like Java. In Cuba, Spaniards imported Chinese indentured workers.

In this chapter, we explore how people resisted these post-slavery coercive systems. Some rebelled to protest conditions or fears of reenslavement. Sometimes workers organized armed revolts. As during slavery, everyday forms of resistance often complemented armed mobilizations. Workers proclaimed rights as colonial subjects and challenged employers in courts. Workers of African and Asian descent sometimes joined forces; more often, they did not. Women challenged male privilege within their own communities, fled plantation work, led protests and anti-tax revolts, and encouraged men to take up arms. The working masses also embraced cultural resistance by practicing traditional religions (Afro-Caribbean, Hinduism, Islam), resisting Europeanization of their children in colonial schools, holding traditional festivals, and challenging authorities when they tried banning such celebrations.

HAITI AND RESISTANCE DURING THE BOYER YEARS

Postindependence Haitian governments were experiments in political centralization and largely undemocratic. The masses had little political say, and the state largely tried to coerce the nation to do what central governments wanted. People resisted by fleeing to remote areas, evading taxes, and living their lives with as much decentralized local autonomy as possible. As Johnhenry González notes, the "masses pursued land and liberty by extra legal means" because the legal system represented structural violence against their interests (González 2019, p. 43). For instance, while peasants signed labor contracts, they felt no obligation to fulfill those contracts, walking away from them whenever they desired. Other times, coffee workers formed collective organizations to pursue better conditions and pay. Sometimes rural collective organizations rose in armed uprising.

In the early 1840s, a series of political struggles rocked Haiti. Haitian liberals campaigned for more open government, winning elections in 1842. However, Boyer set the military upon them, and democracy was denied again. Liberals then sought alliances with peasants, who pursued land rights they believed were due them as inheritance from their grandparents' struggles. A liberal revolt toppled Boyer in 1843, but the government faced new tensions. Spanish speakers in the east broke away in 1844. Small landowners in the south revolted, demanding racial equality and attacking the lingering dominance of lighter skin privilege. Conflicts also emerged between those seeking constitutional democracy and those seeking strong state-led militarism.

Into this new era emerged "the Army of Sufferers," led by Jean-Jacques Acaau, a former rural policeman who led southern peasants known as The Piquets (so named because of the sharp wooden pikes with which they armed themselves). The Piquets sought land redistribution, limits on mulatto power, elimination of all class and color distinctions, and full recognition of their rights as Haitian citizens. Some claimed that this was a "black" armed protest against a "mulatto" elite. Acaau denied this, proclaiming the Piquets merely sought "respect for the Constitution, Rights, Equality, Liberty" and that the rebellion "is not, nor can it be a question, in any circumstance, of a war of colour" (quoted in Sheller 2000, p. 135).

The Piquets were a rural, class-based movement fighting those—regardless of color—who used martial law to abuse and deny the masses' democratic rights and freedoms. The Piquets "realized that only the exercise of political authority could enable the rural population to protect its rights" for land and against taxes from centralized government abuse (Casimir 2020, p. 64). Ultimately, the Haitian state overpowered and defeated the Piquets. Still, French radicals declared them to be black communists, while others portrayed them as the "farthest 'left wing' of democratic republicanism" in the Francophone world—radical democrats not because they were beholden to the ideas of liberal democracy (though to be sure many Piquet leaders like Acaau were) but because they pursued the interests of the masses and the nation (Sheller 2000, p. 139). In Haiti, then, the masses created counterinstitutions to democratically resist the reach of the nondemocratic state. Sometimes—like the Piquets—they revolted in hopes of protecting these institutions and pushing the nation's concept of democracy toward radical ends.

Resisting British Apprenticeship

Counterinstitutions emerged across the Caribbean as people resisted coercive measures that forced workers to stay on plantations. Perhaps the first anti-apprenticeship action in the British Caribbean occurred in St. Kitts. As Emancipation Day on 1 August 1834 neared, enslaved peoples on St. Kitts proclaimed they would work only for wages, feared apprenticeship would be worse than slavery, and could not understand why there was no apprenticeship system in neighboring Antigua. Emancipation Day brought violence, not celebrations. Strikes erupted across St. Kitts, spreading to 156 estates by 4 August 1834. Some fled to the interior to link with maroon leader Markus, prompting leaders in Dominica to fear that violence would spread to their island, which happened a year later when 1800 workers rebelled on Emancipation Day over rumors that plantation owners and colonial officials plotted to return people to slavery. Workers lacked faith in political and economic systems that denied them full participatory rights in those systems.

Throughout the apprenticeship era, whenever workers feared the creeping return of slavery, they stood up and fought back. Trinidad's workers declared a strike, marching on the governor's house to demand to know why the king made them only half free. British Guiana's workers occupied a church for three days, proclaiming that since they were only half free, they would only work half as much as during slavery. Jamaican workers also went on strike. As Gad Heuman puts it, "Apprentices were concerned about any aspect of the system which could be perceived as a continuation of slavery" and made sure that colonial officials heard about it (Heuman 2000, p. 145). Rebellions signaled that they were masters of their own freedom, and they would fight any attempt (real or rumored) to return them to bondage.

Caribbean women found their post-emancipation political and economic freedoms even more constrained than that of men. For instance, across the region, colonial officials restricted voting opportunities for black men via property requirements and taxes. Yet, no woman could cast ballots even if she owned property. Throughout the Caribbean, liberal rights were masculinized. During British apprenticeship, women workers lost the few benefits they possessed under slavery. For instance, after the 1807 abolition of the slave trade, neonatalist policies granted pregnant and nursing enslaved women time off from the fields. Plus, enslaved mothers often received clothes, food, medical care for their children, and more. Apprenticeship eliminated these few maternal advantages, though a mother could have some of these if a child worked in her place.

Women often said no to these arrangements. Some fled the fields, posing a serious dilemma for plantation owners because women often dominated the ranks of field laborers. If women had access to provision grounds, they could better resist being coerced back to the plantations. At home, women also resisted. They preserved culture by preparing traditional dishes. Women remained responsible for children's cultural education and shared tales, fables, and songs. Such in-home cultural education countered new colonial public education systems with Eurocentric curricula and taught in the language of empire. Some mothers refused to send children to colonial schools. As Bridget Brereton puts it, women demonstrated "they were not prepared to subordinate their own and their families' welfare to the needs of the plantation" and thus embarked on their own set of "rational family strategies" to live on their own terms (Brereton 2005, pp. 144, 157).

RESISTING SPANISH APPRENTICESHIP

Spain was the last empire to abolish slavery. In the next chapter, we see how the struggle for abolition overlapped with emerging anti-colonial struggles in Spanish islands. For now, we consider how formerly enslaved peoples in Puerto Rico and Cuba challenged their new intermediary positions between slavery and freedom. Between 1873 and 1876, Spain imposed an apprentice and contract system in Puerto Rico. However, as in the British Caribbean decades earlier, Puerto Rican workers believed apprenticeship infringed on their freedom and rights. They assumed identities as workers, pressing bosses for labor rights and better conditions. Men did not hesitate to flee lands (and thus contracts) when they wished. Women disobeyed orders, engaged in work slowdowns, feigned illness, and missed work. Like apprentices in the British Caribbean, women in Puerto Rico claimed that new work regulations "interfered with their female duties" (Rodríguez-Silva 2005, p. 207). Both men and women confronted employers, destroyed property, and fled to towns and cities. In short, they brought the tools of resistance from the era of slavery to press for better conditions and rights as Spanish subjects.

Cuban apprentices often resisted through legal mechanisms—a strategy learned during slavery. For instance, they appealed in Spanish courts to collect back pay and force officials to prevent physical abuse. As Rebecca Scott argues, "challenge to the master, resistance of a sort, became safer and more likely to yield results" because the worker now could level charges of employer abuse and increase chances of being awarded immediate freedom. The new reality also created more opportunities for workers. While enslaved Cubans long had opportunities to purchase their freedom, few did. Now, workers could give wages to officials to hold and more easily save the needed funds to become totally free in a couple of years. In a sense, if they worked hard (a benefit to the boss) they earned more pay (a benefit to them). As Scott says, this was "a hybrid activity, neither wholly accommodating nor wholly resistant" but it benefitted workers (Scott 2008, pp. 170, 171).

FREE WORKER REVOLTS, PROTESTS, AND STRIKES

Across the Caribbean, newly freed peoples and those born into freedom remained vigilant, protesting perceived slights and demanding full legal protections through courts, strikes, protests, and armed uprisings. This resistance revealed "the people's discontent with the terms of freedom" (Heuman 2014, p. 127). In Martinique and Guadeloupe, free workers found little free about their lives: post-emancipation pass laws and taxation schemes meant workers were under constant threat of violating the law if they tried to improve their conditions. Yet, as much as one-fifth of workers fled Martinique's sugar estates, exacerbating labor shortages for planters. The French realized they had problems, so in the 1850s authorities created an award system for "model workers." Workers could receive a medal reading, "Reward for morality and zeal of work." Workers largely scoffed at the effort. By 1867, Martinique's governor deemed the medal system "impotent" as workers increasingly defied pass laws and engaged in passive resistance. Emboldened workers also attacked police. When officials incarcerated people for vagrancy, fellow workers stormed jails to liberate comrades. In fact, in the decades after abolition, prosecutions soared for physical attacks on Martinican police.

Political discontent was common too. In 1844, Dominica had the Caribbean's only legislature dominated by men of African descent, but that did not mean poor workers trusted their leaders. That year, the government launched an island-wide census. Workers feared this could mean just one thing: counting people as a first step toward reenslaving them. People picked up arms in violent protest known as the *Guerre Nègre*. They threatened to beat, rob, and kill census takers while women ambushed and stoned census workers. The government unleashed the full force of the militia on protestors, killing many, arresting some 300, convicting 90, and hanging 1 ringleader. The revolt and repression reflected ongoing class-based skepticism that poor people had of better-off black and brown men and vice versa. It also reflected how free people were ready to rebel to protect their freedom when they felt threatened.

Gender could complicate politics even before the formal end of slavery. For instance, in 1830s Jamaica, free, middle-class people of African descent pushed for political and social recognition, promoting themselves as respectable British subjects through their newspaper *Watchman*. The newspaper asserted that free women of color embodied this respectability and condemned free women of African descent who freely chose to have relations with whites. The *Watchman*'s writers and readers accused such women of exchanging sex for economic gain that cast a stigma on all free people of African descent. As Meleisa Ono-George puts it, middle-class liberals considered such women "tainted and dangerous," deserving ostracism (Ono-George 2017, p. 369). So, even women who freely chose to be with a white man for whatever reason—economics, love, erotic desire, survival—found themselves attacked by middle-class peoples of African descent who themselves fought whites for power and respect.

In the years immediately following British apprenticeship, women of African descent increasingly took to the public sphere. In 1838, they protested British officials who attacked Baptist and other non-Conformist ministers. In 1839, newly freed women led a rent strike on Jamaica's Spring Hill plantation, pelting officials with stones. Women led anti-tax rebellions in the 1840s and 1850s. In 1840 and 1841, officials attempted to ban the popular Christmas time

Junkanoo street parades and masquerading. Some Christians saw them as pagan religious festivals. Public authorities believed that Junkanoo threatened the new post-slavery order with its masquerading and mass gatherings marked by celebration and defiance. The mayor of Kingston issued a proclamation banning the practice in 1841. The move did not sit well with revelers who responded by clashing with the colonial militia. Jamaican women led the escalating violence, forcing the mayor to take refuge on a ship.

Grievances over low pay and benefits, desires for land, and fears of reenslavement motivated people to rebel throughout the Caribbean. In 1859, Jamaicans protested toll roads, demanding their removal since such roads impeded free movement while draining pocketbooks. During these rebels' trial, crowds of poor people virulently protested, forcing an adjournment. In 1862, St. Vincentian workers declared a strike, assaulted managers and overseers, burned houses, fields and provisions, plundered shops, and looted plantation houses. Workers created a document outlining their complaints. The island's economic decline led plantation owners to reduce what they saw as "privileges" but what workers saw as "rights." These included time on provision grounds, plus rum and molasses rations to workers. Planters revoked these with no warning. "These 'privileges' were," as Woodville Marshall describes, "a part of the labourers' remuneration, which was not protected by the law but which, as far as the labourers were concerned, was sanctified by long custom" (Marshall 1983, p. 97). Bands of between 200 and 2000 people swept across the eastern and southern parts of St. Vincent, attacking planters linked to the allowance withdrawals until colonial militia pacified the situation. More revolts sprouted in Tobago (1876) and Barbados (1876). In 1878, workers in the Danish Virgin Islands rebelled against continued poor working and living conditions. Led in part by three women (the Three Rebel Queens, as they became known), workers looted plantations, burned fields, mills and businesses, and destroyed half of Frederiksted in a two-week wave of unrest known as Fireburn.

In 1851, Colombia abolished slavery. Many newly freed workers found jobs in the Caribbean coast's important transport sector. Coastal workers used their leverage so effectively that the elite sought to liberate capital from the "tyranny of labor" (McGraw 2014, p. 74). The *bogas* comprised a key part of this powerful post-emancipation labor force. Bogas paddled riverine systems between Caribbean ports and interior towns, transporting goods, mail, and people. The bogas represented a large peasant and working-class constituency that resisted the elite economically and culturally. They refused to pay tithes to the Catholic Church, freely engaged in civil marriage and free unions, and attacked elites during Carnival. Throughout Colombia, poor people resisted the privileged. By 1885, thousands of poor Colombians followed El Enviado de Dios—a millenarian preacher who attacked land enclosures, the rich, falling living standards for the poor, and increasing hunger. After authorities arrested him, a leaderless Enviadista Rebellion emerged, building defenses, repelling army attacks, and assassinating officials, priests, and soldiers.

RESISTING INDENTURED SERVITUDE

With the end of British apprenticeship in 1838, the first indentured workers from India arrived in the Caribbean. Over the next 80 years, Europeans transported as many as a million people (mostly from India but also Africa, China, Europe, Indonesia, and Mexico) to their Caribbean colonies. British labor recruiters scoured the Indian subcontinent looking for workers who signed contracts often with just their thumbprint. The contracts outlined seven- to ten-hour workdays, six-day work weeks, pay rates, and benefits like employer-provided housing, food, and healthcare. If an indentured worker labored for five years, they were responsible for their return home, but passage was paid for them if they worked ten years. Indian indentured workers spoke different languages and came from different castes, different regions, and different religions. One thing they had in common: desperate poverty. For most, this was too good of a deal to turn down. However, the long journey to the Caribbean in cramped quarters exposed people to disease and women to sexual violence. Upon arriving in the Caribbean, authorities numbered, deloused, and distributed workers to different sugar plantations, with the largest numbers sent to British Guiana (200,000) and Trinidad (150,000).

Some colonial officials and planters believed East Indians were more docile than peoples of African descent, especially as the latter increasingly challenged authorities to demand better conditions and rights. Officials discovered that was not true. Indians used the court of public opinion to challenge employers who violated contracts. For instance, in 1894, the indentured servant Bechu arrived in British Guiana from Calcutta. Having learned English in his childhood orphanage, Bechu understood the contracts and how employers abused them. In 1896 and 1897, he wrote letters to the editor and testified in royal hearings about how workers faced trial for even the slightest violation of their contracts, but employers never suffered such consequences if they failed to pay legal wage rates or reneged on other contractual obligations: "In this colony, however, an agreement appears to be binding on one side only, for we constantly see coolies being brought up for 'neglecting to attend work,' for 'not completing their task,' and for many such trivial breaches of contract, but in not a single instance have I seen a protector charge an employer for not fulfilling his part of the contract towards an indentured immigrant. Is this fair play?" (quoted in *The Caribbean History Reader* 2013, p. 192).

Indentured workers also employed quotidian resistance and outright militancy. Between 1873 and 1916, the Dutch imported over 34,000 workers to Suriname. The initial wave of Indian workers caused problems for Dutch planters. Because they were British subjects, Indian workers appealed to the British Consul for assistance whenever Dutch employers violated contracts. In response, the Dutch turned to their Indonesian colony, especially the island of Java. This did not really help them though. Both Indian and Javanese workers perfected the art of "foot dragging," disrespectful attitudes toward whites, and flight. As Rosemarijn Hoefte describes it, "contract labourers tried to shy away from open confrontation as much as possible and preferred avoidance protests and secretive everyday forms of resistance to express their dissatisfaction and undermine the system of indenture" (Hoefte 2005, p. 155).

For employers, such behavior reinforced stereotypes of "lazy Asians." However, indentured workers undermined such stereotypes when they led strikes and revolts. In 1869, Indians in British Guiana protested white male sexual exploitation of Indian women. The government sided with protestors and blamed the disturbances on white overseers who used their positions to rape indentured women and, according to the government, fostered "the laxity of morals" supposedly inherent among the indentured (quoted in Bahadur 2013, p. 134).

Labor exploitation and contractual shortcomings also sparked armed resistance. In 1870s Suriname, workers sabotaged trains and crops, stole from employers, and burned fields and buildings. In 1891, violence arose around a Muslim religious holiday, resulting in the killing of a plantation director. In 1902, violent uprisings swept across Surinamese plantations as Indian and Javanese indentured workers went on strike. Employers slashed worker pay, prompting 137 Indian and Javanese workers in Mariënburg to leave the plantation without passes to demand shorter hours, more pay, and dismissal of a brutal overseer. After strikers peacefully put down weapons, police arrested their leader, causing workers to rampage and attack an officer. A manager was replaced and wages increased, but three weeks later the city erupted again as workers cut phone lines and killed a director. The militia responded, killing 17.

A year later, an Indian shovel gang complained of low wages and refused to clear a field for new sugarcane. The next day, 100 Indian workers marched to a courthouse, impaled their shovels in the ground, and waited for an agent to help negotiate wage increases. Instead, police arrived, read the Riot Act, and ordered protesters to disperse. Workers responded by marching toward police, who then shot into the marchers, killing four. More deaths followed the next day when militia arrived. When colonial officials saw Asians acting thusly in their own interests, the previous notion of "lazy" and "docile" Asians quickly changed to that of "barbarous" Asians. According to officials, Indian predisposition to unruliness (not wage issues) triggered the unrest. Such racist stances fed the fire of resistance in places like Suriname's Mariënburg plantation where workers rebelled six times between 1884 and 1932.

Indentured women faced unique problems related to their low numbers. Importers brought mostly men, which placed women indentured workers in sometimes advantageous, though dangerous, circumstances. Through polyandry and moving from male partner to male partner in search of ever-better living conditions, women "used their scarcity to survive as best they could in an exploitative environment" (Bahadur 2013, p. 92). The case of "Baby"—an Indian woman in British Guiana—is illustrative: she took five lovers and had two houses. Baby found a way to exploit the imposed gender imbalance to her favor, undermining the very colonial system of control designed to restrict indentured workers. Other women used similar strategies to improve their conditions, but such practices brought danger, especially from Indian men who sought to control wives, daughters, and lovers in their own households. When women stepped out of both legal and patriarchal control—that is, they went from being victims to agents—men often responded violently. In fact, between 1859 and 1890, jealous men murdered 103 Indian women in British Guiana.

While the Dutch and British introduced Asian indentured servitude after slave emancipation, the Spanish brought it to Cuba during slavery. Thus, enslaved Cubans often toiled with low-wage Chinese indentured workers, who appear not to have engaged in the kind of labor actions seen in British Guiana or Suriname. They resisted though. During Cuba's first war for independence in 1868, 2000 Chinese joined rebels, hoping to liberate themselves from brutal labor contracts if Cuba became free. Legal appeals, though, were the most popular form of resistance. Chinese contracted laborers regularly filed legal complaints against employers for physical abuse and violating contracts.

Intra-Class Resistance: Workers Fighting Workers

Maybe the reader is asking this question: If working people comprised the majority of post-slavery populations, then why were they unable to gain political and economic power? Without a doubt, we cannot underestimate the power of European imperial rule, white supremacy, and mostly white-dominated colonial power in maintaining minority rule in the Caribbean. There is another factor we can consider: workers fighting each other, whether that was black workers fighting one another or Asian and African-descended workers fighting each other.

In March 1858, Antiguans came to believe that Barbudan dockworkers were taking Antiguan jobs. One day, two stevedores (one Barbudan, one Antiguan) began fighting in a rum shop apparently because the Barbudan got a coveted dockworker job that the Antiguan thought should be his as an Antiguan. That night, a mob of Antiguans attacked the Barbudan working-class neighborhood in St. Johns, destroying the home of the Barbudan stevedore and looting other Barbudan homes. Antiguan women surged to the front lines and attacked Barbudan women. Police arrived, fired into the crowd, and killed several people. Over the next three days, more Antiguan-Barbudan violence erupted in the city, with Antiguan police again shooting into crowds. Antiguan xenophobia fueled the rage, but so did the Antiguan notion that they had suffered more than Barbudans during slavery and thus Antiguans had fought harder to earn their freedom. They did not want Barbudans undermining their progress. The violence against Barbudans had little impact other than to play into elite goals of "divide and conquer." As Antiguan workers pursued a nativist agenda (our jobs, our freedom), they alienated any broader transnational support from fellow workers born on an island less than 40 miles away.

Everywhere, antagonism erupted between Asian indentured workers and free workers of African descent. In Cuba, for instance, whites manipulated racial tensions between Asians and Afro-Cubans, contributing to popular notions among the Chinese of their racial superiority or of Afro-Cuban notions that the Chinese were separatists and aloof. Such ethnic hostilities—fueled by white efforts to divide and rule as well as basic difficulties in bridging language barriers—led to a history of assaults and murders between Chinese and Afro-Cuban plantation workers.

In the British Caribbean, some workers of African descent believed Asian indentured workers drove down wage rates or took their jobs. Indentured servants had their own complaints. While drivers and overseers on plantations could be from any race or ethnicity, most were men of African descent. Thus, many Asian workers believed black overseers profited from exploitation of Indian labor. None of this sat well with either group. As a result, tensions fed into ethnic violence like that which erupted on Jamaica's Bogue Estate in 1847 where workers of East Indian and African descent attacked each other. Much of the violence stemmed from mistrust between the two groups, but Afro-Jamaicans offered a rationale like Antiguans who attacked Barbudans years later: nativism. Because Indians lived in separate communities with distinct cultural patterns and gender relations, Afro-Jamaicans felt threatened and defined themselves as "we black nega" versus "foreign coolies." The "we" was defined by who was the better worker (Afro-Jamaicans, said the Afro-Jamaicans) and who could "legitimately exercise political rights." While both were British subjects, only one could claim identity and status as Jamaicans (Sheller 2005a, p. 85). Consequently, across the Caribbean, ethnic and nativist tensions between workers undermined potential working-class alliances that would have enabled workers to better resist the ever-worsening conditions of plantation capitalism.

MORANT BAY, JAMAICA, 1865

Nevertheless, across the region, rebellious workers largely resisted because they were being exploited as second-class colonial peoples. Perhaps the most famous of these actions occurred in 1865 when hundreds of laborers followed Baptist deacon Paul Bogle against Jamaica's colonial government and sugar planters. Nearly two decades of activism, especially the efforts of Bogle's friend George William Gordon, planted the seeds for the uprising.

Born into slavery in 1815, the mixed-race Gordon's white father freed him at age ten. He became a successful landowner and businessman in the 1820s. At 29, voters elected him to Jamaica's legislative assembly. Before and after emancipation, he advocated for the poor who lacked farmland to rent, depended on planters for wages that could be reduced or delayed at any time, lived in unsanitary conditions, and lacked political representation due to a series of property-owning requirements, literacy tests, and poll taxes that disenfranchised most free black voters. By 1852, the island had over 400,000 residents but only 753 registered voters. Using his personal wealth, Gordon loaned money to people to purchase land and plant crops or gave cattle to peasants, making such men property-owning taxpayers and more likely eligible to vote.

By the 1860s, Gordon again served in Jamaica's assembly but now he rejected Anglicanism, became a Baptist, opened several Baptist chapels, and ordained Paul Bogle as a deacon in early 1865. Bogle leveraged his religious position into a political one in eastern Jamaica. He appealed to the Queen to distribute some of her fallow lands to landless peasants. She rejected his appeal. Fed up with the planter-controlled court system that denied their complaints, Bogle and his followers established their own legal system with police, court clerks, and judges. Meanwhile, Bogle created a free militia separate from the colonial militia.

Tensions soon rose. On 7 October 1865, crowds formed at the Morant Bay courthouse. As the magistrate pronounced punishments in one case, people shouted him down; others told the young defendant not to pay the fine. When police went to seize him, a crowd attacked and beat the policemen. The defendant and his protectors escaped. Two days later, the court convicted another defendant of trespassing, but Bogle and associates urged an appeal, only to be shouted down by the magistrate, who then issued arrest warrants for Bogle and 27 others.   When police arrived in Stony Gut to arrest Bogle, 350 armed men emerged from surrounding cane fields, captured some policemen, and beat them. The next day, Bogle and supporters marched with cutlasses and sharpened sticks to the Morant Bay courthouse. Sympathizers from around the area joined in what had become a well-organized movement. Feeling threatened, the magistrate and landowner Baron von Ketelhodt read the Riot Act to disperse. Women in the crowd began throwing stones, chanting "Colour for Colour!" and "No peace. Hell today." Then von Ketelhodt ordered officers to shoot into the crowd.

In response, Bogle's supporters attacked the courthouse, freed 51 prisoners, and targeted many whites for death. Women urged men to burn a schoolhouse, which then caught the courthouse on fire. Women also urged men to continue the fight and pursue whites wherever they fled. Women and men liberated more prisoners and searched for weapons. Von Ketelhodt was later found dead with his head smashed and two fingers cut off. Violence quickly spread. Taking advantage of the melee, many looted and plundered white properties though Bogle urged them not to loot. Others implored people not to plunder, claiming "we don't want clothes…we come to kill" (quoted in Heuman 1994b, p. 21). Such actions, though, suggest the uprising had taken on a life of its own without central leadership and reflecting peasants' broadscale anger. Ultimately, the revolt did not target London or the Queen. Rebels instead targeted colonists who daily exploited them economically, legally, and politically.

On 13 October 1865, Governor Eyre proclaimed martial law, declaring violence threatened to turn Jamaica into another Haiti. Fighting continued, with each side taking reprisals against the other. Bogle believed that if the maroons joined him, it would increase his likelihood of victory. He traveled to nearby maroon communities to make the appeal. However, the maroons rejected

Bogle, captured him, and turned him over to authorities. Why? Since a 1739 treaty, eastern maroons had been loyal to the colonial government, capturing fugitives from slavery and returning them to plantations. Though by 1865, slavery was over, the maroons captured Bogle anyway and handed him to Jamaican authorities. On 24 October 1865, officials hung Bogle. The day before, authorities convicted Gordon—even though there is no evidence that he knew of Bogle's planning—and hung him too.

In the end, rebels torched a thousand homes, and somewhere between 500 and 1500 died—most were peoples of African descent. Many in the British upper and middle classes supported Eyre's repression, though some British intellectuals thought that Eyre himself should stand trial for the butchery in Jamaica. Meanwhile, the British working class sided with Bogle; after all, they sought the same economic and political goals as Jamaican workers. In fact, British workers burned Eyre in effigy. Many Jamaican peasants undoubtedly wished they could do it for real. Instead, Bogle became a martyr and eventually a Jamaican national hero.

Cultural Resistance

People also employed cultural resistance against their oppressors through language, religion, and festivals. Individuals used slang and curse words in their daily speech as forms of resistance against imperially deigned "appropriate" language. Brian Moore notes how British Guianans engaged in a "verbal dexterity" whereby working-class people verbally abused employers and whites with frequent public cussing and vulgarities. In essence, the masses used their everyday speech to challenge elite Victorian values of respectability (Moore 1995, p. 91). Meanwhile, indentured workers retained their languages. Javanese remained the dominant language on Dutch plantations. In the British Caribbean, the majority came from Hindi-speaking regions of Northern India, and Bhojpuri was the leading dialect. While Indian workers came from numerous linguistic areas of India, Bhojpuri became the lingua franca for Indian laborers. Chinese indentured servants in Cuba largely spoke Cantonese. Language allowed workers to speak among themselves, keeping cultures alive and at times facilitating organization under the noses of bosses and overseers. Kreyol in the French Caribbean, Papiamento in Dutch colonies, and various creole languages in the British Caribbean reflected how working peoples adopted aspects of colonial languages, adapted them to local conditions, incorporated other linguistic influences, and created unique languages for daily expression. These hybrid languages—transnational popular creations resulting from the global transfer of different languages across the region—were the peoples' idioms and created a verbal space removed from the linguistic power of the elite.

Religion functioned similarly. In British Guiana, people continued practicing Obeah and Cumfo (worshipping water gods). As syncretic religions, Vodou and Santería blended reverence for Catholic saints and African deities. Through these Caribbean creations, people kept alive ancestral beliefs while accommodating and resisting Christian proselytizing. Yet, in post-slavery Haiti, officials began banning Vodou. The Boyer government in 1835 made practicing Vodou a punishable offense when Catholicism returned as the only legal religion on the island. Still, thousands of Haitians continued to worship Vodou in secret, practicing a spiritually rebellious act against the power of the church, the state, and Francophone-leaning mixed-race Haitians then gaining power in Haiti.

Meanwhile, indentured servants brought Hinduism and Islam to the Caribbean. Around 85% of Indian workers were Hindu and 14% were Muslim. The Dutch imported Indian and then Javanese Muslims to Suriname. Javanese and Indian Muslims acted together in religious brotherhood against their exploiters in waves of uprisings on Surinamese plantations. Like people who practiced Afro-Caribbean religions, Muslim and Hindu workers kept alive their ties to the home country by continuing to practice their religions, worshipping in traditional ways, and retaining a cultural identity that rejected Christianity. On plantations in British Guiana, for instance, Hindu priests and Muslim imams engaged in religious warfare against Christian missionaries by providing spiritual aid to indentured workers.

People also employed public areas as sites of cultural resistance. Religiously inspired festivals allowed people to celebrate their identities and cast aspersions and insults on those who exploited them. Take Carnival and masquerading on St. Vincent: during slavery, planters allowed enslaved peoples time off for Carnival, believing these few days allowed people to "let off steam" and reduce simmering tensions that could lead to revolt. However, enslaved men and women saw Carnival differently. For a few days a year, they controlled the streets of colonial towns. Dressing as dangerous characters filled with the threat of violence (a far cry from much of the prettification and bikini-ization of modern Carnival), they mocked authorities, voiced discontent, and expressed their own creativity in ways illustrating their distinctiveness from Europeans. After emancipation, Carnival remained popular with the poor, but now authorities believed its animated threats of violence and rampant sexuality threatened the colonial social hierarchy and Victorian values. When authorities tried banning Carnival in the 1850s and 1870s, people rebelled. Carnival revelers made the streets a site of popular resistance.

Sometimes workers forged alliances across ethnic lines during festivities. In nineteenth-century Suriname, Indian and Javanese Muslims came together for Islamic celebrations, especially Eid-al-Fitr at the end of Ramadan and Eid-al-Adha several weeks later. Sometimes peoples of African descent joined Islamic festivals while Muslims and Hindus enjoyed Carnival. In Trinidad, Indian Shia Muslims celebrated Hosay—a ten-day event in Muharram (the beginning of the Islamic lunar calendar) commemorating the martyrdom of Prophet Muhammad's grandson Hussein at the Battle of Karbala in 680. During Hosay, people paraded beating drums and carrying elaborate models of mosques while young men engaged in ritualistic stick fighting symbolizing the battle. From the 1850s to 1880s, many non-Muslims (Christian and Hindu, Afro-Caribbean and East Indian) participated in Hosay in what David Trotman calls an "Afro-Asian working-class alliance" (Trotman 2005, p. 139). As Hosay grew in cross-ethnic popularity, authorities grew concerned. For instance, in 1884, Trinidadian authorities issued a decree banning Hosay. Celebrants ignored the ban and paraded through the streets. While Port-of-Spain police did not stop marchers, police elsewhere fired into crowds, killing 22 people in what became known as the Muharram Massacre (the Muslim version of the story) or the Hosay Riots (the British version). "Carnival and Hosay expressed in horrifying ways the fears of revolt and the potential for mayhem which were the constant preoccupation of the elite" (Trotman 2005, p. 137).

Workers of diverse ethnicities used Caribbean yards and streets to express identities through language, religion, dress, food, music, and more. Officials often viewed these as security threats. Not only could such cultural practices reinforce identity and challenge colonial rule, but also, as Brian Moore puts it, "cultural links threatened to transcend the primary racial divisions upon which the whites had placed so much emphasis on preserving the status quo" (Moore 1995, p. 225).

Conclusion

Slavery's end brought neither equality nor total freedom. New coercive labor systems, taxes, and laws forced people to work on plantations designed to export crops to the global capitalist marketplace. While people now earned wages, they also lost the few protections they had under the slave system. In addition, newly freed workers encountered political systems that refused to give them political power by creating voter suppression measures to disenfranchise workers. As Mimi Sheller concludes, "Former slaves were ready for democracy from the first day of emancipation, but democracy was not ready for them" (Sheller 2000, p. 243). Elites then imported men and women from around the world in a new form of colonial servitude. Indentured workers often battled peoples of African descent in the labor market. Ethnic, racial, and nationalist tensions—despite periodic ethnic alliances during strikes or festivals—undermined working-class unity. Gender tensions further undermined this unity as women of all ethnicities found themselves victims of class bias, male aggression, and patriarchal attitudes.

"Freedom" continued to be a troubled concept in the Caribbean. As Natasha Lightfoot notes, these transitory times "took place in the yawning gap between what [men and women] believed freedom should mean and what freedom actually allowed" (Lightfoot 2015, p. 16). Still, Caribbean workers continued to fight back. They employed quotidian resistance, armed uprisings, labor strikes, protests, language, religious expression, flight, sexuality, and demands for rights to claim justice in systems where injustice existed on multiple levels. Yet, all of this occurred in colonial realms. While slavery ended everywhere in the 1800s, most of these places remained European colonies. Freedom had come only part way. In the next chapter, we explore Dominican, Puerto Rican, and Cuban efforts in the second half of the 1800s to sever the colonial yoke—struggles that overlapped efforts to abolish slavery.

WORKS CITED AND FURTHER REFERENCES

G. Bahadur (2013) *Coolie Woman: The Odyssey of Indenture* (University of Chicago Press).

H. McD. Beckles (2011) "Taking Liberties: Enslaved Women and Anti-Slavery Politics" in Verene A. Shepherd (ed.) *Engendering Caribbean History: Cross-Cultural Perspectives* (Ian Randle), 369–80.

S. Boa (2005) "Young Ladies and Dissolute Women: Conflicting Views of Culture and Gender in Public Entertainment, Kingstown, St. Vincent, 1838–1888" in Pamela Scully and Diana Paton (eds.) *Gender and Slave Emancipation in the Atlantic World* (Duke University Press), 247–66.

B. Brereton (2005) "Family Strategies, Gender, and the Shift to Wage Labor in the British Caribbean" in Pamela Scully and Diana Paton (eds.) *Gender and Slave Emancipation in the Atlantic World* (Duke University Press), 143–61.

J. Casimir (2020) *The Haitians: A Decolonial History* (University of North Carolina Press).

R.E. Chace, Jr. (1989) "Protest in Post-Emancipation Dominica: The 'Guerre Negre' of 1844," *Journal of Caribbean History*, 23, 118–41.

The Caribbean History Reader (2013) Nicola Foote (ed.) (Routledge).

S.A. Diouf (1998) *Servants of Allah: African Muslims Enslaved in the Americas* (New York University Press).

J. González (2019) *Maroon Nation: A History of Revolutionary Haiti* (Yale University Press).

G. Heuman (2005) "'Is This What You Call Free?': Riots and Resistance in the Anglophone Caribbean" in Gad Heuman and David Trotman (eds.) *Contesting Freedom: Control and Resistance in the Post-emancipation Caribbean* (Macmillan Caribbean), 104–17.

——— (2011) "Peasants, Immigrants, and Workers: The British and French Caribbean after Emancipation" in Stephan Palmié and Francisco Scarano (eds.) *The Caribbean: A History of the Region and Its Peoples* (University of Chicago Press), 347–60.

——— (1994a) "Post-emancipation Resistance in the Caribbean: An Overview" in Karen Fog Olwig (ed.) *Small Islands, Large Questions: Society, Culture and Resistance in the Post-emancipation Caribbean* (Frank Cass), 123–34.

——— (1994b) *The Killing Time: The Morant Bay Rebellion in Jamaica* (University of Tennessee Press).

——— (2000) "Riots and Resistance in the Caribbean at the Moment of Freedom" in Howard Temperley (ed.) *After Slavery: Emancipation and Its Discontents* (Frank Cass), 135–49.

——— (2014) *The Caribbean: A Brief History*. 2nd edition (Bloomsbury).

G. Heuman and D. Trotman (2005) "Introduction" in Gad Heuman and David Trotman (eds.) *Contesting Freedom: Control and Resistance in the Post-Emancipation Caribbean* (Macmillan Caribbean), xv–xxx.

R. Hoefte (1987) "Control and Resistance: Indentured Labor in Suriname," *New West Indian Guide*, 61/1&2, 1–22.

———— (2005) "Different Modes of Resistance by British Indian and Javanese Contract Labourers Suriname?" in Gad Heuman and David Trotman (eds.) *Contesting Freedom: Control and Resistance in the Post-emancipation Caribbean* (Macmillan Caribbean), 142–55.

———— (1990) "The 'usual barbarity' of the Asians?: Indenture and Resistance in Suriname" in Gary Brana-Shute (ed.) *Resistance and Rebellion in Suriname: Old and New*, 137–58.

E. Hu-Dehart (1994) "Chinese Coolie Labor in Cuba in the Nineteenth Century: Free Labor of Neoslavery," *Contributions in Black Studies*, (Special Issue 12), 38–54.

C. Hutton (2011) "Women in the Morant Bay Rebellion: A Force in the Struggle for the Definition of Post-Slavery Society" in Verene A. Shepherd (ed.) *Engendering Caribbean History: Cross-Cultural Perspectives* (Ian Randle), 460–64.

N. Lightfoot (2015) *Troubling Freedom: Antigua and the Aftermath of British Emancipation* (Duke University Press).

W. Marshall (1983) "'Vox Populi': The St. Vincent Riots and Disturbances of 1862" in Barry Higman (ed.) *Trade, Government and Society in Caribbean History: Essays Presented to Douglas Hall* (Heinemann Educational), 83–115.

J. McGraw (2014) *The Work of Recognition: Caribbean Colombia and the Postemancipation Struggle for Citizenship* (University of North Carolina Press).

B. Moore (1995) *Cultural Power, Resistance, and Pluralism: Colonial Guyana, 1838–1900* (McGill/Queen's University Press).

M. Newton (2005) "Philanthropy, Gender, and the Production of Public Life in Barbados, ca. 1790-ca. 1850" in Pamela Scully and Diana Paton (eds.) *Gender and Slave Emancipation in the Atlantic World* (Duke University Press), 225–46.

M. Ono-George (2017) "'By Her Natural and Despicable Conduct': Motherhood and Concubinage in the *Watchman* and *Jamaica Free Press*, 1830–1833," *Slavery & Abolition* 38/2, 356–72.

D. Paton (2011) "The Abolition of Slavery in the Non-Hispanic Caribbean" in Stephan Palmié and Francisco Scarano (eds.) *The Caribbean: A History of the Region and Its Peoples* (University of Chicago Press), 289–301.

S. Peabody (2005) "Négresse, Mulatresse, Citoyenne: Gender and Emancipation in the French Caribbean, 1650–1848" in Pamela Scully and Diana Paton (eds.) *Gender and Slave Emancipation in the Atlantic World* (Duke University Press), 56–78.

L. Putnam (2013) *Radical Moves: Caribbean Migrants and the Politics of Race in the Age of Jazz* (University of North Carolina Press).

I. Rodríguez-Silva (2005) "Libertos and Libertas in the Construction of the Free Worker in Post-Emancipation Puerto Rico" in Pamela Scully and Diana Paton (eds.) *Gender and Slave Emancipation in the Atlantic World* (Duke University Press), 199–222.

R. Scott (2008) *Degrees of Freedom: Louisiana and Cuba after Slavery* (Belknap).

M. Sheller (2000) *Democracy after Slavery: Black Publics and Peasant Radicalism in Haiti and Jamaica* (University Press of Florida).

———— (2005a) "Acting as Free Men: Subaltern Masculinities and Citizenship in Post-Slavery Jamaica" in Pamela Scully and Diana Paton (eds.) *Gender and Slave Emancipation in the Atlantic World* (Duke University Press), 79–98.

———— (2005b) "'You Signed My Name, but Not My Feet': Paradoxes of Peasant Resistance and State Control in Post-Revolutionary Haiti" in Gad Heuman and David Trotman (eds.) *Contesting Freedom: Control and Resistance in the Post-emancipation Caribbean* (Macmillan Caribbean), 89–103.

"Sugar Cane Alley" (1983) Euzhan Palcy (dir.) NEF Diffusion.

D. Trotman (2005) "Lapping the Volcano: Riots and Their Repression in Post-Emancipation Trinidad" in Gad Heuman and David Trotman (eds.) *Contesting Freedom: Control and Resistance in the Post-emancipation Caribbean* (Macmillan Caribbean), 118–41.

S. Wilmot (2011) "'Females of Abandoned Character?': Women and Protest in Jamaica, 1838–65" in Verene A. Shepherd (ed.) *Engendering Caribbean History: Cross-Cultural Perspectives* (Ian Randle), 449–59.

CHAPTER 5

Anti-Colonial Awakenings: The Dominican Republic, Puerto Rico, Cuba, and Panama, 1820s–Early 1900s

Except in Haitian-controlled Santo Domingo and the new independent mainland countries of Spain's old empire, Caribbean slavery ended during European colonial rule. In Puerto Rico and Cuba, slavery also ended during Spanish rule; however, antislavery activities coincided with anti-colonial wars for independence first launched by Dominicans in the 1860s. That war was based in part on fears that Spanish officials would reimpose slavery. As Robert Whitney puts it, "(f)reedom from slavery and freedom from colonialism were inseparable in the minds of many Cubans and Dominicans" (Whitney 2011, p. 363).

This chapter explores nineteenth-century liberation struggles in the Spanish-speaking Caribbean, illustrating the intertwining of antislavery and anti-colonial battles, the anti-Spanish forces' trans-Caribbean actions, and the resulting emergence of the United States as a new imperial power. We first examine efforts to free Cuba from Spanish rule in the wake of other Latin American independence movements in the 1810s and 1820s. Then, we analyze Santo Domingo's struggles against Spain in the 1860s and the resulting transnational anti-colonialism in Puerto Rico and Cuba. Cuba fought three wars for independence in the 1800s. In the first two, slavery and its abolition were at the forefront of the struggle, while the third—waged a decade after emancipation—illustrated the shortcomings of "political independence" in an era when US political and economic influence was growing. The last Cuban war ended in 1898 after Washington declared war on Madrid. The war illustrated to US policy makers the need for a transoceanic canal across the Central American isthmus—something achievable only after Colombia's province of Panama broke free from Bogota in 1903, with Washington's help.

© The Author(s), under exclusive license to Springer Nature
Switzerland AG 2022
K. Shaffer, *A Transnational History of the Modern Caribbean*,
https://doi.org/10.1007/978-3-030-93012-7_5

EARLY ANTI-SPANISH EFFORTS IN THE CARIBBEAN: *EL ÁGUILA NEGRA* AND FILIBUSTERS

By the mid-1820s, Spain's mainland Caribbean colonies had won independence. In 1822, Haiti conquered Spanish Santo Domingo and abolished slavery. Puerto Rico and Cuba remained Spain's last colonial outposts in the Americas. In Mexico, anti-Spanish politicians linked to Masonic organizations formed the Gran Legión del Águila Negra (Great Legion of the Black Eagle) in May 1823. Liberal reformers—led by Mexican president-elect Guadalupe Victoria—wanted to create republican governments, limit the Catholic Church's influence, and seek freedom of all "Americanos" (especially Cubans) from Spanish rule. After assuming the presidency, Victoria's government planned a joint military expedition with Colombia to invade Cuba and drive out the Spaniards. General Antonio López de Santa Anna—known later as the victor at the Battle of the Alamo in the Mexican state of Texas—would lead the assault from the Yucatán peninsula.

Meanwhile, Cuban exiles fled the island. Many went to the United States while others settled in Mexico where they cooperated with Victoria. In Cuba, a secret branch of the Black Eagle formed in 1826, expecting Mexican and Colombian support via an invasion or in some other material way. However, by 1828, Simón Bolívar, believing that the operation would create a "new Haiti" in Cuba, pulled Colombian support from the expedition. Then, Mexico abandoned the invasion plan. Finally, Spanish officials discovered the Cuban plotters and arrested nearly 20 conspirators.

Other anti-Spanish forces emerged in Cuba between the 1820s and 1850s, including the filibuster Narciso López. Filibusters were groups of irregular armed forces—sometimes supported by a government, usually not—comprising exiles and foreigners who waged wars against governments they opposed. By 1849, the Venezuela-born López had developed anti-Spanish sentiments while living in Cuba, forcing him to flee into exile in the United States. López's anti-Spanish, pro-republican ideas did not mean he supported Cuban independence though. In the United States, he developed a plan to invade and liberate Cuba, but the ultimate goal went further: Cuba, with its thriving slave-based economy that was as attractive to US enslavers in the South as it was to US merchants and manufacturers in the North, would then abandon independence and be annexed to the United States like Texas revolutionaries liberated themselves from Mexico, formed the Texas Republic in 1835, and then joined the United States in 1846. López said his goal was "to strike from the beautiful limbs of the Queen of the Antilles the chains which have too long degraded her in subjection to a foreign tyranny" and "to add another glorious star to the [US] banner which already waves, to the admiration of the whole world, over 'The land of the Free and the home of the Brave'" (quoted in Chaffin 1995, p. 98). López garnered military and financial support from politicians and economic leaders throughout the United States. Between 1849 and 1851, López led three expeditions. The US government blocked the first. The second two landed in Cuba but failed to generate popular support. Though the Black Eagle conspiracy and López's ventures failed to end Spanish rule in Cuba, they signaled the presence of persistent transnational political forces throughout the region determined to liberate Spain's last colonies.

THE 1860s WAR FOR RESTORATION IN THE DOMINICAN REPUBLIC

While anti-Spanish conspiracies consumed many Caribbean liberals, Spanish-speaking residents on Hispaniola faced a different issue. The 1822 Haitian occupation (or unification, depending on one's perspective) brought the entire island under Haitian rule. Popular Dominican lore often treats the 1822–1844 era as a time when a foreign, barbarous Haiti controlled the eastern part of the island. It was more complex than that. Haitians had liberated enslaved peoples in Santo Domingo. Afro-Dominicans enjoyed unparalleled freedoms under Haitian as opposed to Spanish rule. And for a generation, families blended. Nevertheless, there was considerable opposition among the eastern white elite who wanted their own country.

In 1844, mostly lighter-skinned, propertied Dominicans formed a secessionist movement in the east and split the island in two again. These Dominican independence forces (or secessionists—again depending on one's perspective) then invited Spanish investors and immigrants to the country. Soon Spanish influence dominated Santo Domingo, leading to Spain formally annexing it in 1861. New Spanish policies offended average Dominicans. Officials imposed forced labor, leading Afro-Dominicans to fear Spain would reimpose slavery or capture Afro-Dominicans for export to Cuba and Puerto Rico where slavery was still legal. Officials also sponsored more Spanish migration to the island in a bid to whiten and Hispanicize the population. Meanwhile, Spanish officials held most Dominicans with contempt, seeing Dominicans—especially rural Dominicans as morally lax with open displays of prostitution, public drinking, and concubinage. Spaniards felt these too had to be suppressed. Soon, Dominicans began resisting Madrid's new colonization.

In 1861, while Haitian president Fabre Geffrard protested the return of Spanish rule, an amalgam of Haitian soldiers, Dominicans in Haiti, families now divided by and living around a new international border, and Dominican officers organized an armed opposition to Spanish rule. This "collection of republican, nationalist, anti-colonial alliances with military leadership," as Anne Eller describes it, tore down Spanish flags and cut them into pieces, raised the Haitian flag, assaulted Spanish officers, and treated Spanish soldiers with disgust and disdain (Eller 2016, p. 117). Spain responded by sending more soldiers, financed by new taxes on Dominicans. When rural people refused to pay taxes, the government confiscated crops and livestock. Anti-Spanish animosity escalated when the government demanded people turn over livestock to the military without guarantee of compensation.

In 1863, colony-wide guerrilla warfare erupted in the War of Restoration, that is, a war to restore Dominican sovereignty. In February, day laborers and farmers confronted Spaniards. Though government forces repressed the first uprising around Neiba, more towns revolted. Wives, daughters, and lovers managed households and small farming plots, while men joined the ranks of independence leaders like Gregorio Luperón. With men in the hills, women remained in towns or continued to journey to local markets where they heard official information and relayed news to guerrillas. Exiles and refugees, guerrillas and bandits mingled together along the border and in northern Haitian cities where the Haitian government provided protection.

On 16 August 1863, the rebel army under Santiago Rodríguez issued the Grito de Capotillo and raised the new Dominican independence flag in Dajabón. By September, a rebel army of over 6000 men under Gaspar Polanco, Luperón, and others advanced across the north. This was also a transnational conflict. Haitians continued to aid guerrillas and joined the fight. Dominican exiles and allies in Dutch Curaçao, Colombia, Venezuela, and Cuba sent assistance. In 1865, Spain surrendered, and Dominicans proclaimed independence. The War of Restoration also impacted neighboring Puerto Rico and Cuba, where activists launched anti-colonial wars for independence in 1868.

TRANSNATIONAL ANTI-COLONIALISM: THE ANTILLES FOR ANTILLEANS

Transnational anti-colonial relations between Cuba, Puerto Rico, and the Dominican Republic began even before war's end. In 1861, the abolitionist and advocate for Puerto Rican independence Ramón Emeterio Betances fled Puerto Rico, taking refuge in the northern Dominican city of Puerto Plata. There, he met and worked with Luperón and one of the ideological leaders of the Dominican independence movement—the Catholic priest Father Fernando Arturo de Meriño. The Luperón-Betances relationship grew as Luperón offered Betances haven and a base of operations to coordinate anti-Spanish activities in Puerto Rico. Radicals made Puerto Plata a "strategic and ideological center" where Caribbean exiles, freemasons, and anti-Spanish Cubans and Puerto Ricans organized to build an Antillean Confederation. Puerto Plata was "full of inveterate anticolonial activists, who spoke of Caribbean unity in affective and military vocabulary equally" (Eller 2016, p. 230). In fact, people like Betances, Luperón, Máximo Gómez, and Eugenio María de Hostos saw themselves as "Antilleans," as much as Cubans, Puerto Ricans, or Dominicans. Betances regularly signed his writings with the name "El Antillano." He and comrades called for the end of all Caribbean colonialism, translated works into English, French, and Spanish for trans-Caribbean readers, and spoke about "the Antilles for Antilleans."

By 1867, Betances organized an armed expedition to invade his homeland; however, the new Dominican government of Buenaventura Báez ordered Betances' arrest. Betances fled, and by 1868, he and Luperón went into exile in Danish St. Thomas, where they plotted new rebellions. During this exile, Betances wrote *The Ten Commandments of Free Men*. In it, he urged Puerto Ricans to demand Spain abolish slavery; grant the right to vote; provide freedom of religion, speech, press, trade, and peaceful assembly; grant Puerto Ricans the right to bear arms; and more. He closed by suggesting that of course Spain would never do this, so "Puerto Ricans—HAVE PATIENCE! For I swear that you will be free."

In September 1868, Puerto Ricans launched their long-awaited uprising, flying a rebel flag modeled after the Dominican flag. The Grito de Lares—the proclamation launching the Puerto Rican insurrection—mobilized peoples across Puerto Rico, including the *jíbaros* of the interior. The jíbaros were peasants—often mixed-race descendants of native Taínos who continued to practice ancient healing arts, language, and customs in their daily lives. For many jíbaros, this was more than a war for independence as imagined in the minds of leaders from the upper classes, but instead was another chapter in a centuries-long struggle against Spanish colonialism dating to the early 1500s. At the same time, Betances hoped to recruit fighters from across the Caribbean. He purchased a ship to ferry volunteers to the island; however, when the ship arrived in the Virgin Islands, Danish authorities confiscated it. The rebellion then floundered as Betances himself was sailing between Curaçao and the Virgin Islands in desperate efforts to find recruits for the rebellion. The Grito de Lares was the last significant pro-independence movement in Puerto Rico until the 1930s.

CUBA'S TEN YEARS WAR, 1868–1878

While rebellion in Puerto Rico fizzled, it exploded in Cuba. In the mid-1860s, Spanish conservatives began imposing new taxes on Cubans while reversing various liberal policies that had granted limited political representation, labor organizing, and freedoms for Cubans. Spanish repression led to widespread discontent, especially from white, Cuban-born elites in the east who plotted rebellion and sought support from farmers, the middle class, and free peoples of African descent. They called for free trade, republican democracy, universal suffrage for free males, and ending unjust taxation.

By the 1870s, 40,000 rebels (including enslaved and newly freed peoples) fought Spanish rule in the Ten Years War. The 1865 victory in the Dominican Republic showed nationalists in Cuba that Spain could be defeated, and both Dominican and Puerto Rican activists joined Cubans' war for independence. One Dominican was Máximo Gómez. Following Dominican independence, Gómez moved his family to Cuba and soon sympathized with Cuban rebels. His leadership in the eastern Cuba campaigns drove back Spaniards, many who were just poor Spanish draftees and feared Gómez's patented "machete charges" where hundreds of otherwise poorly armed Cuban fighters known as *mambises* charged Spanish lines waving machetes and hacking to death Spanish soldiers.

In Cuba, slave labor still drove the island's sugar economy though abolitionist ideas were on the rise. Abolitionism and anti-colonialism had overlapped before. Slaves rebelled nearly 30 times between the 1820s and 1840s—the exact time that anti-colonial movements like the Black Eagle conspiracy and other anti-Spanish plots emerged. Officials believed anti-Spanish elements in Cuba encouraged the La Escalera slave conspiracy discussed previously. Such overlapping occurred in Puerto Rico too where an 1822 slave conspiracy coincided with a mercenary expedition against the Spanish in a failed attempt to create a Boricua Republic. They coincided again in 1868 when Spanish officials blamed abolitionists for the Grito de Lares because it occurred on a day of rest for enslaved workers.

Most Cuban independence leaders supported gradual abolition of slavery but only after winning independence. Meanwhile, Spanish officials portrayed Cuban revolutionaries as rabid abolitionists, who would unleash a race war that would turn Cuba into another Haiti if victorious. The leader of the Cuban rebellion—Carlos Manuel de Céspedes—contributed to this Spanish fear mongering. On 10 October 1868, he issued the Grito de Yara declaring Cuban independence, freed his own enslaved workers, and invited them to join the anti-Spanish revolt. Not all Cuban rebel leaders agreed with this move, though, as many white pro-independence leaders wanted to separate colonial and slavery issues. In their minds, freedom for enslaved peoples could wait. As it turned out, independence leaders convinced Céspedes in November to proclaim that any anti-colonial supporter who incited slave rebellions against sugar estates would be executed.

However, that did not dissuade enslaved peoples or other separatist leaders. In February 1869, the Cuban Revolutionary Assembly called for complete abolition. Two months later, rebels declared that enslaved peoples in rebel territory were now *libertos*—no longer enslaved, but not completely free because they had to do whatever their former owners or rebel officers deemed was necessary for the war effort. This reflected the conservative backgrounds of most of the rebel leadership who either supported continuation of slavery or believed in the necessity of some transitory system from slavery to freedom as they had seen in the British Caribbean decades earlier.

As Rebecca Scott puts it, "while it is clear that many rebel officers intended to keep treating libertos like slaves, it is equally clear that many libertos had no intention of continuing to behave like slaves" (Scott 2000, p. 50). As they waged war against Spain, libertos increasingly rejected the notion that they were not completely free. Many fled to form palenques. Meanwhile, conservative rebel authorities often were uncertain how to treat libertos and were uncertain as to the libertos' loyalty. Due to this hesitation, many insurgent leaders refused to free people, rebel officers often refused to arm Afro-Cuban soldiers, and some white officers questioned whether formerly enslaved peoples should technically count as "Cubans."

Cuban conservatives further feared rebel leaders Máximo Gómez and Antonio Maceo: Gómez because he was Dominican and Maceo because he was

Afro-Cuban. General Gómez believed it essential to incorporate peoples of African descent into the rebel army and abolition was the morally right thing to do. He advocated destroying plantations to undermine the Spanish colonial economy—something that many rebel leaders rejected since their lands too could have come under assault. As for Maceo, his troops admired him (calling him the Bronze Titan) as he fought in over 500 skirmishes, skillfully employed Gómez's machete charges, and suffered at least 25 battle-related wounds. However, conservative rebel leaders mistrusted Maceo because he saw Cuban independence and slave emancipation as synonymous.

Women played key roles in the *mambí* army by advocating independence, abolition, and women's rights. Maceo's mother Mariana Grajales—a leading abolitionist voice since the 1850s—reflected the growing cult of "revolutionary motherhood" among the mambises where "obedient daughters, devoted wives, admiring girlfriends, but above all…mothers" used their domestic duties for clearly political ends (Prados-Torreira 2005, p. 62). Female revolutionaries were transnational too. In 1869 in New York, Emilia Casanova founded the League of Cuba's Daughters—the first political group organized by a Cuban woman—and raised money for rebel supplies. That same year, rebels held the First Constitutional Assembly at Guáimaro. Ana Betancourt took the stage, giving what Prados-Torreira calls "among the first feminist speeches" in Caribbean history. Betancourt linked women's emancipation with slave emancipation and anti-colonialism, noting, "the time has come to free women" (quoted in Prados-Torreira 2005, p. 84). Spaniards captured Betancourt in 1871 and sent her to Spain, where she died in 1901. After 1959, the Castro government created the Order of Ana Betancourt Award for women who dedicated their lives to revolutionary, internationalist, and anti-imperialist struggles.

By the 1870s, women led workshops producing weapons, horseshoes, and other war supplies for rebel forces. Their homes became secret meeting spots and storage sites for rebel resources. With men under arms, it fell to women and children to harvest crops and create food supplies for rebels. As war-related injuries mounted, rebel forces needed hospitals. Women ran them, including Bernarda Toro (Máximo Gómez's wife) and María Cabrales (Antonio Maceo's wife), who both ran a hospital where black-and-white nurses worked side by side.

Ultimately, the rebels were outgunned, even though in 1871 Betances had given them caches of weapons he had stored in the Virgin Islands, Curaçao, and Haiti. Haiti—in the type of Antillean support pushed by people like Betances—aided the rebels by selling them firearms. Yet, it was not enough, prompting some rebel leaders to enter secret peace negotiations with Spain in 1874. After discovering this, an outraged Emilia Casanova exposed the negotiations, shaming rebel leaders for undermining the independence struggle. Nevertheless, by 1878, both sides acknowledged that the war had reached a stalemate. Both sides were exhausted from a decade of struggle that had destroyed Cuba's economy. Only around 200 of nearly 600 sugar plantations and mills survived, while 500 coffee plantations had been burned down.

THE LITTLE WAR IN CUBA, 1879–1880

The government and rebels signed the Pact of Zanjón, which promised to give Cuba political representation in the Spanish parliament, grant amnesty to combatants, free all enslaved peoples who fought in the war, grant freedom from indenture to Chinese war participants, provide political liberties like freedom of the press and assembly, and place 1888 as the date for full slave emancipation (though that date would move to 1886). Plus, numerous political openings emerged in newly legal mutual aid societies, newspapers, and labor unions.

Rebel leaders were forced to leave the island. General Calixto García settled in New York City. However, he came to believe that the treaty was a mistake. He then organized the Cuban Revolutionary Committee and issued a new declaration of war against Spain on 26 August 1879. Sectors of the rebel army took up García's call and fought until 1880 in the Guerra Chiquita (the Little War). Popular portrayals of the war cast it as a struggle by Afro-Cubans, who refused to lay down weapons because the Pact of Zanjón did not grant total and immediate abolition. Without doubt, Afro-Cubans drove the continued fighting, but it was more complicated and transnational than this. Transnationally, García arrived from New York in early 1880. Many people in the United States supported continued hostilities and aided rebels. On the island, thousands of rebels refused to disarm and continued fighting. One of their leaders was Antonio Maceo's brother José, who, along with Quintín Bandera and others, formed a multiracial rebel leadership pushing for immediate abolition and independence. Spanish officials portrayed the rebellion as "black" and not "Cuban," but poor whites joined free and enslaved peoples. However, the small, scattered movement could not withstand the onslaught of Spanish repression, lack of military leadership experience, and perpetual shortage of weapons. Ultimately, authorities arrested most rebel leaders, and the war ended in September 1880 (Fig. 5.1).

THE CUBAN WAR FOR INDEPENDENCE, 1895–1898

During the 1880s, broad support for a new liberation struggle emerged. Middle-class nationalists sought political independence, while working-class labor unions sought social revolution. These two driving forces coalesced under José Martí's political leadership in the early 1890s. A former political prisoner of Spain, the anti-imperialist Martí rejected both Spanish rule and any potential annexation of Cuba to the United States. By the 1890s, US influence penetrated throughout the Spanish colony. US-Cuban trade relations expanded as over 90% of Cuban exports went to the United States by the early 1890s. US culture and fashion arrived in great waves. Cuban students whose parents increasingly sent their sons to university in the US northeast brought US values, products, and culture. While Spain grew weary of the United States' growing "soft power", Martí did as well. He acknowledged admiring much about the United States but argued that Washington's violent westward

Fig. 5.1 Battle of Desmayo—multiracial mambises fighting Spanish troops (Getty Images)

expansionism diminished any early virtues of the country. The United States might be growing powerful but look what it did to its own natives, its formerly enslaved peoples, and its teeming industrial work force. Martí had resided in the United States, having "lived in the monster and I know its entrails." Martí aimed to "demonstrate two useful truths to our America: the crude, uneven, and decadent character of the United States, and the continuous existence there of all the violence, discord, immorality, and disorder blamed upon the peoples of Spanish America." As a result, he warned Cubans to avoid "Yankeemania"—an overwhelming admiration for the United States that glossed over its brutality. Cuba's answers and its destiny should be found on the island and in its people—rich and poor, African and European—not pursued by mimicking the United States (quoted in *Latin America and the United States*, pp. 63–64).

In New York, wealthy and middle-class Cuban nationalists hoped to create a politically free, Catholic, capitalist country. By the late 1880s and early 1890s, growing numbers of tobacco workers in Havana and Florida had a very different vision for a post-Spanish Cuba. They formed transnational anarchist labor organizations seeking a radical socialist agenda for an independent Cuba: sweeping land redistribution, better pay, and more working-class power. Martí united these groups around the central idea that, first, the island had to be free from Spain and only then could further transformation of Cuba be discussed. In 1892, Martí formed the Partido Revolucionario Cubano (Cuban Revolutionary Party, or PRC) to unite these disparate camps into an organized liberation movement.

In February 1895, Martí declared war on Spain in the Grito de Baire. By late 1895, rebel forces moved into western provinces, and within a year rebellion spread to every part of the island, disrupting sugar and tobacco harvests, and bringing economic woes to elites. General Máximo Gómez—who one remembers fled the Dominican Republic and became a leader in Cuba's Ten

Years War—again led rebel forces, proclaiming that unlike the 1868 war that was led from "the top down," the current rebellion "surges from the bottom up, that is why it will triumph" (quoted in Pérez 1995, p. 160).

That meant waging war not just against Spain but against wealthy, exploitative Cubans too. As a result, the new mambises engaged in scorched earth campaigns, burning sugar and tobacco properties of the rich. As Louis Pérez puts it, the "most devasting weapon in the insurrectionary arsenal became *la tea*—the torch" (Pérez 1995, p. 162). Poor whites joined rebels of African descent. They gladly followed Gómez's decrees to wage total war to halt all economic activity and deprive wealthy planters of profits and Spanish officials of taxes. If the mambises could destroy the elite's economy and source of wealth creation, then upon victory, these lands could be redistributed, and economic power transferred from the pre-insurrection elite to the revolutionary masses. Rebel forces received a wide array of help in these endeavors ranging from local bandits and professional baseball league officials to exiles and anarchists abroad.

Banditry, Baseball, and Resistance

Just who is a "bandit" or a "criminal"? Is it a person who breaks the law? Of course, but what if that law is unjust and benefits exploiters? The person is still an outlaw, but is that necessarily a bad thing? When people rebelled against Spain, colonial officials quickly labeled them bandits and outlaws—which they were, but aren't all revolutionaries by definition? In the years after emancipation, thousands of formerly enslaved peoples became wage laborers looking for work. Basic capitalist economics tells us that as labor pools expand, wages decline. This happened just as Cuba entered an economic recession. At the same time, economic pressures forced small landowners to sell or abandon their lands as industrial-scale sugar plantations expanded across the countryside. Small landowners could not compete. Economic losses and barely survivable wages drove people to make different choices. Some joined growing ranks of people looking for a day's wage. Others moved to cities or crossed the Florida Straits looking for work. Many, though, held a grudge and began waging their own economic war on the very Spanish elite they blamed for their financial difficulties. Some in rural Cuba turned to petty theft, sabotage, burning fields, and kidnappings for ransom as ways to extort money and to protest deteriorating conditions. While Spanish authorities called these people criminals and bandits, Imilcy Balboa Navarro refers to their acts as "everyday survival strategies"—not done with any explicit political agenda but to survive against the actions taken by elites (Balboa Navarro 2015, p. 84).

In the years leading to the 1895 declaration of independence, such acts continued to reflect many rural Cubans' desperation. Bandits turned to "taxing" property owners and railroads. While some outlaws did this solely for the money and quickly withdrew once they had been paid, others developed blatant political agendas behind their actions. These social bandits operated throughout rural Cuba where rebels dominated the countryside during the war. It did not take long for the actions of the two to coincide. Manuel García is one example. Following a youthful career of juvenile delinquency that led to later assaults on Spanish police and cattle rustling, García's banditry in the 1890s overlapped with the rebel army's activities. He eventually sympathized with their anti-Spanish actions, merging his own hatred of Spanish authorities with theirs. As a result, García gained wealth through extortion, robbery, and ransom against planters who remained loyal to Spain. Yet rather than keep all his gains, he gave much to the mambí army, which in turn protected him. Until his death in 1896, García regularly financed rebel causes. By no means did all bandits support the rebel army, but even those with no explicit political agenda committed crimes for survival, and in so doing undermined the stability and legitimacy of the Spanish colonial system.

While banditry in rural areas contributed to the mambises' financial strength, survival of rural peoples and the destabilization of the Cuban economy, the independence movement also received financial help from urban Cuba and from a rather unlikely source: professional baseball. The first professional baseball league in the United States began in 1871, and, from its earliest days, Cubans played in the major leagues. Baseball quickly gained popularity in Cuba. Sons of wealthy Cubans returned from US universities with bats, gloves, balls, and a growing enthusiasm for the game. American seamen expanded this transnational cultural influx by playing this new sport in parks and open spaces. Baseball spread in popularity among Cuba's masses—much to the consternation of Spanish officials who saw yet another American cultural import vying for influence with Spanish culture. In 1878—just seven years after professional baseball emerged in the United States—Emilio Sabourín launched the first professional baseball league in Cuba.

Baseball, though, proved to be more than just a pastime. For many Cubans, the sport symbolized "modernity" because it originated in the United States. Yet, some nationalists feared baseball as another North American cultural intervention and thus another dangerous form of Yankeemania. The sport spread, nonetheless. Over the years, Spanish officials attempted to reign in baseball. During the Ten Years War, they banned baseball on grounds that it was anti-Spanish. In the last years of that war, officials prevented a Havana team from calling themselves "Yara" (after the Grito de Yara of 1868) and a team from Remedios from calling themselves "Anacaona" (the early 1500s Taíno resistance leader). After war began in 1895, officials arrested Sabourín for anti-colonial activities, including a scheme to take money from professional baseball and give it to insurgents. Officials deported him to a Spanish penal colony where he died. The founder of Cuban professional baseball perished as a pro-independence political prisoner.

Transnational Support for Independence

Support for the liberation cause emerged in Europe and the United States. Ramón Emeterio Betances—the anti-Spanish agitator in Puerto Rico and the Dominican Republic in the 1860s and independence activist during the Ten Years War—also had a European history. He joined the 1848 revolution in France when he was a medical student in Paris, served as a French diplomat in the Dominican Republic in the 1880s, and became a PRC representative while living again in Paris. In the 1890s, he gave refuge to anarchists fleeing Spanish persecution because of their opposition to the monarchy and their pro-Cuban independence stances. Betances counseled the anarchist Michele Angiolillo to assassinate Spanish prime minister Antonio Cánovas del Castillo. Betances blamed the prime minister for sending General Valeriano Weyler to Cuba in 1896 where Weyler imposed martial law, deported political prisoners, and imposed a policy that drove thousands of rural Cubans into urban concentration camps where they died from famine and disease. Shortly after meeting Betances in 1897, Angiolillo traveled to Spain, tracked down Cánovas del Castillo, and killed the prime minister with a bullet to the head.

Meanwhile in Cuba, anarchists detonated bombs across Havana and attempted to assassinate Weyler, who responded to anarchist violence with arrests and deportations. Anarchists in Florida collaborated with their Havana comrades. When war broke out in 1895, Florida's anarchists quickly aided the struggle, invoking a transnational call to arms that defied nationalist identity and brought together Spaniards, Cubans, Italians, and African Americans working in Florida. As one anarchist put it, "The flag of independence that waves in the countryside is not just the flag of one determined party; it does not represent only the protest against Spanish domination of Cuba. Rather, it represents the virile protest of all tyrannized and exploited people who make a supreme effort to attain their freedom" (quoted in Shaffer 2020, p. 54). Florida-based anarchists declared strikes against Spanish-owned tobacco factories in Florida, halting production and undermining Spanish profits and wealth. With money raised by cigar rollers in Tampa and beyond, they bought weapons and boats, then sailed across the straits, landed in Cuba, and joined the mambises.

The Spanish-American War and Its Aftermath

Then Washington became involved and thus began to reshape imperial relations and designs in the Caribbean. Certain forces throughout US and Cuban history had seen Cuba as a "natural" extension of the US mainland and envisioned annexing Cuba to the United States. In mid-1896, prominent Cuban conservatives and Spanish businessmen decided that their economic livelihoods rested with substituting one imperial power for another. As they saw it, their own Spanish rulers were incapable of winning the war, and they feared independence would bring a massive redistribution of their wealth and land. So, they unsuccessfully petitioned US presidents Grover Cleveland and William McKinley to militarily intervene in the war with hopes that a victorious Washington would annex Cuba.

Then, their dreams appeared to come true. The battleship *USS Maine* exploded in Havana's harbor in February 1898, killing over 200 sailors and intensifying growing popular sentiment in the United States for Washington to declare war on Spain—a demand generated by sensationalist news coverage in the US press. Newspapers reported on Weyler's concentration camps, Spaniards abusing Cuban women, and theories blaming Spain for planting a mine that sank the *Maine*. In April, the United States declared war on Spain, and US troops sailed for global ports of the Spanish empire in Guam, the Philippines, Puerto Rico, and Cuba. The Cuban War for Independence continued, but now it also become the Spanish-American War.

Dreams of US annexation came crashing down when the congressional resolution authorizing war included the Teller Amendment that said the United States would not annex Cuba. Still, the arrival of US troops changed the dimension of the war. US troops routed Spaniards, and Washington claimed that it—and not Cubans—had primary responsibility for ending Spanish colonialism. In late 1898, Spain and the United States signed a peace treaty with no representatives from any Spanish colony, including Cuba. Just like that the island switched from Spanish control to US military occupation.

From January 1899 to mid-1902, the US military ruled Cuba as US corporate investment poured onto the island to resurrect and expand sugar and tobacco plantations rather than redistribute land the mambises expected as reward for fighting Spain. Various groups challenged US rulers and their Cuban collaborators. Anarchists launched a newspaper in Havana the same week as official US occupation began. For two years, they railed against foreign businessmen, Cuban officials who did Washington's bidding, and the US military government. As rebel leader Aguinaldo in the Philippines resisted US rule, anarchists urged Cubans to follow Aguinaldo's lead

Some Cubans did fight back. Displaced peasants and landless veterans began a wave of social banditry by attacking plantations and their mostly American owners. Banditry grew so threatening that occupation chief General Leonard Wood organized a new rural guard to fight bandits. However, when arrested bandits went before trials of their peers, those peers refused to convict their desperate comrades. In response, Wood ordered the guard to execute captured bandits without trial. Were the bandits "outlaws"? Sure, but were the postwar environment and laws designed to protect that environment "just"? Of course not. As before and during the war, banditry had a political edge that targeted perceived exploiters.

The US occupation ended in 1902 when Washington handed the island to Cubans (something they did not do in Puerto Rico). As Cubans created a new constitution during the last year of occupation, Washington again intruded. The US Congress passed the Platt Amendment prohibiting Cuba from going into debt to foreign countries, requiring Cuba to lease a coaling or naval station to the United States, and allowing Washington to militarily invade the island whenever Washington saw the need to preserve stability. Before Cuba could be released from American control, Cubans had to insert this amendment into their own constitution. By one vote, the Cuban constituent assembly approved the Platt Amendment, setting the stage for the United States to leave—but enabling US troops to return as they did in 1906, 1912, and 1917.

PANAMANIAN INDEPENDENCE

The war had another transnational impact on the Caribbean. Since the Spanish Conquest, the Panamanian isthmus had been a transit point between the Caribbean and the Pacific. For centuries, pack animals and humans carried goods on their backs across the isthmus. In the mid-1800s, a railroad linked the Pacific and Caribbean. Americans and Europeans long dreamed of building a canal across the isthmus. In the 1880s, the French tried to build a canal using mostly French Caribbean laborers. Worker-killing disease, scandal, and bankruptcy brought that project to a halt. But the 1898 war convinced Washington that the time was right to build its own canal as emerging US economic, political, and military power required quick movement of goods, men, and naval vessels around the world.

But where to build the canal? Washington saw two potential locations: a canal cut across the isthmus of Colombia's Panamanian province or along the San Juan River that separated Costa Rica and Nicaragua, then across Lake Nicaragua and to the Pacific via a new canal. Into the mix stepped the Frenchman Philippe Bunau-Varilla, former general manager of the French Panama Canal Company. When the French project went bankrupt in 1888, he remained in Panama to avoid fraud charges. Over the next dozen years, he attempted to lure investors, especially US politicians. The confluence of US victory in Cuba in 1898 and Bunau-Varilla's tenaciousness led to the so-called Panama Revolution.

In 1901, the New Panama Canal Company based in the United States owned the tract of land in Panama through which the French project had failed. The company and Bunau-Varilla lobbied the US Congress to build a canal through this land. When the price to build a canal was shown to be cheaper in Nicaragua, Bunau-Varilla and the Company lowered their asking price and reminded congressmen that Nicaragua was full of active volcanoes. Did congressmen really want their canal to be destroyed by seismic eruptions? Washington chose Panama. However, Panama was still part of Colombia, and, in 1903, the Colombian Senate rejected the treaty with the United States to build the canal.

Bunau-Varilla and the Company fumed. Furious times called for furious actions. Panamanian separatists organized in New York City. Bunau-Varilla helped them draft a constitution, create a flag, and bankroll an armed uprising against Colombia to liberate Panama. Meanwhile, secessionists in the isthmus had been mobilizing for years, including the pro-separatist provincial governor

José Domingo de Obaldía, who began plotting with Washington to build a canal after the Colombian Senate rejected the treaty. In late 1903, Panamanians launched their independence war. A coalition of liberals, separatists, and US controllers of the railroad worked together to slow Colombian troops advancing to put down the rebellion. At the same time, the battleship *USS Nashville* prevented the Colombian navy from aiding its soldiers in Panama. On 3 November 1903, rebels declared creation of the new Republic of Panama without hardly firing a shot. Ten days later, Washington recognized the new country and immediately signed a treaty with Bunau-Varilla, Panama's new ambassador to Washington. With that, Washington launched construction of the Panama Canal, which opened in 1914 after a decade of herculean labor performed mostly by Spanish and West Indian workers. One separatist cause in Cuba facilitated another in Panama, resulting in a US-run canal in the western Caribbean guarded by a US military presence in the eastern Caribbean.

CONCLUSION

In 1898, Spanish colonialism ended in the Caribbean, but a new era of US expansionism and the beginning of the United States as a new imperial power in the region ushered forth. The US government now owned Puerto Rico (and then the Danish Virgin Islands purchased in 1917), shaped the constitutions of Cuba and Panama to facilitate a new type of indirect political control, regularly threated and executed military intervention if Washington did not like what it saw, and promoted expansion of US economic and cultural influences across the region. US "neocolonialism" became a new form of imperial rule in the Caribbean, soon spawning waves of anti-American resistance.

The Haitian Revolution had launched the Caribbean's anti-colonial struggles when Jean-Jacques Dessalines cast off French colonial rule and declared Haitian independence in 1804, making Haiti the first free country in the Caribbean. Throughout the nineteenth century, antislavery and anti-coercive labor struggles emerged everywhere, but only in the Spanish Caribbean did peoples strive for independence and national freedom—the short-lived Republic of Cartagena; the Caribbean Basin countries of Central America, Mexico, and northern South America; the Dominican Republic in 1844 and again in 1865; Puerto Rico and Cuba from 1868 to 1898; and Panama in 1903. Everywhere else, people from all walks of life struggled to acquire the rights they believed that Great Britain, France, the Netherlands, and Denmark owed them. In short, they struggled to enjoy rights they were entitled to as "colonial" subjects.

Events in the first decades of the twentieth century changed that. Radical working-class organizations began challenging colonialism and neocolonialism. Armed groups resisted US military intervention in Haiti, the Dominican Republic, and Nicaragua. Meanwhile, political struggles grew in British colonies as the emergence of black consciousness ideas and the impact of the Great War in Europe gave rise to a wave of anti-imperialism across the Caribbean. That is our next story.

Works Cited and Further References

I. Balboa Navarro (2015) "Bandits, Patriots or Delinquents? Social Protest in Rural Cuba (1878–1902)," *International Journal of Cuban Studies* 7/1, 79–98.

G.A. Baralt (2007) *Slave Revolts in Puerto Rico* (Markus Wiener).

J. Casanovas (1998) *Bread, or Bullets!: Urban Labor and Spanish Colonialism in Cuba, 1850–1898* (University of Pittsburgh Press).

T. Chaffin (1995) "'Sons of Washington': Narciso López, Filibustering, and U.S. Nationalism, 1848–1851," *Journal of the Early Republic* 15/1, 79–108.

K. Chaar-Pérez (2013) "'A Revolution of Love': Ramón Emeterio Betances, Anténor Firmin, and Affective Communities in the Caribbean," *Global South*, 7/2, 11–36.

A. Eller (2016) *We Dream Together: Dominican Independence, Haiti, and the Fight for Caribbean Freedom* (Duke University Press).

A.K. Finch (2005) *Rethinking Slave Rebellion in Cuba: La Escalera and the Insurgencies of 1841–44* (University of North Carolina Press).

P.S. Foner (1972) *The Spanish-Cuban-American War and the Birth of American Imperialism, 1895–1902*, Two Volumes (Monthly Review Press).

Latin America and the United States: A Documentary History (2011) R.H. Holden and E. Zolov (eds.) (Oxford University Press).

D. Paton (2011) "The Abolition of Slavery in the Non-Hispanic Caribbean" in Stephan Palmié and Francisco Scarano (eds.) *The Caribbean: A History of the Region and Its Peoples* (University of Chicago Press), 289–301.

L.A. Pérez (1995) *Cuba: Between Reform & Revolution* (Oxford University Press).

——— (1999) *On Becoming Cuban: Identity, Nationality, & Culture* (Ecco).

T. Prados-Torreira (2005) *Mambisas: Rebel Women in Nineteenth-Century Cuba* (University Press of Florida).

R. Schwartz (1989) *Lawless Liberators: Political Banditry and Cuban Independence* (Duke University Press).

R. Scott (2008) *Degrees of Freedom: Louisiana and Cuba after Slavery* (Belknap).

——— (2000) *Slave Emancipation in Cuba: The Transition to Free Labor, 1860–99* (University of Pittsburgh Press).

K.R. Shaffer (2020) *Anarchists of the Caribbean: Countercultural Politics and Transnational Networks in the Age of US Expansion* (Cambridge University Press).

R. Whitney (2011) "War and Nation Building: Cuban and Dominican Experiences" in Stephan Palmié and Francisco Scarano (eds.) *The Caribbean: A History of the Region and Its Peoples* (University of Chicago Press), 361–72.

CHAPTER 6

Working-Class Resistance and Anti-Imperialism, 1900–World War II

In the first half of the twentieth century, imperial and colonial rule intensified throughout the Caribbean with the United States alone militarily intervening over 20 times from 1898 to the early 1930s. The United States never formally held colonies in the Caribbean, though Washington purchased the Virgin Islands from Denmark in 1917, owned Puerto Rico to this day, and controlled the Panama Canal until 1999. Instead, Washington substituted direct colonial rule with neocolonialist policies. For instance, both the Cuban and Panamanian constitutions allowed the United States to invade whenever Washington decided. More broadly, Spanish-speaking islands, Haiti, and the Caribbean's Central American countries grew dependent on US sugar and fruit corporations. Governments repressed unions and kept workers in poverty so US corporations could export cheap foodstuffs to US markets. In the process, these countries' presidents and the corporations enriched themselves handsomely, forging what came to be known as "Banana Republics." Meanwhile, European governments strengthened their hold on Caribbean colonies such as during the Great War when Caribbean soldiers fought for Great Britain. When the Great Depression spread throughout the region in the 1930s, colonial governments did little to help the masses and then fought working-class efforts to improve their situations.

This chapter explores numerous examples of working-class resistance to this colonialism and neocolonialism in the early 1900s. In Cuba, Puerto Rico and Panama, anarchists challenged governments, capitalists, and growing US control. During the US occupations of Haiti (1915–1934) and the Dominican Republic (1916–1924), rural and urban citizens resisted occupiers and domestic officials with whom they colluded. In Nicaragua, Augusto César Sandino led rebels against the Nicaraguan government and US marines who supported it. In the 1920s, Communists formed anti-imperialist leagues. The UNIA linked peoples of African descent into a movement fighting exploitation. Finally, in the 1920s and 1930s, workers in the British Caribbean—often including men radicalized as soldiers during the Great War—created the first major trade unions to fight for better conditions and self-rule. Ultimately, these were decades of growing popular, working-class mobilization against various forms of colonialism and the capitalist system sustaining them.

TRANSNATIONAL ANARCHISM CONFRONTS US EXPANSION

By the early 1900s, anarchists in Cuba, Florida, Puerto Rico, and Panama challenged local and national power structures and sought to create free, egalitarian societies for all regardless of ethnicity, gender, nationality, or race. These were transnational organizations in which anarchists saw their local and national activism as part of a trans-Caribbean network linked to a larger global movement. The network hub was in Havana with nodes throughout Cuba and reaching to Puerto Rico, Florida, and the Panamanian isthmus, with smaller links to the Mexican Yucatán, Colombia, and Venezuela. Native-born and immigrant anarchists moved across the network to attack political, economic, and military power in the region.

In the early 1900s, anarchists spread around the Caribbean simultaneously with US economic, military, and political expansion. Anarchists challenged labor exploitation and US rule in Puerto Rico beginning in 1899, the 1906–1909 US occupation of Cuba and US neocolonialist policies toward Cuba in general, and labor abuses during construction of the Panama Canal from 1904 to 1914. The canal opened in 1914, and in 1916 anarchists organized canal workers into the multinational, multilingual Maritime Workers Union with members from the Caribbean, South America, and Europe. Multilingual workers from these regions attended rallies and the union printed bilingual manifestoes in Spanish and English to reach West Indian workers: "West Indian Comrades: bear in mind that with *your* cooperation we will be victorious," read one manifesto (quoted in Shaffer 2020, p. 193). Over 1500 marchers paraded through Panama City when the US canal governor refused to negotiate. On 15 October 1916, the anarchist union declared the first general strike against the US canal, and 10,000 workers walked off the job. Many Panamanian police sided with strikers, refusing to prevent protesters from blocking trains taking workers into the Canal Zone to work. Ultimately, US-Panamanian government repression, arrests, and attacks on demonstrators undermined the strike, and the Panamanian government deported radicals from multiple countries.

Six months later, anarchists in Puerto Rico and Cuba confronted different dilemmas related to US control. In April 1917, the United States declared war on Germany. The next day, Cuba did too, implementing a military draft nearly identical to that of Washington. In Puerto Rico, a month earlier, islanders became US citizens and eligible for military service. Caribbean anarchists protested the war, resisted military service, helped workers avoid registering for the draft, organized strikes against US-owned businesses, and took their anti-war campaigns to the cultural realm. Anarchist Adrián del Valle published his novel *Jesús en la guerra* (Jesus in the War) in Havana in 1917 just as Cuba declared war on Germany. The novel portrays Jesus (protected by anarchists) preaching anti-nationalism on Europe's battlefields. Captured by Germans, Kaiser Wilhelm executes Jesus. The execution convinces anarchists that only a violent struggle against all nationalisms could free humanity—exactly what governments in Washington and the Caribbean feared and exactly what anarchists in Puerto Rico began supporting.

By the late 1910s, the debate over Puerto Rico's political status divided people across the island. The Socialist Party (founded in 1915) rejected political independence and instead sought US citizenship for Puerto Ricans. Anarchists rejected both US colonialism and an emerging independence movement, arguing that even if Washington granted independence to Puerto Rico, it would be an independence ruled by capitalists who would exploit the island's masses. Inspired by Russian Bolsheviks, anarchists called for a proletarian revolution against US and Puerto Rican capitalism first, and then the new revolutionary society would fight for political independence from Washington.

Anarchist women joined the fray. In Cuba and Puerto Rico, women organized and led Sunday evening gatherings where anarchists gave speeches and women led in singing radical songs and staging revolutionary plays. Women taught in anarchist schools and supported strikers both on picket lines and from their kitchens. Like men, they faced all the dangers of imprisonment and deportation. When governments deported women's partners, they faced the daunting prospects of raising children alone.

The Puerto Rico-born Luisa Capetillo advocated for men and women living together in free union instead of state- or church-sanctified matrimony. She promoted both women's and workers' issues, which to here were inseparable. As an activist in the Puerto Rican Free Federation of Labor, she led campaigns against US-owned tobacco corporations on the island. In New York, Florida and Cuba, she wrote, spoke, and organized workers against capitalism and US expansion. By 1917, she and other women led or participated in labor strikes across Puerto Rico such as a dockworkers' strike in Puerta de Tierra, where police shot indiscriminately into the crowd. Several leftist women fought back with the only weapon at their disposal: hatpins, which they stabbed repeatedly into police horses, which reared and threw off their baton-wielding, pistol-shooting cops.

Caribbean anarchists also attacked US militarism. They condemned US hypocrisy, noting that Washington defended freedom and democracy during the Great War, but afterward the United States undermined Caribbean democracy. US policy turned countries into US economic colonies ruled by dictators who repressed workers so US corporations could exploit cheap labor and gain immense profits. Case in point was Cuba in the 1920s. Anarchists portrayed the island as an American corporate feudal estate. The Gerardo Machado dictatorship unleashed unprecedented repression in 1925—jailing, deporting, and assassinating leftists. Such actions, one anarchist wrote, showed how Machado and his enforcers were "the servants of the industrial fortresses that Wall Street established in this colony of *Yanquilandia*" (quoted in Shaffer 2020, p. 211). When a government could not stop working peoples' resistance, Washington intervened like in 1917 when the US military invaded Cuba during a wave of labor strikes or in 1925 when the US military entered Panama from the Canal Zone to put down a rent strike led by leftists.

Caribbean anarchists fought battles on numerous local and national fronts, but they also had to confront US imperial expansion. Anarchists saw through the charades of "democracy," "independence," "making the world safe for democracy," and other empty words and phrases. As a result, anarchists resisted the United States and struggled to create a Caribbean free from the reach of *Yanquilandia*.

RESISTING US IMPERIALISM IN HAITI, 1915–1934

In the late 1800s, European governments began using their navies to collect debts owed to Europeans. Washington tried to prevent European interference in Caribbean affairs by militarily intervening in indebted countries, establishing receiverships to collect money owed to Europeans, and then paying the debts. By 1915, European creditors were demanding payments from Haiti. At the same time, the population revolted against Haitian president Vilburn Guillaume Sam. When Sam ordered the execution of nearly 170 political prisoners, the masses chased him into the French embassy. The next day, they drug him out of the embassy grounds and tore apart his body. The political and economic turmoil threatened Washington's desire for a stable region to conduct trade but also to preserve the eastern entrance to the Panama Canal that opened the previous year. President Wilson—with one eye on the growing conflagration in Europe and another in his own backyard—also feared instability might allow Germany to infiltrate Haiti. These factors led Wilson to send US marines to occupy Port-au-Prince. Later that year, Haiti's Congress chose Philippe Sudré Dartiguenave as president. Occupation forces issued Dartiguenave an ultimatum: accept a new treaty with Washington or US marines would establish a military government. The treaty allowed the United States to collect debts, create a new police force under US command, and do anything necessary to "protect" Haitian independence, life, liberty, and property. After the Haitian Congress rejected a new constitution, marines put it to a vote among the largely illiterate population who deposited color ballots in voting boxes guarded by US marines. The constitution passed.

Such heavy-handed tactics violating Haitian sovereignty, along with new measures creating a forced labor system, generated immense resentment. Urban youth and media criticized the occupation, workers declared strikes, and students demonstrated. Haitians cast insults upon marines or met occupiers with stares and silence, refusing to cooperate. In the north, peasants, landowners, and elements of the disbanded Haitian army took up arms and formed *cacos*—private militias of poor peasants against the occupation. True to the historic transborder nature of resistance on Hispaniola, they acquired most of their arms from the Dominican Republic. However, this initial armed resistance was ineffective; no marines were even harmed.

By 1918, a landowner and demobilized army officer—Charlemagne Péralte—led a new caco guerrilla army. In his call to arms, Péralte declared to the US minister that "we reclaim our rights ... ignored by the unscrupulous Americans, who by destroying our institutions deprive the people of Haiti of all its resources and devour our name and our blood .... We demand the liberation of our territory and all the advantages given to free and independent states by international law .... We are prepared to sacrifice everything to liberate Haiti, and establish here the principles affirmed by President Wilson himself: the rights and sovereignty of small nations." To fellow Haitians, Péralte declared that "the people are poor, and the Occupation still oppresses us with taxes. It spreads fires and forbids us to rebuild wooden houses under the pretext of keeping the city beautiful .... Let's get rid of those savage people, whose beastly character is evident in the person of their President Wilson—traitor, bandit, troublemaker, and thief" (quoted in *Bandits or Patriots*).

The occupation government's economic program of roadbuilding and public works projects included the despised *corvée* system where people paid taxes to support construction. However, because most poor Haitians could not pay, they had to work it off. This forced labor system led 15,000 people to flee their homes and join the cacos in mountain hideouts where maroons had also escaped to in the 1700s. Cacos fought the marines for two years, communicating in the maroons' traditional ways through drumming and blowing conch shells. People joined Péralte for different reasons. Certainly, the corvée system ranked high in their motivations, but they also saw Péralte standing up for their rights, fighting political corruption, and opposing the US-created police force's brutality. Péralte also let them plunder estates and offered protection for those who refused to cooperate with authorities. In 1919, Péralte formed a provisional government to challenge the occupation government. However, in November, marines killed Péralte, and his successor died the following year.

Marines and Haitian police continued tortures and executions, destroyed property, forced people into concentration camps, and raped women. By 1927, US owners had taken over 43,000 acres of land. People resisted the abuses. Some tried to fight off the illegal transfer of their land to US buyers. For instance, someone burned aerial photos of a US-backed dam and irrigation project. Other Haitians fled the island to work in Cuba's expanding sugarcane plantations where they earned far more than in Haiti, enabling them to send money home to relatives. Vodou practitioners fought for the religion's survival against occupation efforts to eliminate it. Since 1915, new musical styles like US jazz and Cuban son had entered Haiti. Haitian musicians adopted these genres, Haitianized them, and created new rhythms with Haitian instruments and lyrics speaking to Haitian reality. Such musical opposition to the occupation could be heard during Carnival when bands performed anti-American songs. Meanwhile, Haiti's elite led a conservative resistance to the occupation. Poets promoted pure French poetry to stop the influx of American English words and phrases. The elite also resisted US attempts to create technical training schools, seeing them as "African American" and "black" and thus "backward" in their eyes.

In the United States, politicians, Garvey's (Universal Negro Improvement Association) UNIA, the NAACP, Marxists, and anarchists formed transnational, anti-imperialist campaigns that attacked US military interventionism in Haiti. Ultimately, a combination of armed resistance, protest, and transnational activism forced the United States to withdraw. However, the occupation radically changed Haiti's economy. Now, US sugar corporations transformed Haitian agriculture into something not seen since the Haitian Revolution: largescale, export-oriented, foreign-owned sugar plantations.

Resisting US Imperialism in the Dominican Republic, 1916–1924

The eastern side of Hispaniola fared little better when the United States invaded the Dominican Republic in 1916—only nine months after invading Haiti. US intervention was nothing new. Washington invaded in 1905 to establish a receivership for international debt payments. In 1912, Washington invaded following the assassination of the Dominican president. In 1914, President Wilson forced the resignation of a president that Washington hated; and then in 1915, the United States again demanded greater control of the country's finances to pay off growing debt burdens. President Juan Isidro Jiménez accepted this new demand and another that led to creation of a new rural police force (or constabulary) under US control. In December 1916, Dominicans revolted. Washington responded by invading, replacing the Dominican government with one run by the US navy.

As Ellen Tillman puts it, "Dominican resistance to the imposed military presence was a foregone conclusion" (Tillman 2016, p. 77). Opposition spread far and wide. Abroad, émigrés—especially in Cuba—publicly protested and raised funds for their homeland's liberation while Dominican diplomats asked London to intervene. On the island, many former rural policemen attacked the new constabulary. Other Dominicans protested the loss of sovereignty, American paternalism, and the occupation forces' racism that treated almost all Dominicans as "black" even though few Dominicans—no matter how dark their skin—considered themselves "black" since they associated the term with poverty, backwardness, and "Haitian."

Additional factors contributed to the opposition. Throughout history, Dominicans had resisted central governments in Santo Domingo. In fact, the United States intervened during a civil war between regionalists and centralists. The United States wanted a strong central government administered by the navy. The navy did not help its cause when it issued an island-wide disarmament order. Rural male masculine identity often centered around guns, so this was a cultural affront. While many surrendered their weapons, apparently they gave up old, often-unusable relics and kept the good stuff, continuing their resistance to Santo Domingo.

Throughout the north and in the Samaná peninsula, armed resistance coincided with anti-US/anti-Santo Domingo publications, speeches, meetings, and sabotage. People deserted the constabulary by the droves—some out of conscience, some because local merchants refused to cash constabulary checks, and others because opposition newspapers published their names as collaborators, and thus they faced ostracism or even death. Meanwhile, guerrilla groups in Haiti and the Dominican Republic cooperated against simultaneous US occupations. One teenager—Gregorio Urbano Gilbert—could not go to Haiti to join the cacos. Instead, he took a pistol, strolled to a group of lounging marines, and opened fire, shouting "Long Live the Dominican Republic" (quoted in Tillman 2016, p. 105).

Marines crushed this initial challenge, but a new resistance emerged from 1918 to 1922 following numerous abuses, including torture, land grabs, modernization efforts that insulted the middle and upper classes, taxes, and more. The best-known opponents were the *gavilleros* (gunmen), who roamed the island since around 1900 and often worked with local leaders to resist centralized control. Gavillero violence surged in response to US marines overseeing local affairs, occupation campaigns to disarm the rural population, and marine racism against local populations. In 1921, Dominicans protested the occupation by shouting "Eradicate the White Blood of the Republic," that is, the US occupiers (quoted in Dubois and Turits 2019, p. 173). Gunmen attacked plantations, demanded ransom, sabotaged railroads to prevent movement of marines, and cut telegraph lines. In response to land grabs, rebels burned land titles and submitted forgeries to gain title to land. They also resisted efforts to enclose and fence lands that undermined the tradition of communal cattle raising on open pastures.

Other sectors of Dominican society resisted occupation. Dominican elites wore only European fashion to avoid styles from the United States. The elite opposed the arrival of US popular culture and despised US dances like the foxtrot. A strong morality mixed with anti-imperialist feelings led many to see American dances and movies as promoting sexuality that threatened Dominican women. In education, elites and the middle class challenged attempts by the military government to reconfigure the education system along US lines as Americans had done in Haiti, Puerto Rico, and Cuba.

An international coalition of leftists, the UNIA, the NAACP and other US-based groups protested the occupation as they did the Haitian one. Meanwhile, in the early 1920s, the Dominican labor movement grew and blamed the occupation for a faltering economy. Labor leader Eugenio Kunhardt attempted to assassinate an occupation-friendly provincial governor. In the countryside, Ramón Nateras' armed guerrillas fought US marines and the constabulary, aided by cross-border assistance from Haiti. By 1924, the United States had enough, and US president Harding—himself critical of the occupation—withdrew the marines.

CARIBBEAN ANTI-IMPERIALIST LEAGUES IN THE 1920s AND 1930s

Communist parties emerged across the Caribbean in the 1920s and 1930s. Within two years of the 1917 Bolshevik victory in Russia, the Communist International (aka, the Comintern) formed to foment world revolution. As part of its strategy, it helped emerging Caribbean Communists organize anti-imperialist movements to challenge US expansionism. Both Mexico City and New York City became sites for Caribbean Marxists to organize and communicate with one another. Two examples are illuminating: Cuba linked to Mexico City and Puerto Rico linked to New York City.

Activists like Julio Antonio Mella formed the Partido Comunista Cubano (Cuban Communist Party, or PCC) in 1925. The PCC advocated a radical anti-imperialist nationalism that opposed President Geraldo Machado and US allies who propped him up. "Nationalism" was not always a "radical" position though. Machado called himself a "Cuban nationalist" by repressing radical labor unions to keep the United States from invading. Some nationalists worked peacefully to oppose Machado. For Mella, though, the real liberating nationalists were those "who respond to violence with violence. Included in this last group are nationalist university students; the other important movement is the workers" (quoted in Whitney 2001, p. 51).

Machado's government arrested, deported, and killed numerous leftists. For his part, Mella fled into exile. After radical organizing in Guatemala, he went to Mexico City, working with other exiled Cuban radicals. In 1928, Mella founded the Asociación de Nuevos Emigrados Revolucionarios Cubanos (Association of New Cuban Revolutionary Emigrants, or ANERC), a transnational anti-imperialist organization of anarchists and Marxists. Mella used ANERC to rally support for an exile invasion of Cuba to overthrow Machado and beat back US expansion. However, in January 1929, one of Machado's thugs assassinated Mella in the streets of Mexico City.

The transnational anti-imperialism of early Caribbean Communists also existed in links between Puerto Rico and New York City. The Comintern established the Caribbean Bureau in New York in 1930 to coordinate Caribbean Communist organizations with the American Communist Party (CPUSA). The CPUSA was based in New York, where Puerto Ricans had increasingly migrated after being granted US citizenship in 1917. Numerous Puerto Rican leftists circularly migrated between the city and the island over the years. In 1934, islanders organized the Puerto Rican Communist Party, solidifying relations with the CPUSA.

Transnational Radical Support for Sandino's Anti-Imperialism

Communist-inspired transnational solidarity connected Caribbean leftists with Augusto César Sandino in Nicaragua. US marines had left Nicaragua in August 1925, only to return in May 1926 to suppress a Mexican-armed Liberal Party uprising against the Conservative government. Though marines soon withdrew, they returned in January 1927 supposedly to protect US citizens and property. Liberals and Conservatives signed a new peace treaty that May, but one Liberal general—Sandino—refused to sign and led a new uprising.

Working with anarchists in Mexico's coastal oil fields in the 1920s radicalized Sandino. He returned to Nicaragua, infused with a hatred of the Conservative government, the United States, which backed it, and US companies. While US foreign investment paled in comparison to Cuba, Haiti, Mexico, the Dominican Republic, or the Panama Canal, US corporations owned large agricultural plantations and mines in Nicaragua. Sandino attacked them all, prompting the government, Washington, and the companies to label him a "bandit." "We," Sandino replied, "in our own house, are fighting for our inalienable rights. What right have foreign troops to call us outlaws and bandits, and to say that we are the aggressors? …. We declare that we will never live in cowardly peace under a government installed by a foreign Power …. And when the invader is vanquished, as some day he must be, my men will be content with their plots of ground, their tools, their mules, and their families" (quoted in Latin America and the United States 2011, p. 128). For six years, he fought Nicaraguan and US troops—the latter of which attacked with airplanes.

An array of Caribbean leftist networks aided his resistance. In Mexico City, Mella's Liga Antiimperialista de las Américas (Anti-Imperialist League of the Americas) led the transnational "Hands Off Nicaragua" campaign supporting Sandino's armed resistance. The Comintern's Caribbean Bureau coordinated Caribbean Marxists aiding Sandino. Supporters from Mexico, Colombia, and the Dominican Republic (a group known as the Latin American Legion) took up arms and joined Sandino in Nicaragua. Until his assassination in 1934, Sandino responded to this internationalist support by calling for an Indo-Latin American Continental and Antillean Confederation to stand up to Washington.

Transnational Resistance in Imperial Black Contact Zones: Central America and Cuba

In the first decades of the twentieth century, numerous West Indians migrated to London, New York, and Paris. They also migrated for work in US neocolonial countries like Cuba and Panama. Winston James calls these sites "black contact zones" where "people of African descent from different geographic spaces met, interacted, and commingled with one another, often for the first time" (James 2011, p. 450). On the canal and plantations, workers resisted the racist and poor workplace conditions they encountered. Sometimes they appealed to colonial officials as when West Indian workers beseeched British consuls for protection from US employer abuse. In 1916, West Indians joined the Canal Zone strike discussed earlier. In 1920, Barbadian labor leader William Stoute organized a violently repressed strike of West Indians in Panama that brought together Caribbean veterans returning from the battlefields of Europe, West Indian workers, and a growing sense of black nationalism. Meanwhile, the UNIA spread throughout the greater Caribbean, uniting peoples of African descent from around the region who found themselves working side by side in Cuba and Panama.

Transnational Resistance in Imperial Black Contact Zones: The Great War and at Home

The Great War from 1914 to 1918 served as an imperial black contact zone shaping racial and working-class militancy. The war reached into the British Caribbean in different ways. For instance, by 1916, Great Britain stopped importing Asian indentured workers partly due to colonial opposition but also because London needed all the ships it could muster for war. Meanwhile, nearly 16,000 West Indians served in the British West Indies Regiment in the Middle East, Italy, France, and East Africa. The war brought together West Indians from around the colonies, making these fronts into new black contact zones. Rarely, though, were BWIR soldiers given guns to fight, and always they served under white officers. Caribbean soldiers largely served in support positions such as digging ditches for trench warfare or carrying and loading explosives.

When war ended in November 1918, BWIR soldiers increasingly realized that white and black troops did not equally share the tasks of demobilization. Black soldiers performed the hardest tasks and received less pay than whites. On 6 December 1918, some in the BWIR revolted, assaulted officers, and planted at least one bomb. Though quickly crushed, rebel soldiers soon formed the Caribbean League, calling for black self-rule in the Caribbean by any means necessary.

When veterans returned home to the Caribbean in 1919, they brought with them an intensifying black, working-class radicalism forged during the war years. In 1897, Trinidadians had organized the Trinidad Workingmen's Association—a middle-class and working-class alliance first headed by Walter Mills, a mixed-race pharmacist. Until 1919, the TWA had little success. However, radicalized veterans returned to Trinidad and joined the TWA, causing a split in union ranks between those pushing constitutional reforms and those pursuing black nationalist, working-class agendas. Increasingly, black consciousness newspapers like Marcus Garvey's *Negro World* circulated among sailors and dockworkers. From October to December 1919, Trinidadian dockworkers—many of whose leaders were UNIA members—declared a strike, forcing employers to grant an eight-hour workday, overtime pay, and higher wages. UNIA influence ran high among TWA radicals, and speakers at strike meetings read Garvey's editorials. At the same time, East Indians increasingly joined the strike, and for one of the first times, workers of Asian and African descent forged a temporary united front. As Kelvin Singh concludes, "objectively the unrest had taken on a trans-ethnic working-class character" (Singh 1994, p. 31). However, unity was short-lived as a strong black consciousness orientation soon dominated West Indian labor movements.

The Trinidadian labor unrest of 1919 was also a transnational affair. Much of the TWA leadership came from other British colonies. Migrant women from British Guiana, Jamaica, and Barbados held leadership positions in the 1919–1920 Trinidad protests. Albertha Husbands from Barbados led the TWA's domestic workers in the 1919 strike while serving as vice president in the women's branch of the UNIA. Elma Constance Francois migrated to Trinidad from St. Vincent in 1917. She joined the TWA, rising to a leadership role. By the 1930s, she dedicated herself to interlocking issues of racism, sexism, nationalism, and capitalist exploitation.

Labor actions spread around the Caribbean. For instance, returning veterans rebelled in British Honduras. A strong UNIA presence shaped one of the main leaders—S.A. Haynes—a Garveyite who soon moved to the United States and became a UNIA official. Throughout the 1920s, the UNIA shaped working-class Antilleans at home and abroad where "the UNIA often performed the function of a quasi-political party as well as mutual aid organization" (Martin 1993, p. 360). Strikes spread to Jamaica, the Bahamas, St. Lucia, Anguilla, Tortola, St. Kitts, and British Guiana between 1920 and 1924. The veterans' black consciousness, working-class uprisings found transnational favor in the words of Marcus Garvey, who after the war had called on Europe to decolonize the African world and return rule to African peoples. For some, this meant the Caribbean too, leading to new calls for black majority self-rule.

ORGANIZED LABOR AND RESISTANCE TO BRITISH RULE

Compared to the Spanish-speaking Caribbean, organized labor was weak or nonexistent in the British, French, and Dutch West Indies in the early 1900s. As O. Nigel Bolland points out, whereas working-class organizations in Spanish-speaking lands created labor unrest, British Caribbean "trade unions were generally the result, rather than the source, of the labor protests and rebellions" (Bolland 2011, p. 462). Workers sporadically organized in the British colonies: the Trinidad-based TWA or Herbert Critchlow's British Guiana Labor Union in 1919. However, not until the 1930s did West Indians begin forging substantive labor unions.

The Great Depression sparked labor organizing in British colonies. Workers responded to growing unemployment, wage reductions, and no government safety net by mobilizing to safeguard their rights, improve working and living conditions, and develop a new political consciousness. In 1933, several unemployed workers in Trinidad staged the first of many regionwide labor disturbances. In 1934 and 1935, workers struck sugar industries in British Guiana and Trinidad. In Trinidad, black and Indian women sugar workers led militants. In British Honduras, the Unemployed Brigade marched to protest unemployment, poverty, and housing shortages. In January 1935, a recently formed Workers' League on St. Kitts launched a general strike. Hundreds of workers refused to plant sugarcane and attacked a plantation with heavy sticks and stones. That October, workers on St. Vincent—outraged by the increasingly unaffordable state of life on the island—took to the streets protesting high prices, especially on imported goods. Average men and women rose to leadership roles. Bertha Mutt led demonstrators, as did a man who took the name "Selassie" and a woman named "Mother Selassie" after the recently crowned Ethiopian leader—a development reflecting the growing link between black consciousness and working-class organizing. Demonstrators forced their way into St. Vincent's Town Council, assaulted the governor, ransacked neighboring businesses, freed local prisoners, cut telephone wires, and destroyed bridges to hamper arrival of police and militias. In 1935, coal loaders in St. Lucia went on strike. On May Day 1937, Clement Payne issued the first May Day propaganda in Barbados, hoping to create a trade union movement. Though colonial governments suppressed these challenges, British authorities increasingly feared what they symbolized: masses of workers mobilizing against colonial capitalism at a time when Britain also faced nationalist challenges to its rule in Ireland and India and the growing threat from fascism in Germany and Italy. The empire was threatened both from without and within.

Trinidad 1937

Oil dominated Trinidad and Tobago's economy. Oil workers received the highest pay on the island, but even they suffered when cost of living outpaced wages. Oil workers also faced job insecurity and lack of transportation between homes and refineries. They likewise complained about white privilege in an industry where most managers were white, with many coming from apartheid-era South Africa. If oil workers struggled, one can imagine the difficulties for lower-paid workers in other industries.

After the 1919 strike, the TWA became the Trinidad Labor Party, but party politics seemed incapable of solving workers' dilemmas. Then, Grenadian migrant and BWIR veteran Uriah Butler arrived. Butler was an oil worker, but after being injured, he became a Baptist minister. Butler preached a volatile concoction of working-class politics, black nationalism, and radical Baptist invective. In 1936, he formed the British Empire Workers and Citizens Home Rule Party—an organization dominated by workers of African and Indian descent in oil and sugar. Over the next year, he spoke across the island, launching petitions demanding better pay in all sectors, unemployment benefits, a moratorium on taxes, promotion of nonwhites to managerial positions, and self-rule by the colony's nonwhite majority. Butler forged a relationship with East Indian lawyer Adrian Cola Rienzi, who worked for East Indian rights in

Trinidad and had a record of uniting African and Asian descended sugar workers. Rienzi was a transnational radical, having returned to Trinidad in 1934
after working with the Irish Sinn Fein and the Indian Nationalist Movement—
two leading anti-British organizations.

From 1935 to 1937, Butler spoke and wrote in support of Trinidad's workers, arguing that worker mistreatment was un-British and unconstitutional.
Referring to the crown, corporations and the colony's governor, Butler,
declared in a speech that "It is the Fascist Imperialist Band that is sinking us
into slavery. They are the enemies of the British Constitution in Trinidad."
Butler claimed his followers were prepared to revolt, armed "with the British
Constitution and under the Union Jack to move manfully forward to kill or be
killed in their fight for the enjoyment of the fullest constitutional rights and
privileges" (quoted in Jacobs 1987, pp. 368, 376). On 19 June 1937, Butler
led oilfield workers on strike.

Working-class women from across the island attended meetings on the eve
of the June uprising. Once protests began, Butler told them to return home to
serve mainly support roles for strikers. Yet, while Butler believed women's roles
in the uprising should be domestically supportive (i.e., bring food to the men),
Butlerite women had other ideas, and participated in strikes, marches, and even
violence. In response to strikers' demands, oil companies pressured the government to ban meetings and arrest Butler. As officers grabbed Butler one day,
workers rushed to help him escape. The crowd set upon one of the arresting
officers—Corporal Charles King—and beat him. Then, Butlerite women took
over. Locals hated King, accusing him of framing men and then raping their
women partners. When King fled the angry mob, he jumped out a window and
broke his legs. As he lay unable to move, a group of women approached,
doused him with fuel, and set him alight. He burned to death before help
arrived. In response, the government mobilized more troops to pacify
the region.

Yet, the strike spread. Within days, workers across Trinidad's oil fields
declared strikes. Workers from outside the area arrived in buses to support
strikers, block roads, attack stores, impede trains full of sugarcane, and close
plantations. Encouraged and emboldened, sugar and oil workers armed with
guns, axes, machetes, and stones attacked the phone exchange, cut phone lines,
and fired on police patrols. On 22 June 1937, the violence reached Port of
Spain. There, the Communist-inspired Negro Welfare Cultural and Social
Association (NWCSA)—which merged racial consciousness and working-class
issues—paraded throughout the city, closing shops, and attacking the railroad
yard before troops forced them back. NWCSA women like St. Vincent-born
Elma Francois led or participated in strike actions across the island. Authorities
arrested Francois and tried her for sedition. After giving an impassioned speech
in her defense, the jury acquitted her.

Eventually, dockworkers, public works laborers, factory workers, and bus
drivers joined the strike. In Tobago, workers joined their Trinidad compatriots.
As Singh notes, the strike—while more spontaneous than planned—"had cut

across the barriers of race within the working-class population and was affecting every major sector of the economy" (Singh 1987, p. 66). However, protestors lacked a centralized labor organization to coordinate labor actions. Ultimately, the government used its strong centralized force of arms and military personnel to crush strikers.

JAMAICA 1938

Depression-era privations also rocked Jamaica's peasantry and working class. Yet here another factor contributed to the masses' growing radicalization. For decades, Jamaicans traveled to work in Cuba's expanding sugarcane fields where Cuban police and Rural Guardsmen tormented them with impunity. When protestors challenged this treatment, plantation officials evicted them. West Indians fought back against this racist and nationalist violence. They appealed to colonial officials, but often with few results. They then wrote letters to newspapers highlighting Cuban mistreatment of British war veterans and colonial officials' unwillingness to assist British subjects. They formed mutual aid societies and self-reliance initiatives to resist abuse. However, the Great Depression in Cuba forced thousands of laborers and their families to return to Jamaica—a move exasperating already intense unemployment and contributing to growing unrest. As contemporary observer Arthur Lewis suggested, these repatriated Jamaicans, whose worldview had expanded due to their experiences in the radicalized cane fields in Cuba, were "quicker to protest against bad conditions" (Lewis 1993, p. 383).

Before 1938, a few small unions existed to channel some of this energy, but nothing island wide or spanning the array of occupations. Then, in April 1938, construction workers rebelled. Dock, transportation, and public works laborers in Kingston launched sympathy strikes in May. Strike actions spread across Jamaica, penetrating the sugar and fruit exporting sectors while the colonial government mobilized troops to suppress them. If authorities thought they could crush this surge of radicalized workers, they were woefully mistaken. On 21 May 1938, a waterfront workers-led general strike swept across Jamaica. Over the coming days, demonstrators paraded through streets, threatened store owners to close or face violence, attacked trolleys, blocked streets, and brought the economy to a halt for nearly three weeks. Women threw projectiles during marches and, as it turned out, were the main victims when police fired into crowds. Violence resulted in the Moyne Commission inquiry into the Jamaican disturbances particularly and larger labor unrest in the British Caribbean generally. Moyne recommended new laws to protect labor unions, new workplace regulations, social welfare benefits, universal adult suffrage, and self-rule.

Two key figures emerged from the Jamaican labor rebellion: Alexander Bustamante and Norman Manley. Bustamante organized mass meetings on strikers' behalf. Authorities arrested him as a seditious agitator and inciter of riots. Manley—a lawyer and Bustamante's distant cousin—defended Bustamante while offering to negotiate with officials and employers on behalf of strikers. For a time, the two men worked together. Bustamante formed the Bustamante Industrial Trade Union—the largest of its kind in Jamaican history, uniting skilled and unskilled laborers and strengthening the hand of Afro-Jamaican workers against employers. Meanwhile, Manley formed the People's National Party that by 1940 adopted a democratic socialist platform and at first served as the political wing of Bustamante's union. However, by 1942, the two split and Bustamante formed the Jamaican Labour Party. By the end of World War II, Jamaica had two working-class political parties that became key in transitioning the island from campaigns for self-rule to independence in 1962. As Arthur Lewis wrote in the immediate wake of the 1938 violence, the Jamaican masses gained two things: "the rise of trade unions, and the entry of the working classes into West Indian politics" (Lewis 1993, p. 386).

Conclusion

Working-class mobilization in the early twentieth century challenged not only working conditions and low wages around the Caribbean but also political systems that perpetuated colonial and neocolonial capitalist exploitation. Barry Carr has called these "The Red Years of the Caribbean and Central America" (Carr 2012, p. 233). "Red" as in "socialist" primarily, but one could also think of the Spanish meaning of the word "red:" network. Transnational networks linking working-class radicals against colonial and imperial capitalism spanned the Caribbean. Anarchists fought US expansion, exploitation in Banana Republics, conditions on the Panama Canal, and more. Workers in Haiti and the Dominican Republic challenged US marines occupying their countries while aiding one another across Hispaniola's political border. By the 1920s and 1930s, the USSR developed relations with Communists in the Western Hemisphere. The Comintern's Caribbean Bureau linked Marxist organizations around the region with headquarters in New York City, where Caribbean migrants increasing moved and interacted.

As US neocolonialism spread across the Caribbean from Cuba and Puerto Rico in the east to Central America in the west, West Indians migrated in large numbers to work on the canal or on sugar and fruit plantations. In these black contact zones—along with another in the war trenches of Europe—West Indians from different places met, shared experiences, and developed black, working-class identities. They took these transnational identities with them as they journeyed around the Caribbean where labor uprisings triggered new attacks against British colonial capitalism after the Great War and during the Great Depression. Colonial government repression of these movements provoked "people to question the legitimacy of the colonial system that defended injustices" (Bolland 2011, p. 461). Thus, as racial and class consciousness grew in the minds of the British colonial masses, they also began questioning colonial rule.

Throughout the region, women played important roles in these labor-based, anti-colonial actions. From support roles to leadership roles, female activists sometimes adopted traditional feminine household roles like cooking for demonstrators and strikers. They also left the private sphere of the household and engaged in political activity in the streets. As Rhoda Reddock concludes, "the anti-colonial struggle was at the same time a class struggle and a nationalist struggle, and within this broad variegation, women workers, housewives, self-employed and unemployed women found a place" (Reddock 1987, p. 236).

WORKS CITED AND FURTHER REFERENCES

G. Averill (1997) *A Day for the Hunter. A Day for the Prey* (University of Chicago Press).

Bandits or Patriots?: Documents from Charlemagne Péralte http://historymatters. gmu.edu/d/4946

O.N. Bolland (2011) "Labor Protests, Rebellions, and the Rise of Nationalism during Depression and War" in Stephan Palmié and Francisco Scarano (eds.) *The Caribbean: A History of the Region and Its Peoples* (University of Chicago Press), 459–74.

――― (2001) *The Politics of Labour in the British Caribbean* (Ian Randle/ Marcus Wiener).

L. Braithwaite (1987) "Introduction" in Roy Thomas (ed.) *The Trinidad Labour Riots of 1937.* (University of the West Indies, St. Augustine Press), 1–20.

B. Carr (2012) "'Across Seas and Borders': Charting the Webs of Radical Internationalism in the Circum-Caribbean, 1918–1940" in Luis Roniger, James N. Green and Pablo Yankelevich, (eds.) *Exile and the Politics of Exclusion in the Americas* (Sussex Academic), 217–41.

J. Casanovas (1998) *Bread, or Bullets!: Urban Labor and Spanish Colonialism in Cuba, 1850–1898* (University of Pittsburgh Press).

L. Dubois and R.L. Turits (2019) *Freedom Roots: Histories from the Caribbean* (University of North Carolina Press).

J. Franks (1995) "The *Gavilleros* of the East: Social Banditry as Political Practice in the Dominican Sugar-Growing Region, 1900–1924," *Journal of Historical Sociology*, 8/2, 158–81.

J.L. Giovannetti-Torres (2018) *Black British Migrants in Cuba: Race, Labor, and Empire in the Twentieth-Century Caribbean, 1898–1948* (Cambridge University Press).

R. Hart (1993) "Labour Rebellions of the 1930s" in Hilary Beckles & Verene Shepherd (eds.) *Caribbean Freedom: Society and Economy from Emancipation to the Present* (Ian Randle), 370–75.

G. Heuman (2014). *The Caribbean: A Brief History* 2nd edition (Bloomsbury).

R. Jacobs (1987) "The 1937 Sedition Charge against Butler" in Roy Thomas, (ed.) *The Trinidad Labour Riots of 1937* (University of the West Indies, St. Augustine Press), 367–90.

W. James (2011) "Culture, Labor, and Race in the Shadow of US Capital" in Stephan Palmié and Francisco Scarano (eds.) *The Caribbean: A History of the Region and Its Peoples* (University of Chicago Press), 445–58.

――― (1998) *Holding Aloft the Banner of Ethiopia: Caribbean Radicalism in Early Twentieth Century America* (Verso).

Latin America and the United States: A Documentary History (2011) R.H. Holden and E. Zolov (eds.) (Oxford University Press).

A. Lewis (1993) "The 1930s Social Revolution" in Hilary Beckles & Verene Shepherd (eds.) *Caribbean Freedom: Society and Economy from Emancipation to the Present* (Ian Randle, 376–92).

T. Martin (1993) "Marcus Garvey, the Caribbean, and the Struggle for Black Jamaican Nationhood" in Hilary Beckles & Verene Shepherd (eds.) *Caribbean Freedom: Society and Economy from Emancipation to the Present* (Ian Randle), 359–69.

A. McPherson (2016) *The Invaded* (Oxford University Press).

R. Reddock (1987) "The Women in Revolt" in Roy Thomas (ed.) *The Trinidad Labour Riots of 1937* (University of the West Indies, St. Augustine Press), 233–64.

B. Samaroo (1987) "Precursor to 1937" in Roy Thomas (ed.) *The Trinidad Labour Riots of 1937.* (University of the West Indies, St. Augustine Press), 21–56.

H. Schmidt (1995) *The United States Occupation of Haiti, 1915–1934* (Rutgers University Press).

K.R. Shaffer (2020) *Anarchists of the Caribbean: Countercultural Politics and Transnational Networks in the Age of US Expansion* (Cambridge University Press).

―――― (2013/2020) *Black Flag Boricuas: Anarchism, Antiauthoritarianism, and the Left in Puerto Rico, 1897–1921* (University of Illinois Press).

K. Singh (1987) "June 1937 Disturbances" in Roy Thomas (ed.) *The Trinidad Labour Riots of 1937* (University of the West Indies, St. Augustine Press), 57–80

―――― (1994) *Race and Class Struggles in a Colonial State: Trinidad, 1917–1945* (University of Calgary Press).

E. Tillman (2016) *Dollar Diplomacy by Force: Nation-Building and Resistance in the Dominican Republic* (University of North Carolina Press).

M.-R. Trouillot (1990) *Haiti: State against Nation* (Monthly Review). *Voices of Women in Jamaica, 1898–1939* (1993) Linette Vasse (ed.) (University of the West Indies Press).

R. Whitney (2001) *State and Revolution in Cuba: Mass Mobilization and Political Change, 1920–1940* (University of North Carolina Press).

―――― (2011) "War and Nation Building: Cuban and Dominican Experiences" in Stephan Palmié and Francisco Scarano (eds.) *The Caribbean: A History of the Region and Its Peoples* (University of Chicago Press), 361–72.

J.A. Zumoff (2013) "Black Caribbean Labor Radicalism in Panama, 1914–1921," *Journal of Social History*, 47/2, 429–57.

CHAPTER 7

Fighting Tyranny, Colonialism, and Imperialism at Mid-Century

By the mid-twentieth century, the Caribbean remained the center of colonialism and neocolonialism in the Western Hemisphere. In the 1930s, the United States stopped using direct military intervention in the region. However, through political influence, economic domination and cultural penetration, Washington maintained considerable control. Nevertheless, popular resistance emerged against US influence and US-backed dictators in Cuba and the Dominican Republic. In the late 1940s, Caribbean exiles and opponents of authoritarianism formed the Caribbean Legion—an armed transnational force attacking dictatorships. In the 1950s, armed Puerto Rican nationalists attacked US military and political targets on the island and in Washington. Meanwhile, the French West Indies transitioned from colonies to *départments*, giving the French Caribbean representation in Paris. However, discontent with this change led to demands for autonomy and even independence by the 1960s, with armed groups emerging in the 1970s. London avoided large-scale violence by gradually awarding self-rule and then independence to its larger colonies—a move celebrated by nationalists but then mocked for the lingering neocolonialism that followed. Finally, violent uprisings in Curaçao in 1969 ushered in new relationships between the Netherlands and Dutch Caribbean possessions.

Resisting Dictators: Machado in Cuba

By 1925, the United States had politically dominated Cuba for over two decades via the Platt Amendment to the Cuban Constitution. Sugar exports to the United States and US investment in utilities, transportation, and tourism firmly tied Cuba's economy to the United States more than ever. Meanwhile, working people saw little benefit. Anarchists, Socialists, and Communists rose again in the early 1920s, inspired by the 1917 Bolshevik Revolution. War for

K. Shaffer, *A Transnational History of the Modern Caribbean*, https://doi.org/10.1007/978-3-030-93012-7_7

independence veterans and leftists created radical alternative schools for children and workers. University of Havana students worked with leftist labor unions to challenge the government and US interests. As Robert Whitney puts it, what "made these people 'radical' was that they set themselves against the values of oligarchic rule"—those elites who dominated the state and economy since the 1890s and who believed the masses were incapable of leading the country (Whitney 2001, p. 36).

As noted in the last chapter, in 1925 the Machado government responded to radical mobilization by crushing unions, killing or deporting leftists, and forcing radicals to flee. Machado's repression stabilized Cuba for US economic interests, but repression did not kill the resistance. Some leftists fled into exile. From Mexico City, the Asociación de Nuevos Emigrados Revolucionarios Cubanos (ANERC) coordinated a transnational effort to attack Machado in the court of public opinion while planning to invade Cuba and topple the regime. Meanwhile, anarchists in New York surreptitiously sent radical newspapers into the island while publishing reports smuggled out of Cuba. Beginning in 1930, armed students and workers confronted Machado's police and bombed homes of army and police officers. Union-led and independent strikes shut down the urban economy while plantation workers across rural Cuba took over sugar mills. Almost daily throughout 1933, workers and students violently confronted police.

Women played important roles in the anti-Machado movement. Socialist Ofelia Domínguez Navarro and other feminists formed the Unión Laborista de Mujeres (Union of Women Workers, or ULM) that promoted anti-imperialism and women's suffrage. While Machado publicly supported women's suffrage to deflect accusations that he was a dictator, the ULM accused Machado of corrupting the democratic process. Some feminists like Rosa Pastora Leclerc of the ULM's student wing joined guerrillas fighting Machado. Others like Domínguez Navarro urged ULM feminists to put suffrage on the back burner and instead focus on "poverty, gender exploitation, and North American capitalist imperialism as the sources of women's oppression," as K. Lynn Stoner writes (Stoner 1997, p. 192). In 1931, police arrested Domínguez Navarro. They released her after several months, and she fled to Mexico in 1933 where she worked with Cuban exiles against the dictatorship.

As the anti-Machado coalition grew, Antonio Guiteras led an attack on a military barracks in April 1933. That summer, a general strike spread across Cuba. Then in September, lower-ranking soldiers joined students and workers. This "Sergeants Revolt" forced the United States to abandon Machado, who left and was replaced by Ramón Grau San Martín. Whitney calls this 1933 Revolution "the first time in Cuban history the country was governed by people who did not negotiate the terms of political power with Spain (before 1898) or with the United States (after 1898)" (Whitney 2001, p. 2).

However, the government was fragile. Washington hated it while leftist, centrist, and rightest factions soon emerged. In January 1934, US sugar corporations threw their support behind rightists in the military led by Fulgencio Batista. The military toppled Grau, and a right-wing government came to power, unleashing a new wave of anti-worker repression. Yet, workers refused to be silent. In March 1935, half a million staged the largest general strike in Cuban history. At one point, they burned Batista in effigy. Still, Batista's forces proved too strong, broke the strike, and killed Guiteras. For much of the next 20 years, Batista ruled overtly or behind the scenes, brutally repressing challengers while cozying up to US mafiosos and corporations. It took the Cuban Revolution to topple him. We turn to those events in Chap. 9.

RESISTING DICTATORS: TRUJILLO IN THE DOMINICAN REPUBLIC

There is no shortage of authoritarian rulers in Caribbean history. A particularly notorious example is Dominican president Rafael Trujillo. Trujillo came from lower middle-class, mixed-race origins. Growing up, he hated the rich and their country club airs, which is ironic since he used his power to become perhaps the richest person in the Caribbean. During the 1916–1924 occupation, Trujillo joined the US-created National Guard, eventually being promoted to general. In 1930, Trujillo refused to attack rebels who rose against the sitting president. Trujillo ran in the subsequent presidential election, winning 95% of the vote. He then ruled with brute force, with spies everywhere and enforcers killing opponents or compelling them to flee.

Despite his brutality, plenty of people supported Trujillo. The US backed him because his iron rule protected the Caribbean first from German Nazis in World War II and then from Communists during the Cold War. Meanwhile, he showered favors on the military, making it a key ally. For the very poor, he provided schools, healthcare, jobs, and sanitation—all real material benefits for a population largely ignored by central governments since 1865. For decades, rural areas resisted the state which they saw as doing little more than exploiting them for Santo Domingo's benefit. However, Trujillo elevated these rural masses as allies and beneficiaries of the centralized state, enabling, as Robin Derby puts it, "non-white, lower-class men to identify with the regime" (Derby 2009, p. 174). Many women supported Trujillo, who placed Dominican feminists in government posts to promote the concerns of children, education, and social welfare. "Trujillist feminists" worked transnationally with feminists in the United States and Latin America. They leveraged this transnational support into political influence when the Acción Feminista Dominicana (Dominican Feminist Action) worked with Trujillo to enact women's suffrage in 1942. Though women now could vote for Trujillo, this feminist activism also cast a façade of democracy over his omnipotent dictatorship.

Adopting the title Father of the Fatherland, Trujillo embarked on a "defense" of the Dominican Republic as he exploited long simmering racial tensions. In the 1930s, the mixed-race Trujillo launched campaigns to "De-Africanize" and "Hispanicize" the country, aiming to eliminate Haitian undercurrents within

Dominican society while glorifying Catholicism, Spain, and light skin. As he tried to "whiten" the country, he also whitened himself by wearing gloves and makeup in public to hide his complexion.

Trujillo's "De-Africanization" campaign came to a head with the Massacre of 1937. In July, the government created a new foreign registry to identify Haitian workers and Dominican-born descendants of Haitian migrants. In October, Trujillo arrived on the border and heard complaints that Haitians were "stealing jobs" from Dominicans, willing to work for less than Dominicans, refusing to speak Spanish, and driving up demand and prices for housing. Trujillo then ordered the deportation of Haitians. During the roundup, Dominican soldiers and vigilantes attacked Haitian men, women, and children with machetes. They also butchered descendants of Haitian workers born in the Dominican Republic, Dominican spouses, and Dominicans who stood up to defend Haitians who were their neighbors, friends, and coworkers.

Trujillo denied any massacre, and Haitian president Vincent said nothing. In 1938, Trujillo gave around $525,000 (about $9.4 million in 2020) to Haiti to disperse to survivors and victims' families, but corrupt Haitian officials siphoned off most of the money. Trujillo held a few show trials, convicted a handful of people, and then freed them. Meanwhile, the League of Nations absolved Trujillo of wrongdoing. It appeared to the international community that Trujillo had done nothing wrong. Adding to his "clean image," he invited East European Jews fleeing Hitler to resettle in the Dominican Republic.

The massacre, the international community's failure to condemn Trujillo's abuses, and murders of as many as 50,000 Dominicans generated widespread domestic and transnational opposition. By the 1940s and 1950s, small groups of mostly Dominican youth organized underground cells to oppose Trujillo. Among these anti-Trujillo activists were women like Josefina Padilla, Bolívar Kunhardt, and Carmen Natalia Martínez Bonilla. While at university, they joined the opposition, helped publish anti-government newsletters, gave talks, and organized cells. As Trujillo cracked down on dissent, people—including many of these young women—fled to New York, Puerto Rico, Cuba, and Venezuela. In Cuba, exiles formed the Unión Democrática Antinazista Dominicana (Dominican Anti-Nazi Democratic Union or UDAD). Wherever they went, exiles testified to Trujillo's crimes, protested at Dominican embassies, served as spies, and smuggled items. Women exiles stressed, as Elizabeth Manley puts it, "Trujillo's inability to maintain the morality and dignity of the nation"—a reference to Trujillo's security forces violating scores of girls and women (Manley 2017, p. 102).

Inspired by the Cuban Revolution (which had just come to power), the Dominican Liberation Movement began guerrilla warfare training in Cuba. On 14 June 1959, they launched a failed uprising in the Dominican Republic, but their failure inspired the leftist 14th of June Movement led by Minerva Mirabal, her sisters, and Manolo Tavárez Justo. The movement's 300 members stretched across the country and became the most organized internal resistance force confronting Trujillo. The movement met clandestinely, distributed information, and cautiously recruited people. Then, the Catholic Church (a longtime Trujillo supporter) publicly condemned the government's use of torture and other human rights abuses.

At some point, tyrants cross the line, taking their repression one step too far. For the United States, that occurred in mid-1960 when Washington severed diplomatic relations with Trujillo and the CIA sent weapons to the opposition (something that continued into 1961 under the Kennedy Administration). For Dominicans, Trujillo crossed the line on 25 November 1960 when government agents assassinated the Mirabal sisters. Public opinion shifted for good against Trujillo. On 30 May 1961, assassins attacked Trujillo's car, killing him in the roadway. His sadistic son Ramfis ruled for a brief spell before fleeing, ending the Trujillo regime.

THE CARIBBEAN LEGION WAGES TRANSNATIONAL WAR AGAINST DICTATORS

Considerable transnational opposition emerged against Trujillo. Between 1946 and 1950, pro-democracy Caribbean exiles living mostly in Cuba and Venezuela formed the Caribbean Legion to overthrow regional dictatorships. Many Dominicans and Cubans had fought against fascists during the 1930s Spanish Civil War. Allied victory over fascism in 1945 encouraged Caribbean pro-democracy advocates. In the postwar years, guns, planes, and landing craft could be readily purchased on the open market. Surely, if large, nondemocratic governments like Italy, Japan, and Germany could be toppled, then dictatorships in small Caribbean countries could fall too. However, the United States backed these dictatorships, so to attack a dictatorship in Costa Rica, Nicaragua, or the Dominican Republic meant challenging Washington's neocolonial power in the region.

From exile in Havana in mid-1947, Juan Bosch—a fervent opponent of Trujillo and an UDAD leader—plotted Trujillo's demise. He purchased weapons in the United States with money from Cuba's Department of Education. Some 1200 men from nearly every Spanish-speaking country in the Caribbean— though Dominicans comprised the majority—trained on a small Cuban key called Cayo Confites for an invasion of the Dominican Republic. One of the 1200 was a law student and political activist in Havana: Fidel Castro. The United States heard about the plan and pressured Cuba's government to stop it, arrest its leaders, and confiscate the guns. As legend has it, Fidel escaped arrest by jumping off the ship full of detained combatants and swimming eight miles through shark-infested waters to Cuban shores.

This was a temporary setback for the Legion. Juan Arévalo, the new democratically elected leftist president of Guatemala, convinced the Cuban government to release the weapons to him, which he turned over to the Legion's combatants then relocating to Guatemala. There, they signed the Caribbean Pact, announcing, "All groups representing the oppressed peoples of the

Caribbean are invited to join this pact, so that they too—with our help—can liberate their own countries [and] pledge to establish a Democratic Alliance of the Caribbean....to strengthen democracy in the region...liberate the European colonies that still exist in the Caribbean...[and] promote the creation of the Republic of the Lesser Antilles" (quoted in Gleijeses 1989, p. 108).

Castro reflected this internationalism in explaining why he joined the Legion. He told Bosch, "Cuba was liberated through the great efforts of a Dominican, General Máximo Gómez. And that we Cubans have a debt of honor with Santo Domingo. I want to pay this debt, and it is because of this that I want to fight against Trujillo" (quoted in Geyer 1991, p. 56). As one recalls, there had been numerous occasions for trans-Caribbean support to fight tyranny over the centuries: privateers aiding Haiti and the Republic of Cartagena, the Black Eagle trying to liberate Cuba, "Antilleans" aiding Dominicans against Spain, Dominicans and Puerto Ricans aiding Cuban independence fighters. Fidel's transnational activism had a long history.

The Legion turned its attention to Teodoro Picado's government in Costa Rica. When Picado rejected results of the 1947 elections, the Legion provided men and weapons to support an uprising against Picado. They overwhelmed the small Costa Rican army, toppled Picado, and installed exiled businessman José Figueres as president. Then the Legion tried a second time to topple Trujillo in what they called Operation Luperón—the name derived from the nineteenth-century Dominican independence general. Trained in Guatemala, the Legion invaded by air this time, but Trujillo's forces quickly captured them. While the Caribbean Legion failed to topple Trujillo, they reflected a Pan-Caribbean desire to eliminate authoritarianism. They also aimed to eliminate Caribbean colonialism once and for all as the Caribbean Pact envisioned a unified and independent Lesser Antilles republic rather than the smattering of French, English, and Dutch colonies that divided the islands.

PUERTO RICAN NATIONALISTS AND ANTI-COLONIAL RESISTANCE, 1930S–1950S

In the 1940s, much of the Caribbean remained under some form of colonial control, but times were changing. Anne MacPherson outlines five eventual outcomes for places that were still colonies in 1940: (1) Puerto Rico became an "associated free state" of the United States; (2) some British colonies became independent countries; (3) other British possessions as well as the US Virgin Islands remained colonial territories; (4) France incorporated the French West Indies; and (5) Dutch lands entered partnerships with Holland (MacPherson 2011, p. 477). Except for the British colonies that became independent, all remained controlled by a mother country. In response, many Caribbean peoples continued advocating for independence.

In 1917, the United States granted US citizenship to Puerto Ricans. However, Puerto Rican residents still lacked voting representation in the US

Congress, and the US president appointed their governor and Supreme Court. While many on the island sought closer relationships with the United States, others wanted an independence that had eluded Puerto Rico since Christopher Columbus arrived in November 1493. One of those seeking independence was Pedro Albizu Campos.

A Great War US army veteran, Albizu Campos developed an interest in Irish and Indian independence movements while studying law at Harvard University. He turned his new interests in anti-colonialism to his native Puerto Rico: "Puerto Rico and the other Antilles constitute the battlefield between Yankee imperialism and Ibero-Americanism. Ibero-American solidarity demands an end to all Yankee interference in this archipelago to restore the continental equilibrium and assure the independence of all Columbian nations. Our [Puerto Rican] independence is an essential part of this supreme necessity" (quoted in *Pedro Albizu Campos*).

Albizu Campos returned to the Caribbean to promote anti-imperialism and Puerto Rican independence. In 1927, he traveled to the Dominican Republic and spoke against the effects of US occupation. In Haiti, he took great risks to visit Haitian nationalists. He traveled to Cuba and witnessed Machado's brutal repression. Everywhere he saw the same conditions: Cuban, Haitian, Dominican, and Puerto Rican sovereignty undermined by US machine guns. Upon returning to Puerto Rico, he edited a nationalist newspaper, writing columns calling for Caribbean independence and an end to dictators.

In 1930, members of the Puerto Rican Nationalist Party elected him their president. After the party failed miserably in the 1932 election, he refused to participate further in a US-created electoral system. Instead, nationalists engaged in direct action, marches, and demonstrations. Violence soon immersed the island in blood. In 1935, police assassinated five nationalists at the University of Puerto Rico. The following year, members of the nationalists' youth movement assassinated a US military officer. Police killed the young assassins while in jail. In 1937, nationalists in the southern city of Ponce marched to commemorate the end of slavery and advocated strikes against US corporations. While marchers sang the movement's anthem "La Borinqueña," police opened fire, killing 19 and injuring over 200 men, women, and children.

Albizu Campos declared war. Repression would stop only when islanders understood that "the nation cannot exist without possessing all of its material wealth: agriculture, industry, commerce, communications, businesses. All forms of wealth have to be in native hands to assure the life of the nationality" (quoted in *Pedro Albizu Campos*). He also aimed his war message at the United States, noting that Puerto Ricans had read their Bibles: an eye for an eye and an American killed for every nationalist murdered. Nationalists attempted to put that into action. In Ponce in 1938, as the US-appointed governor Blanton Winship oversaw a parade commemorating the US invasion of Puerto Rico in 1898, nationalists opened fire, attempting to assassinate Winship who had ordered the previous year's attack.

In 1950, Washington changed Puerto Rico's status to an Associated Free State. Puerto Ricans now could vote directly for the island's governor. Nationalists viewed the new status as colonialism with a new name and launched armed attacks across the island. They took over the town of Jayuya in central Puerto Rico for a few days, declaring the Free Republic of Puerto Rico. Blanca Canales, a college-educated social worker who joined the Nationalist Party in 1931, unfurled the island flag and shouted, "Long Live a Free Puerto Rico." In fact, women played key roles in the party. Pedro Albizu Campos viewed women as physical and moral mothers of the nation who could defend Puerto Rico. Two women served as his bodyguards. Island authorities jailed ten nationalist women for their roles in the 1950 attacks. In addition, the party had women's branches across the island engaging in political education and fundraising. As Margaret Power concludes, "the party defined women as more than wives and mothers and formally recognized women as an important component of the anti-colonial, nationalist movement" (Power 2018, p. 135).

Nationalists attacked seats of power too. In 1950, they assaulted the governor's San Juan residence. One of their most notorious attacks occurred in the United States. Two New York-based nationalists took the train to Washington in October. They attacked the residence where US president Truman lived during White House renovations. The failed assassination attempt illustrated nationalist willingness to strike the seat of empire, but it also led to arrests of Albizu Campos and thousands of independence supporters on the island.

On 1 March 1954, nationalists took their war against the United States to the halls of colonial power itself. Lolita Lebrón led a small group to Washington, DC. The goal: draw global attention to Puerto Rico's colonial status by attacking the US Congress. The group sat in the visitor's gallery overseeing the House of Representatives (the lower house of the US Congress), then rose from their seats. Lebrón shouted, "Long Live Free Puerto Rico," as the nationalists emptied their pistols into the congressmen below, wounding five before being arrested. Police discovered Lebrón's purse which contained notes reading in part: "I state that the United States of America are betraying the sacred principles of mankind in their continuous subjugation of my country, violating their rights to be a free nation and a free people, and in their barbarous torture of our apostle of independence, Don Pedro Albizu Campos." Convicted of conspiracy charges, the court sentenced the nationalists to 50 years in prison. US president Jimmy Carter commuted their sentences after 25 years (Fig. 7.1).

Popular support for Puerto Rican independence fell over the last half of the 1900s, but militancy remained as the Young Lords in the United States took up the cause in the 1960s and 1970s, followed in the 1980s by *Los Macheteros* (The Machete Wielders), who early in the decade sat atop the US FBI's Public Enemy Number One list. Yet, violent opposition was not the only way Puerto Ricans resisted domination. People continued to speak Spanish, no matter how

Fig. 7.1 Mural of Lolita Lebrón crucified in life among other Puerto Rican nationalist martyrs (Creative Commons/Seth Anderson)

much American overseers tried making English the island's primary language. Catholicism continued strong despite efforts to spread Protestantism via churches, schools, hospitals, and orphanages. Islanders resisted Americanization and kept their identity by eating Puerto Rican food, celebrating Christmas on December 24 and Three Kings Day in January, dancing island dances and singing island songs. So, while nationalists failed to liberate Puerto Rico from US control, Puerto Ricans continued to live as "Puerto Ricans." Yet, Puerto Rico remains the oldest colony in the Caribbean.

ANTI-AMERICANISM AT MID-CENTURY

In the 1950s and 1960s, many peoples shared Puerto Rican nationalists' anti-Americanism. The region had plenty of right-wing leaders and followers who benefited from US neocolonialism and trampled the rights of indigenous peoples, peasants, and leftists. There was also an abundance of anti-Yankee nationalism against Washington's foreign policy. As Alan McPherson points out, most Latin Americans with anti-US sentiment during this time lived in the Caribbean (Cuba, the Dominican Republic, Panama, and Venezuela) because this was where US influence was greatest. Nationalists resented US actions that overthrew the democratic government of Guatemala in 1954, Washington's efforts to overthrow the Cuban Revolution in the early 1960s, US responses to Panamanian nationalism and the "Panama Flag Riots" of 1964, the US invasion of the Dominican Republic in 1965, and Washington's continued backing of dictatorships in Haiti, Nicaragua, and Guatemala. When US vice president Richard Nixon arrived in Venezuela in 1958, people pelted his car with stones, and spat on him.

ANTI-COLONIALISM AND DECOLONIZATION IN THE BRITISH WEST INDIES

British Caribbean nationalist parties led their peoples to political independence in 1962 in Jamaica and Trinidad and Tobago, then 1966 in Barbados and Guyana. However, it was a long road to get there. The 1930s labor uprisings spurred growing desires for self-rule in the British Caribbean. As MacPherson concludes, "overall labor organization laid the basis for a mass nationalism in which the popular classes had real, if temporary, clout" (MacPherson 2011, p. 484). Throughout the 1930s and after World War II, numerous independence movements arose across the British Empire from India and Kenya to Malaya and Palestine. Toward the end of World War II and in the years immediately following, London gradually liberalized its colonialism across the Caribbean. For instance, Britain granted universal suffrage to subjects in Jamaica in 1944 and Trinidad in 1945. Universal suffrage coincided with more self-rule, resulting in colonial peoples having ever-increasing say in their representation. Then, in 1948, London's Caribbean colonial subjects became British citizens.

Generations of people in British colonies had absorbed Victorian values of respectability, considered themselves British as well as West Indian, and believed in democracy, capitalism, and moral reform. Some advocated decolonization and eventually independence, but also believed that new independent entities should retain their Britishness. In other words, seeking a decolonial or independent status away from Great Britain did not mean one had to abandon British cultural and political values. This was most common among middle-class West Indians who positioned themselves as leaders in decolonization efforts.

Yet, it was usually working-class West Indians who dominated the frontlines in struggles against colonial capitalism in the 1930s and beyond. In Jamaica, issues of race and color shaped the push to decolonize. Colin Palmer writes that the 1938 labor rebellion started "the process of self-discovery for many, an assault on the bastions of racial mistreatment and denigration" for others (Palmer 2016, p. 23). Racial identity became a driving force for national identity in Jamaica's decolonization and independence drives, thus challenging West Indian middle-class leaders who saw Britishness as a rallying principle for independence. While colonial authorities heavily repressed the Afro-Jamaican religion of Rastafari (explored more in the next chapter) in the 1950s, that repression of a black consciousness group by white and brown colonizers led many Jamaicans to place Africa and thus African cultural elements "central to their imagination," forcing Jamaicans "to look into their ancestral mirror to discover their inner and outer selves" (Palmer 2016, p. 17). So, should an independent Jamaica, for instance, be guided by British/Anglo-Caribbean or African/Afro-Caribbean culture?

By the time London granted full independence to Jamaica in 1962, nearly two dozen black consciousness groups existed on the island. However, the government could exploit black identity for nationalist sentiment. For instance, in 1964 Jamaica's first prime minister Alexander Bustamante named Marcus Garvey as Jamaica's first national hero and had his body relocated from London to Jamaica. Yet, as Black Power advocate Walter Rodney noted a few years later, the government brought back Garvey's body but not his message of black majority rule. Afro-Jamaican culture was central to developing a nationalist identity in Jamaica, but white and light-skinned leaders of independent Jamaica could use someone like Garvey for their own state interests.

While race and class issues predominated nationalist discussions, women's issues lagged. As a result, nationalist leaders rarely discussed women's issues or framed nationalism in terms of gender concerns. In the British Caribbean, most pro-independence organizations lacked women leaders. As Linden Lewis puts it, "the exclusion of women from political responsibility represents a major failing of the nationalist project in the English-speaking Caribbean" (Lewis 2000, p. 274). Women did participate, though mostly on the margins of nationalist political parties. For instance, Jamaicans Rose Leon and Daphne Campbell argued that women's needs would only be met after Jamaica won its freedom. So, West Indian women supported independence, but did so by backing a muted feminism and from mostly rear positions in the movements. Though women might not have influenced nationalist discussions, they could make their voices heard at the ballot box as women gradually gained the right to vote across the British Caribbean: Jamaica 1944, Trinidad and Tobago 1946, Barbados 1950, the Lesser Antilles 1951, British Guiana 1953, and Bermuda 1962.

Early on, leftist politics dominated many nationalist political parties, raising fears in Cold War-era Washington and London of Soviet influence. As a result, when moderate nationalists in Barbados, Jamaica, and British Guiana gained control of the parties in the 1940s and 1950s, they marginalized or purged leftists. For instance, in the early 1950s, the People's Progressive Party (PPP) in British Guiana united workers of African and Indian descent. British intelligence surveilled PPP leader Cheddi Jagan for a decade. Prime Minister Winston Churchill was convinced Jagan was a Communist. In fact, Cheddi's wife Janet—a US citizen from Chicago—was a Marxist. In 1953, the PPP won colonial elections. However, British troops invaded, prevented the PPP from taking power, and ended one of Caribbean history's most successful working-class alliances between peoples of African and Indian descent. In 1962, Cheddi Jagan rose to lead the colony again. However, US president John Kennedy and the CIA—fresh from defeat at the Bay of Pigs invasion designed to topple the Cuban Revolution the previous year—colluded with Jagan's opponent Forbes

Burnham to destabilize the Jagan government. Burnham (Afro-Guyanese) was a former Jagan (Indo-Guyanese) ally in the 1953 election, but now Burnham's mostly Afro-Guyanese followers attacked Indian businesses to undermine Jagan. As the British Guiana case illustrates, anti-colonialism and independence politics reflected not only popular politics and Cold War intrigues but also lingering tensions between Asian- and African-descended peoples.

In Trinidad and Tobago, nationalists deployed one of the colony's great musical traditions—calypso—as a cultural weapon. Rooted in African chants and storytelling, Calypso (or Kaiso) added satirical lyrics with social and political commentary to percussion played on steel drums. Attila's "Commissioner's Report" mocked the Moyne Report's analysis and recommendations of the 1930s uprisings. Other singers attacked civil liberties abuses and corruption. Beginning in the 1950s, calypsonians worked with Eric Williams to promote independence. Williams, independence, and calypso grew inseparable as one hears in calypsonian Mighty Sparrow's 1957 "William the Conqueror." Calypso also reflected ethnic politics. Black Stalin sang of African unity. Lord Baker's "God Bless Our Land" reiterates the notion that all people in the country were equal citizens, mimicking the country's motto of unity that implies racial harmony and solidarity. However, Indo-Trinidadians were less sure, with many claiming that the Trinidad motto of "Together We Aspire, Together We Achieve" was just a way to mask Afro-Trinidadian dominance in society that required Indians to abandon their identities and submit to Afro-Caribbean politics.

FIGHTING A DIFFERENT FORM OF COLONIALISM IN THE FRENCH WEST INDIES

While London granted self-rule and some independence, Paris brought its Caribbean colonies closer into the French orbit in 1946 when it made French Guiana, Guadeloupe, and Martinique *départments* of France to better assimilate these francophone lands. Under the new status, all French laws applied to the départments, including laws that could benefit Caribbean workers like a 40-hour workweek. However, such equality never materialized, leading to growing disenchantment. Some West Indians then pushed for greater self-rule and autonomy, while others looked to parts of France's global empire for inspiration: Indochina (Vietnam) and Algeria, which achieved independence via armed struggle between 1954 and 1962.

Martinican writer Aimé Césaire, whose ideas we explore in the next chapter, joined the French Communist Party in 1945, served as mayor of Fort-de-France, and sat as a Martinican representative to the National Assembly in Paris. In 1946, his efforts helped to change Martinique's status to a départment, though he hoped eventually to see more autonomous rule for the West Indies. However, Césaire grew increasingly disappointed with the new status, seeing how France did not apply the laws fully to the West Indies and that

Caribbean residents remained economically and racially unequal to the metropole. By 1958, Césaire formed the Martinique Progressive Party, advocating self-rule.

Within these debates over the status of the French West Indies, new debates arose about the relationship between nationalism and feminism. West Indian women's rights activists conceived their feminism differently than French feminists. Caribbean feminists focused on the realities of West Indian women's conditions—essentially Caribbeanizing feminism. As Félix Germain writes, their feminism was "connected to France yet rooted in their local experiences" (Germain 2018, p. 63). They formed Women's Unions in 1958 and 1960, advocated workers' rights, and fought to improve daily conditions for Caribbean people. Some activist women challenged the secondary status of the West Indies in the French world after *départmentalisation*. For instance, Gerty Archimède was one of the first women of African descent from Guadeloupe to sit in the French National Assembly. In the late 1940s and early 1950s, she rebuked Paris' approach of passing laws for the French world but carving out exceptions and qualifications for French départments—essentially continuing a form of colonialism even though becoming a département was designed to decolonize the islands. Such bifurcated laws denied Antillean equality with France. Though French Caribbean feminists and people like Archimède did not advocate independence, they continued resisting unequal representation and status in the Caribbean and illustrated that becoming a département was not the same as decolonization.

In the 1960s, some Caribbean students who went to French universities returned radicalized and called for Martinican and Guadeloupean independence. In the 1970s, new nationalist groups emerged in Guadeloupe around the Kreyol language, which nationalists proclaimed gave Guadeloupe a specific identity and thus served as a force of cultural resistance to French assimilation. In the 1970s and early 1980s, armed nationalist resistance movements appeared. Martinique's National Council of Patriotic Committees, the Unification Movement of the Guadeloupean National Liberation Forces, the Popular Union for the Liberation of Guadeloupe, and the Caribbean Revolutionary Alliance launched violent campaigns in the Caribbean and Paris rather than participate in what they saw as illegitimate French elections—similar, one recalls, to Puerto Rican nationalist positions in the 1930s. Like the Puerto Ricans, these French West Indian independence groups wanted the United Nations to recognize them as colonies deserving to be independent. However, the UN did not place them on its decolonization list and Caribbean pro-independence movements failed to generate wide support.

RESISTANCE IN THE DUTCH WEST INDIES

In 1954, the Netherlands Antilles (Aruba, Bonaire, Curaçao, Eustatius, Saba, and St. Maarten), Suriname, and Holland became "equal," autonomous members of the Kingdom of the Netherlands. As self-governing entities, the UN removed the islands and Suriname from its list of colonies. Equality within the kingdom did not translate into unity and equality within Suriname as old ethnic rivalries linked to various positions on independence emerged. In 1958, an alliance between peoples of Indian and African descent came to power, joined years later by a Javanese party, thus forging a unique three-way, multicultural coalition to run Suriname. However, the two largest ethnicities (Afro- and Indo-Surinamese) increasingly fought over the spoils of government patronage while disagreeing over independence: Johan Pengel (Afro-Surinamese) supported a slow approach to independence, while Jagernath Lachmon (Indo-Surinamese) rejected independence, believing Indians benefited from Dutch rule. A black nationalist movement also emerged among leaders who often had lived in or studied at universities in Holland and might have been influenced by Indonesia's nationalist victory against the Dutch Empire. Meanwhile, Dutch public opinion increasingly rejected colonialism, while political nationalism grew among Surinamese both abroad and at home. In 1975, Suriname became independent.

In 1969, violence erupted in the largest populated island in the Netherlands Antilles. Papiamento-speaking, darker-skinned workers in Curaçao lived a second-class status as white Dutch residents earned more money and lived in better neighborhoods, something epitomized in Amador Nita's book *Cambionan Social cu un Yiu di Tera ta Sonja Cune den e Partinan Igual di e Reinado Nobo* (Dreams of Social Change by a Son of This Country in the Equal Parts of Our New Kingdom). Events around 30 May 1969 (known as Trinta di Mei in Curaçao) reflected long-simmering dissatisfaction with racial and economic realities on the island. The unrest that May erupted from a slow-burning rise in discontent that periodically sputtered into the open such as when legislators refused to speak Dutch and only Papiamento or as radicalized university students returned home to challenge the status quo.

The Shell oil refinery was the greatest symbol of Dutch colonialism on the island. On 6 May 1969, Curaçaoan workers declared a strike against Shell, demanding equal pay with international Shell workers on the island. Over the coming weeks, slow-paced negotiations frustrated strikers as the main labor union resisted calls for a general strike. However, more radical unions emerged, spurred on by the newspaper *Vitó*, which since 1966 had been a leading anti-colonial publication drawing correlations between South Africa's racist apartheid system and Dutch power in Curaçao. In the year leading to Trinta di Mei, *Vitó* ran columns about workplace inequalities at transnational corporations like Shell and Texas Instruments. The newspaper condemned corporations for hiring Dutch (usually white) workers who received better pay and conditions than Curaçoans. The uprising impacted Holland too. Curaçaoan university students there protested when the kingdom sent marines against people seeking legitimate demands. Students in Dutch cities demonstrated in support of islanders, chanting "Marines Go Home," "No Soldiers but Work," "Holland, Maid of Uncle Sam," and "Independence for the Antilles."

Into the fray stepped Amador Nita and Wilson "Papa" Godett, leaders of the radical dock workers union demanding an end to Dutch colonialism and racial discrimination. On 30 May 1969, 5000 strikers led in part by Godett and his allies marched on the capital to demand governmental action. During the march, more people joined. Marchers crossed the bay bridge to Otrabanda on the working-class side of the bay. There, violence erupted as people threw Molotov cocktails, looted shops, and chanted "Bread and Respect," "Kill the Dutch," and "Just Destroy Capitalist Possessions." Marchers attacked symbols of capitalism like Coca-Cola and Texas Instruments. Women joined the uprising. They wrote for *Vitó*, helped set Otrabanda alight, carried goods looted from Dutch stores, and continued working in the Texas Instruments factory to financially support those in rebellion. Small contingents of Dutch marines and police tried to halt marchers, but the crowd grew angrier when police shot Papa Godett in the back. He survived but the government did not. Pressured by the Chamber of Commerce, which feared more violence, Curaçao's government resigned, and workers received a contract guaranteeing equal pay with foreign workers. After the uprising, the Labor and Liberation Front, 30 May republished Nita's book, adding that all could have been avoided if the Dutch had respected Curaçaoans as equals.

CONCLUSION

Colonialism is not an institution far removed from our contemporary world. While Spanish colonies gained independence throughout the 1800s, the French, English, and Dutch Caribbean remained possessions of Europe deep into the second half of the twentieth century. Some places like Puerto Rico, the US Virgin Islands, and others remain colonial possessions, even if they are not called that. Yet, even where colonialism ended or receded, cultural and capitalist neocolonialism rose to become powerful forces undermining true autonomy and independence. Neocolonialism occurred across the Caribbean, and in some places authoritarian leaders used the power of the state and ties to the United States to destroy their opposition as in Machado's Cuba and Trujillo's Dominican Republic. Such conditions spurred more political, cultural, and armed resistance.

Often, this resistance was transnational. Feminists in Cuba, the Dominican Republic, and the French Caribbean communicated with international feminists. Feminism became central to their notions of national identity. Puerto Rican nationalists found allies in Cuba but especially in New York, where a growing Puerto Rican community had emerged since the 1910s. Radicals in Curaçao and Suriname found support from migrants in the Netherlands, especially Caribbean students studying in Dutch universities at the height of 1960s radicalism. The Caribbean Legion in the late 1940s epitomized this transnational radicalism. Pro-democracy, anti-imperialist progressives from the region united to attack dictatorships with a larger goal of driving out all colonialism and uniting the Lesser Antilles.

From the late 1910s to the 1970s, Caribbean nationalism and anti-imperialism drew on another transnational influence: black consciousness and black power. The UNIA, Caribbean Communists, black consciousness movements, and Black Power radicals emerged throughout the Caribbean and its diasporas. These movements added important racial dimensions to twentieth-century struggles for freedom, and it is to these we turn next.

WORKS CITED AND FURTHER REFERENCES

C.D. Ameringer (1996) *The Caribbean Legion: Patriots, Politicians, Soldiers of Fortune, 1946–1950* (The Pennsylvania State University Press).

B. Carr (1996) "Mill Occupations and Soviets: The Mobilisation of Sugar Workers in Cuba, 1917–1933," *Journal of Latin American Studies*, 28/1, 129–58.

J. Clemencia (2001) "*Katibu ta galiña*: From Hidden to Open Protest in Curaçao" in Albert James Arnold (ed.) *A History of Literature in the Caribbean: Volume 2: English- and Dutch-Speaking Regions* (John Benjamins), 433–42.

R. Derby (2009) *Dictator's Seduction: Politics and the Popular Imagination in the Era of Trujillo* (Duke University Press).

R. Fernández (1987) *Los Macheteros: The Wells Fargo Robbery and the Violent Struggle for Puerto Rican Independence* (Simon & Schuster).

H. García Muñiz (2011) "The Colonial Persuasion: Puerto Rico and the Dutch and French Antilles" in Stephan Palmié and Francisco Scarano (eds.) *The Caribbean: A History of the Region and Its Peoples* (University of Chicago Press), 537–51.

F. Germain (2018) "French Caribbean Feminism in the Postdepartmentalization Era" in Félix Germain and Silyane Larcher (eds.) *Black French Women and the Struggle for Equality, 1848–2016* (University of Nebraska Press), 51–68.

G.A. Geyer (1991) *Guerrilla Prince: The Untold Story of Fidel Castro* (Little, Brown, and Company).

P. Gleijeses (1989) "Juan José Arévalo and the Caribbean Legion," *Journal of Latin American Studies*, 21/1, 133–45.

A.K. Joseph-Gabriel (2018) "Gerty Archimède and the Struggle for Decolonial Citizenship in the French Antilles, 1946–1951" in Félix Germain and Silyane Larcher (eds.) *Black French Women and the Struggle for Equality, 1848–2016* (University of Nebraska Press), 89–106.

L. Lewis (2000) "Nationalism and Caribbean Masculinity" in Tamar Meyer (ed.) *Gender Ironies of Nationalism: Sexing the Nation* (Routledge), 261–82.

L. Lewis (2000) "Nationalism and Caribbean Masculinity" in Tamar Meyer, ed. *Gender Ironies of Nationalism: Sexing the Nation* (Routledge), 261–82.

A. MacPherson (2011) "Toward Decolonization: Impulses, Processes, and Consequences since the 1930s" in Stephan Palmié and Francisco Scarano (eds.) *The Caribbean: A History of the Region and Its Peoples* (University of Chicago Press), 475–89.

E. Manley (2017) *The Paradox of Paternalism: Women and the Politics of Authoritarianism in the Dominican Republic* (University Press of Florida).

A. McPherson (2003) *Yankee No! Anti-Americanism in U.S.-Latin American Relations* (Harvard University Press).

G.J. Oostindie (2014) "Black Power, Popular Revolt, and Decolonization in the Dutch Caribbean" in Kate Quinn (ed.) *Black Power in the Caribbean* (University Press of Florida), 239–60.

——— (1990) "Preludes to the Exodus: Surinamers in the Netherlands, 1667–1960s" in Gary Bran Shute (ed.) *Resistance and Rebellion in Suriname: Old and New* (University of Utrecht), 231–58.

C. Palmer (2016) *Inward Yearning: Jamaica's Journey to Nationhood* (University of the West Indies Press).

J. Parker (2006) "Diaspora against Empire: Apprehension, Expectation, and West Indian Anti Americanism, 1937–1945" in Alan McPherson (ed.) *Anti-Americanism in Latin America and the Caribbean* (Berghahn Books), 165–87.

Pedro Albizu Campos. Escritos (1930) https://horomicos.files.wordpress.com/2018/09/pac_brooking_1930.pdf

M. Power (2018) "Women, Gender, and the Puerto Rican Nationalist Party" in Jon Mulholland, Nicola Montagna, and Erin Sanders-McDonagh (eds.) *Gendering Nationalism: Intersections of Nation, Gender and Sexuality* (Palgrave Macmillan), 129–43.

L. Putnam. "'To Study the Fragments Whole': Microhistory and the Atlantic World," Journal of Social History, 39/3 (Spring 2006), 615–30.

A. Spry Rush (2011). *Bonds of Empire: West Indians and Britishness from Victoria to Decolonization* (Oxford University Press).

K.L. Stoner (1991) *From the House to the Streets: The Cuban Women's Movement for Legal Reform, 1898–1940* (Duke University Press).

——— (1997) "Ofelia Domínguez Navarro: The Making of a Cuban Socialist Feminist" in William H. Beezley and Judith Ewell (eds.) *The Human Tradition in Latin America* (Rowman & Littlefield), 181–204.

R. Whitney (2001) *State and Revolution in Cuba: Mass Mobilization and Political Change, 1920–1940* (University of North Carolina Press).

CHAPTER 8

A Caribbean "Black Lives Matter": Black Consciousness and Black Power, Early 1900s–1970s

Race-based resistance was integral to modern Caribbean history. Europeans constructed an entire political-economic-cultural slave system, and enslaved workers found numerous ways to resist. After slavery, people of African descent defied the repressive tools imposed across the region. Resistance intensified in the twentieth century. After formal independence in 1902, the Cuban constitution promised a race-blind political system, but widespread black disenfranchisement led some to organize their own political party. In 1914, Marcus Garvey launched the UNIA in Jamaica, then relocated its headquarters to New York. Chapters spread throughout the Caribbean, providing black self-help philosophies, a race-proud economic system, and a Pan-Africanist vision. Numerous black consciousness advocates joined Communist organizations in the 1920s and 1930s, adding important race agendas to Communist doctrine. Black consciousness ideas emerged powerfully in Haiti and Jamaica at mid-century. Books, poetry, and music reflected and expanded black consciousness, especially around the Jamaica-based Rastafarian religion. Then, by the late 1960s and early 1970s, Black Power ideas swept across the Caribbean.

AFRO-CUBAN POLITICS AND THE *PARTIDO INDEPENDIENTE DE COLOR* IN THE EARLY 1900s

In 1902, the US military withdrew from Cuba following its four-year occupation after the Spanish-American War/Cuban War for Independence. Afro-Cubans struggled to fit into the new society. They had dominated the ranks of the mambises, fought for independence, and expected to be rewarded with land and opportunities in the new republic. The Cuban constitution embodied the words of José Martí that this was to be a republic for all—easily interpreted as one where peoples of African descent would have equal access to education, be treated equally before the law, and have equal political representation. Again, "legality" and "reality" were two different things.

© The Author(s), under exclusive license to Springer Nature Switzerland AG 2022
K. Shaffer, *A Transnational History of the Modern Caribbean*,
https://doi.org/10.1007/978-3-030-93012-7_8

Recognizing the reality of racial inequality that legal words could not mask, many Afro-Cubans fought for whatever spoils they could. Cuban political parties often ran Afro-Cuban candidates to win black votes, but these candidates also hoped to win office and then share the spoils of patronage with their communities. In essence, white-dominated parties used Afro-Cuban candidates for votes, but after winning office, Afro-Cuban politicians leveraged their power to put public resources like jobs, money, and assets into Afro-Cubans' hands.

Not all Afro-Cubans appreciated this situation and created their own political party instead. Pedro Ivonnet and Evaristo Estenoz formed the Cuban Independent Party of Color. Ivonnet and Estenoz served as mambí officers during the war. They witnessed Afro-Cubans' sacrifices, only to see those sacrifices ignored as voting restrictions, unemployment, and illiteracy grew among Afro-Cubans after Cuban independence. In 1907—one year into the second US military occupation—the *Partido Independiente de Color* (PIC) published the *Manifesto to the People of Cuba and to the Raza de Color*, which charged Cuba's white elite with violating the Cuban Constitution's promise of universal equality. They indicted white Cubans for helping US occupiers discriminate against Afro-Cubans. They also condemned Afro-Cubans, who associated with white-dominated political parties and colluded in discrimination. Rather, they argued, Afro-Cubans needed their own political party to pursue greater access to public education, abolition of the death penalty (used disproportionately more against Afro-Cubans), an eight-hour workday, opposition to the Platt Amendment, and proportional distribution of land and jobs to Afro-Cubans. Neither revolutionary nor socialist, the PIC simply wanted people of African descent to be fully Cuban. As Aline Helg concludes, "pride in being black and Cuban, in sum, was the principal racial message of the *independientes*" (Helg 1995, p. 151).

By 1908, the PIC established branches across the island, published the newspaper *Previsión*, and claimed over 10,000 mostly working-class supporters. While no women led Cuba's PIC, they nevertheless shaped and represented the party. The 1890s independence war widowed many Afro-Cuban women. To survive, they worked for barely livable income as laundresses, seamstresses, prostitutes, and more. As Takkara Brunson puts it, "racial discrimination affected women's economic livelihood and social mobility" every bit as they did men's (Brunson 2019, p. 278). It is no surprise, then, that Afro-Cuban women joined the PIC. For instance, Rosa Brioso portrayed women's realities in her regularly published columns in *Previsión*. Women protested racial discrimination and emphasized their Cuban patriotism and race pride just like men in the party.

The PIC's opponents accused the party of reverse racism and claimed that PIC political victories would turn Cuba into another Haiti. *Previsión* countered by saying Cuba actually was becoming more like the racist United States. The PIC sought to improve all Afro-Cubans' lives, promoted the idea that blacks and people of mixed race were all part of the "Afro-Cuban family" and there should be no skin color prejudice. The party concluded that "we do not long for black supremacy over whites; but neither do we accept, and never will, white supremacy over blacks" (quoted in Helg 1995, p. 149). Across Cuba, mainstream leaders grew irate. In 1910, the government called the PIC racist and antiwhite. That February, the Cuban legislature passed the Morúa Law banning political parties based on race because such parties supposedly violated the constitution. By April, government repression spread, and police arrested PIC leaders, accusing them of fomenting a race war.

Though outlawed and marginalized, PIC supporters continued to operate on the margins of Cuban society. In February 1912, Estenoz threatened that if the government did not revoke the Morúa Law, then the island would face a black uprising. In May 1912, people across the island prepared to celebrate the tenth anniversary of Cuban independence. The outlawed PIC had its own plans. Leaders called on supporters to converge in local plazas across the island in a defiant show of resiliency and strength. Many came armed. The government, press, and perhaps most Cubans reacted with fear to the protests. The press portrayed PIC actions as the beginning of a race war. The government responded with violence. Cuban troops and white vigilantes shot, machine-gunned, and indiscriminately bombarded Afro-Cubans. By July, they had killed Estenoz and Ivonnet along with as many as 6000 mostly Afro-Cuban citizens. The government charged nearly 1000 people with rebellion and began outlawing Afro-Cuban culture. Racist violence decimated the Caribbean's first black consciousness party.

THE UNIA AND TRANSNATIONAL BLACK CONSCIOUSNESS, 1910s–1920s

Black consciousness movements arose across the region as activists organized at home and wherever they migrated. As introduced in the last chapter, black contact zones served as locations where people of African descent from different places met and organized for common purpose. These could be the trenches of Europe's Great War, the Panama Canal, or Cuban sugar plantations. New York City increasingly became an important black contact zone. Over 150,000 Afro-Caribbeans migrated to the United States from 1899 to 1937. These included soon-to-be prominent activists for black consciousness and leftist causes, including Jamaicans Claude McKay, Wilfred Domingo, and Marcus and Amy Jacques Garvey, Trinidadians C.L.R. James and George Padmore, Puerto Ricans Arturo Schomburg and Jesús Colón, Cyril Briggs from Nevis, and Hubert Harrison from the Virgin Islands. Many had been radicalized in Caribbean labor strikes or as returning veterans from the Great War. Others became radicalized in the United States, where they faced intense racial segregation and where they joined militant organizations.

Two years after the 1912 "race war" in Cuba, Marcus Garvey created the UNIA in nearby Jamaica, envisioning it as a black pride/black consciousness/ black self-help organization. Garvey came from a family of Jamaican radicals. His father—also named Marcus—attended meetings that led to the Morant

Bay rebellion in 1865 and claimed to have been a descendent of Jamaican maroons. In 1907, young Marcus joined a Jamaican printer's union while training in his godfather's print shop. There, he heard stories about slavery-era and post-emancipation resistance leaders like Sam Sharpe and Paul Bogle.

Black contact zones also shaped Garvey. From 1910 to 1914, he worked in the Panama Canal Zone and for the US-based United Fruit Company in Costa Rica before traveling to Great Britain to study law. Rather than develop a working-class consciousness, though, Garvey developed a black consciousness, believing peoples of African descent from around the world needed to organize to secure rights and well-being, work in and run their own stores, and shop in those stores. Upon returning to Jamaica in 1914, he established the UNIA as a benevolent aid association. In 1916, he migrated to New York, establishing the UNIA headquarters in Harlem where he transformed it into what Robin Kelley calls "a mass-based, global, black nationalist movement intent on redeeming Africa and establishing a homeland for the black world" (Kelley 2002, p. 24).

Pan-Africanism did not originate with Garvey. Edward Wilmot Blyden is considered the father of the idea. Born in St. Thomas in the Danish Virgin Islands in 1832, he moved to Venezuela and the United States before migrating to the new country of Liberia. There, he taught, edited the country's only newspaper, and by the 1860s served as secretary of state. During these years, he challenged Eurocentric ideas about the supposed inferiority of Africans and people in the African diaspora, seeing instead that all races were equal but had different characteristics reflecting particular climates. The "African Personality" was communal and not individualistic. This was not better or worse than European individualism—just differently equal. He urged Africans and those in the diaspora not to admire Europe because its culture was not suitable for the African Personality. Liberia was created as a place for formerly enslaved peoples in the United States to repatriate, but Blyden expanded the idea and invited skilled workers of African descent from around the Americas to migrate to Liberia in what was possibly the world's first black-driven "Back to Africa" campaign. Decades later, in July 1900, activists held the first Pan-African conference in London and with important transnational Caribbean links. The key organizer was Henry Sylvester Williams, a Trinidad-born lawyer practicing in London at the time. Benito Sylvain from Haiti served as a vice chairman while also advising the emperor of Ethiopia. Nearly 50 participants and observers attacked colonialism and spoke on preserving black identity.

From Harlem, Garvey expanded his Pan-Africanist organization across the United States, created both a women's auxiliary unit and the Black Cross nurses' sector, and promoted black-owned businesses. He urged people to shop only in those stores, so money circulated within the community. While never a paramilitary organization, the UNIA did play at war. The UNIA reflected a symbolic militarism in songs and speeches, military-like drills, uniforms, Garvey dressing up in regalia that made him look like some commodore on a ship, and the UNIA's Universal African Legions—a "military" wing with its own calvary unit that trotted through Harlem's streets.

In 1920, Garvey published the "Declaration of the Rights of the Negro Peoples of the World," a Pan-Africanist manifesto envisioning a unified African diaspora needing to think of itself as "African" first, not African American, African Jamaican, and so on—African as a noun, not an adjective. In the declaration, Garvey outlined how US and European rulers exploited peoples of African descent around the world by denying them rights, exploiting their labor, colonizing their lands, and depriving them of legal protections and an honest justice system. To rectify this, the declaration offered 54 points "to encourage our race all over the world and to stimulate it to overcome the handicaps and difficulties surrounding it, and to push forward to a higher and grander destiny."

Garvey proclaimed that "all men are created equal and entitled to the rights of life, liberty, and the pursuit of happiness" so it was up to him and the UNIA "as the duly elected representatives of the Negro peoples of the world" to proclaim this and fight for its fruition—something possible only if they had taxation with representation (they would pay taxes only if they had representatives of African descent in government), equitable representation in governing bodies and courtrooms, control over their communities, and schools that taught "Negro History." Garvey further insisted that peoples of African descent "should adopt every means to protect" themselves by rejecting colonialism and neocolonialism and securing the right to "give aid to a fellow Negro when thus molested." Finally, if his people were to be free, they would have to do it themselves, not rely on white-dominated governments to pass reforms or laws, and certainly not participate in colonial or neocolonial enterprises that wasted the black masses' organizing energies (Garvey 1920, *Declaration*).

Women played important roles in the UNIA in both the Black Cross Nurses and the Women's Brigade while comprising at least half of the membership in half of the UNIA's chapters. Two women stand out as UNIA leaders, and both were Marcus Garvey's wives. Amy Ashwood Garvey was Marcus' first wife, cofounder of the UNIA in Jamaica, and the organization's first secretary. She followed Marcus to New York, played a prominent role in the head office, and served as secretary of the Black Star Line—a shipping venture created for trade and travel between diasporic communities and countries (one of its ships was named the *SS Antonio Maceo* after the Cuban independence hero). Marcus unceremoniously divorced her in 1922, and then married Amy Jacques Garvey. She wrote for and edited the *Negro World*. Through her women's page in the newspaper, she gave UNIA women a platform to express their views. For several years, she cowrote Marcus' speeches and thus helped shape Garveyism.

The UNIA grew to some two million members in over 1000 chapters worldwide. Most were in the United States, where nearly half of all US-based leaders were Afro-Caribbean. West Indians accounted for nearly half of UNIA leadership and newspaper writers in New York City. Meanwhile, activists created 221 chapters across the Caribbean by 1926. The UNIA presence in Cuba was so large that London briefly considered recognizing the UNIA as the representative of British Caribbean workers in Cuba's sugar plantations. Yet, while the UNIA had branches across the Caribbean and Central America, the UNIA had few Afro-Hispanic members, reflecting the limited appeal of Garveyism to non-English-speaking African-descended populations. Even in Cuba, few Afro-Cubans joined the UNIA.

The UNIA used the *Negro World* to showcase works and commentary by US- and Caribbean-born artists and activists of African descent. Garvey led each week with an editorial, and Amy Jacques Garvey published a column titled "Our Women and What They Think." The paper circulated around the Caribbean, making it one of the region's most widely read newspapers. Though colonial governments prohibited its distribution, Caribbean seamen carried copies of the *Negro World* to Caribbean ports where it inspired and helped organize new UNIA chapters.

However, by the mid-1920s, problems, dissention, and repression undermined the UNIA. Bankruptcy ended the Black Star shipping line. Internal dissent splintered the organization after Garvey met with the Ku Klux Klan, Garveyites killed an opposition leader, and rank-and-file members deserted to join other militant organizations. Then, US officials arrested, convicted, and jailed Garvey for fraud before deporting him to Jamaica. With Marcus imprisoned in the United States, Amy became the de facto leader of the UNIA. Following Marcus' death in 1940, she continued promoting black nationalism and sponsored the African Freedom Charter in the United Nations.

For over a decade, the UNIA functioned as "the largest and most powerful black nationalist organization the world has ever known" (James 1998, p. 136). Its transnational influence was felt for decades. Kwame Nkrumah led the West African country of Ghana to independence in 1957, citing Garvey as inspiration for his ideas of African independence and racial pride. In Jamaica, Leonard Howell organized the new Rastafari religion, seeing Garvey as a prophet. Finally, many of Garvey's proposals in the Declaration served as the starting point for Black Power movements in the 1960s.

BLACK CONSCIOUSNESS MEETS MARXISM, 1920S–1930S

The UNIA was not the only black consciousness organization emerging in the Caribbean-to-New York diaspora. Because the UNIA was first and foremost a black consciousness organization, that narrow focus provided openings for organizations with leftist, anti-capitalist agendas. After all, the UNIA did not oppose capitalism; Garvey believed in the sanctity of private enterprise for the African-descended community. The late 1910s was a heady time for someone with radical inclinations: disillusionment with capitalist democracy; hope for a workers' utopia following the 1917 Bolshevik Revolution; black consciousness; radical unionization efforts of veterans, Communists, and anarchists. Caribbean peoples created and joined organizations to resist the combined threats of racism and capitalism, forging a Caribbean vanguard in US Socialist and Communist organizations from the 1910s to 1930s that united black nationalism with revolutionary socialism.

Hubert Harrison migrated to the United States from Danish St. Croix in 1900. By the 1910s, he was a highly praised speaker in the Socialist Party. However, he left the party over racial divisions. For all its rhetoric about equality, white socialists in the United States (and not just in the South) could be as racist as any other cracker. Harrison moved to Philadelphia where he worked on the docks, joining hundreds of Caribbean seamen and dockworkers belonging to the anarcho-syndicalist IWW labor union. Then, he moved to Harlem. While Harrison moved further left politically, he also became a black nationalist, even helping Garvey get his first speaking engagement in New York shortly after Garvey arrived in 1916. Over the years, Harrison denounced capitalism (as any good socialist would) and attacked capitalism's impact on peoples of African descent (here comes the budding black nationalist). As James notes, Harrison epitomized the experiences of many people of African descent living in the United States: "Harlem's black nationalism was the last resort of a black socialist in a racist land" (James 1998, p. 128).

Harrison grounded his black nationalist socialism not only in his own transnational experiences between the Caribbean and the United States but also as an astute observer of US imperialism in the Caribbean during the 1910s and 1920s: "When we look upon the Negro republics of Hayti [*sic*] and Santo Domingo where American marines murder and rape at their pleasure while the financial vultures of Wall Street scream with joy over the bloody execution which brings the wealth of these countries under their control; when we see the Virgin Islanders in the deadly coils of American capitalism gasping for a breath of liberty…we begin to realize that we must organize our forces to save ourselves from further degradation and ultimate extinction" (*A Hubert Harrison Reader*, 2001, p. 225). The black working masses of the hemisphere needed to organize to defeat white US imperial capitalism.

Meanwhile in 1930s London—another imperial black contact zone—West Indians also engaged in working-class, Pan-Africanist resistance movements. The example of Chris Braithwaite is illustrative. Born in Barbados in 1885, he moved to London. There, he founded the Colonial Seamen's Association that forged a network of maritime workers fighting capitalist imperialism, worked with the British Communist Party, and helped to create Pan-Africanist organizations like the International African Friends of Ethiopia and the International African Service Bureau for the Defence of Africans and People of African Descent. Braithwaite and other West Indians in London like George Padmore and C.L.R. James from Trinidad as well as Marcus Garvey's first wife Amy Ashwood Garvey pursued a socialist Pan-Africanism aimed at opposing racism, attacking British imperialism, and supporting British Caribbean labor strikes of the 1930s.

THE AFRICAN BLOOD BROTHERHOOD, 1919–1922

The merger of black nationalist and socialist politics vividly surfaced in the African Blood Brotherhood, founded by West Indian migrants like Cyril Briggs in 1919. Born in Nevis in 1888, Briggs arrived in the United States in 1905 and, like Harrison, explored the increasingly connected world of leftist politics and black nationalism. In New York, he edited the *Amsterdam News* and *Crusader*. The latter helped launch the ABB in Harlem. In *Crusader*, Briggs focused on links between black workers' realities and the promises of the Bolshevik Revolution. It proclaimed that "we are Bolshevists...but Negro first," and urged readers to join the IWW (quoted in Stevens 2017, p. 27). One historian relates how Briggs merged the two ideologies: he "did not so much abandon his black nationalism as graft onto it revolutionary socialism, and, in particular, Bolshevism" (James 1998, p. 160).

Briggs and other Caribbean radicals in New York like Otto Huiswood (Suriname), Richard B. Moore (Barbados), and Claude McKay (Jamaica) merged socialism and black nationalism as the driving inspiration for the ABB. They saw Russia's Bolsheviks supporting ethnic minorities, anti-colonialism, anti-imperialism, self-determination, antiracism, and anticapitalism. ABB activists also saw themselves as defiant black nationalists, calling for peoples of African descent to arm themselves in self-defense. Ultimately, McKay, Harrison, and Briggs envisioned socialism as the best way to achieve black liberation globally.

By the 1920s, the Communist (Workers) Party was the leading pro-Soviet party in the United States and recruited men and women of African descent. After 1922, West Indians in the ABB leadership joined the Communist Party as its first black members and helped bring peoples of African descent into the party well into the 1930s. In 1919, the Comintern had declared its goal to end colonialism in Africa and Asia. In 1920, Lenin insisted the Comintern address issues of race and nationality. In 1922, ABB members McKay and Huiswood traveled to Moscow to attend the Comintern's Fourth World Congress. While discussing links between capitalism and racism in the United States, McKay noted how racism still existed in the US Communist Party, and it had to stop. The speech shaped Comintern policy on race, and the Comintern published it as a small book. For McKay and other ABB Communists, "the Comintern represented the purest ideals of socialism, untarnished by racism and colonial ambition" (James 1998, p. 181). These Afro-Caribbean Communists hoped to use their influence with the Comintern to push US Communists to respect their nonwhite comrades.

The ABB also was a transnational resistance organization with members across the Caribbean from the Dominican Republic to Trinidad to the Panama Canal Zone. As mentioned earlier, British Caribbean dockworkers and seamen working for the IWW organized along the Atlantic seaboard and into the Caribbean. IWW organizers reached into Cuba, hoping to organize Caribbean sugar cane cutters. West Indian seamen distributed radical US newspapers from the ABB, the IWW, and the Communist Party to workers in the Caribbean. People read *Crusader* throughout the region. Meanwhile, people from around the Caribbean wrote to *Crusader*, sharing their experiences with readers across the transnational distribution network.

Black nationalist Communists also attacked US military intervention. *Crusader* challenged readers to side with those exploited under US occupation in Haiti and the Dominican Republic. In 1925, former ABB leaders headed the Communist-backed American Negro Labor Congress, which called for solidarity with Haiti's masses. When Haitian workers and students rebelled against US marines in late 1929, the ANLC and the Comintern-backed Anti-Imperialist League launched a solidarity movement with the rebels. They coordinated efforts between US and Haitian Communist Parties that called for Haitian self-determination and an end to neocolonialism. As Margaret Stevens puts it, "the Haitian uprising of 1929 provided an important opportunity [for US Communists] for challenging US hegemony by following the lead of black working-class students and laborers in Haiti, just as enslaved Africans across the hemisphere had taken inspiration from the Haitian revolution" (Stevens 2017, p. 51). Ultimately, Caribbean activists in the United States facilitated transnational cooperation between US and Caribbean Marxists and black nationalists.

BLACK CONSCIOUSNESS AND CULTURAL RESISTANCE, 1920s–1950s

As early as 1917, Hubert Harrison understood the emancipatory potential of cultural and literary endeavors. He founded the Liberty League and the newspaper *The Voice* that ushered in the New Negro Movement and the birth of what by the mid-1920s became the Harlem Renaissance in New York. This cultural resistance movement showcased artistic creations of people of African descent while promoting progressive politics. Yet, it was just one of many race-based cultural resistance movements that Caribbean peoples embraced in the 1920s and 1930s. These movements transcended political borders to shape art, culture, and politics from New York to Havana to Port-au-Prince to Fort-de-France.

In Cuba, the *negrismo* and *vanguardia* movements emerged in the mid-1920s. Following the 1912 massacre of Afro-Cubans and the suppression of Afro-Cuban culture, few intellectuals and artists dared to explore Cuba's African heritage. However, by the 1920s, scholars and artists from historian Fernando Ortiz to poet Nicolás Guillén created a new sense of Cuban identity that encompassed the once-banned Afro-Cuban culture. Believing their political leaders were selling Cuba to the highest bidder, artists, poets, and writers began celebrating and incorporating Afro-Cuban culture into their works in what Vera Kutzinksi calls a "cultural alternative to North Americanization and as a political vehicle for national integrity and survival" (Kutzinski 1993, p. 142).

Négritude was a Francophone version of this cultural resistance. Martinican poet Aimé Césaire popularized the term in his 1939 *Cahier d'un retour au pays natal* (Notebook of a Return to the Native Land). The poem tackles anti-colonialism, oppression, and racism. The narrator declares his blackness "is not a stone" that weighs him down but something essential that "takes root in the ardent flesh of the soil." The first step toward liberation was accepting one's blackness and all it entails. Négritude authors explored how the slave trade prevented people from knowing Mother Africa, thus disrupting one's identity, and leading many to reject their African cultural roots in favor of those of European colonizers. Joined by Francophone writers like Léon Damas from French Guiana, négritude writers showcased struggles of people breaking from colonialism by embracing African cultural foundations of their societies.

Women played vital roles in the rise of négritude. Aimé Césaire worked with his wife Suzanne during World War II to edit, write, and publish the Martinican literary magazine *Tropiques*. Previously in the late 1920s, Paris-based Martinican sisters Jane and Paulette Nardal hosted African American, Anglophone, and Francophone black consciousness writers in their literary salons where writers shared and nourished négritude ideas. In the late 1920s, the sisters worked with the French-based *La Dépeche africaine*, which published their short stories and essays on music, sculpture, and black cultural internationalism. Their writings analyzed black consciousness and black internationalism in the African diaspora, providing "an essential kernel of the philosophical foundation for the literary and cultural movement later celebrated the world over as Negritude" (Sharpley-Whiting 2000, pp. 12–13).

In the early 1930s, a new form of political and cultural black nationalism emerged in Haiti thanks in part to the 1928 publication of Jean Price-Mars' *Ainsi parle l'oncle* (So Spoke the Uncle). Price-Mars reflected on the aftermath of the Haitian Revolution when the victors created a system like that which Europeans had imposed on them: plantation labor, export agriculture, European dress, Catholicism, and more. Haitians "had donned the old frock of western civilization." Soon, though, a struggle developed between the state (composed especially of Haitians who wanted to ape Europe) and the nation (the Afro-Haitian rural masses). Toward the end of the US occupation, Price-Mars and his associates developed their ideas into a new form of Haitian nationalism: *indigénisme*. While indigénisme recognized the roles of European and African cultural roots in Haiti, these writers championed rural society, celebrating its racial pride, Vodou, and African-based peasant culture. Indigénisme found its largest support in the countryside, which not coincidentally was where one found the most armed opposition (i.e., the cacos) to US occupation.

Haiti's nationalist movement split into two competing branches: Communists and *noiristes*. The former looked for additional Marxist inspiration abroad. For instance, in his novel *Gouverneurs de la rosée* (Masters of the Dew), Communist Jacques Roumain's characters merge socialist organizing principles and local Afro-Haitian peasant knowledge to overcome their strife. However, noiristes looked only inward for inspiration, criticizing elites who imitated the West and condemned rural culture. For noiristes, nothing good came from Haiti's European roots. Rather, the "true Haitian soul" was African, black, and rural.

In the late 1920s, a group of intellectuals began ethnographic studies of Haiti's rural culture, seeking Haiti's "authentic" cultural and historical identity in the country's African roots. In 1932, they formed the group Les Griots. One member was Dr. François Duvalier—later the infamous dictator "Papa Doc." Over time, Griot noiristes argued that assimilation of French values impaired Haitian development. Only by embracing rural folk culture like Vodou and music could Haitians fully repudiate "foreign" Francophone culture, Catholicism, liberalism, and Marxism. Noiristes further proclaimed that decades of mulatto rule had to end. Haiti needed to be governed by people who represented the Afro-Haitian masses and who knew their Afro-Haitian heritage. The Griots then argued that, as Winston James puts it, "the biology of a racial group determined its psychology, and in turn its 'collective personality'" (James 2011, p. 454). They saw "black" as a biological type imbued with particular characteristics—a view also believed at the time by a man with a little mustache across the Atlantic.

The Cultural Politics of Noirisme in Haiti: The Rise and Rule of Papa Doc

Throughout the 1930s and 1940s, noiristes reshaped Haiti. Black and rural arts reflected black political discontent. Rural music took on nationalist themes. By the 1940s, commercial music played on the radio by bands like Jazz des Jennes incorporated Kreyol language, proverbs, and more that "championed Haitian cultural authenticity" and became an "important vehicle for [Haitian black consciousness] dissemination" (Smith 2009, p. 60). In short, cultural expression became a tool for Haiti's working masses to express pride and anger.

At the same time, the Marxist wing of the indigéniste movement again mobilized. Marxists—as limited as their influence was in post occupation Haiti—complicated racial and color discussions by incorporating class analysis into Haitian radicalism. Roumain organized clandestinely in Haiti, while Max Hudicourt printed an anti-government newspaper. By 1936, the Vincent government brutally repressed their small Communist Party—which Roumain had helped to create with money and support from the Communist Party USA. For Vincent, such foreign Communist support justified the repression. In 1940, Hudicourt, Roumain, and other Communists returned to Haiti from exile, again building on their transnational linkages: Hudicourt with the CPUSA in New York and Roumain with Cuban Communists. Once again, the government quickly crushed them.

In 1946, a new crop of young leftists challenged Élie Lescot's government. Lescot jailed editors of a Communist newspaper and suppressed strikes by students, workers, teachers, and shopkeepers. Meanwhile, Lescot's mulatto government alienated the black-dominated National Guard, which in late January staged a military coup. In August, Haitians elected Dumarsaise Estimé as the first popularly elected black president in Haitian history. He implemented the first income tax, nationalized foreign companies, advocated recognizing labor unions, and proposed making Vodou equal with Catholicism. Estimé promoted black consciousness in politics and the arts, brought Afro-Haitian intellectuals into the government (including François Duvalier as labor minister) and promoted this new leadership as the "Authentiques"—the true inheritors of Jean-Jacques Dessalines' legacy.

While noiristes might have been happy, others were not. A requirement to contribute up to 15% of their pay to buy government bonds angered workers. Estimé isolated Marxists and key unions from the government while unleashing a new wave of anti-Communist violence. Meanwhile, the elite plotted Estimé's removal. The military stepped into the growing instability and deposed Estimé in 1950 and his successor Paul Magliore in 1956.

Into this mix rose Duvalier. In 1957, he ran for president on a noiriste platform, promising widespread social and economic reforms. After easily winning, Duvalier used government coffers to spend on his Afro-Haitian support base, creating a classic populist regime of mass support for an authoritarian leader. Duvalier's state now celebrated black popular culture, praised Vodou, and oversaw the rise of a black middle class. Duvalier also learned a lesson from Estimé: do not trust the military. So, he reduced the military's influence and organized his own private militia—the Tonton Macoutes—to enforce his rule and eradicate opposition at first signs of discontent.

Duvalier created a cult of personality around his leadership, using traditional forms of Afro-Haitian popular culture to forge an authoritarian power structure. Carnival floats celebrated his public works projects and noiriste policies. Carnival music groups and bands used public funds to support this once rebellious art form that now promoted Duvalier's state. Duvalier manipulated Haitian history, portraying himself as the true descendant of Toussaint and Dessalines. He also exploited Vodou, claiming God (Bondye in Vodou) had chosen him while portraying himself as Baron Samedi—the Vodou loa of the dead who can also give life. Thus, as Baron Samedi, Papa Doc literally had your life in his hands, so it was best to appease the loa and thus appease the dictator. Duvalier manipulated other aspects of rural popular culture. The Tonton Macoutes wore denim shirts and straw hats while carrying machetes so that they resembled the Vodou loa of the harvest. The Tonton Macoutes enforced Duvalier's policies, used rape and murder as political weapons, killed as many as 60,000 men, women, and children, and helped Papa Doc—and then his son Jean-Claude—rule Haiti with an iron fist that forced dissidents to flee into exile. With the rise of a fervent noiriste to political power in Haiti, the once-resistance-oriented culture and religion of Haiti's masses had been turned into tools of dictatorship against all who challenged Duvalier. The culture of the nation had been captured by the state to be used against the nation.

Rastafari and Black Consciousness in Jamaica, 1930s–1970s

While black consciousness came to political power in Haiti in the late 1950s, in neighboring Jamaica black consciousness emerged in a new form of religious-based resistance: Rastafari. Rasta's roots go back decades before the 1930s to the emergence of "Ethiopianism." Since the nineteenth century, Jamaican churches and black consciousness advocates promoted Ethiopia's centrality to Christian history, its ability to resist European colonization, and Ethiopia's victory over Italy in 1896. Thus, Ethiopia became a liberation icon in the African diaspora. In Jamaica, Ethiopianism became Rasta due to the importance of three "prophets:" Marcus Garvey, Leonard Howell, and Haile Selassie.

One remembers that Garvey was born in Jamaica, founded the UNIA there in 1914, moved to Harlem in 1916, and expanded the UNIA into the largest Pan-African organization in history. Garvey promoted the uniqueness of Ethiopia and the country's "redemptive" qualities that countered white ideas of African inferiority. The UNIA's official anthem was "Ethiopia, Thou Land of Our Fathers," composed by Arnold J. Ford, a Barbados-born musician. Marcus Garvey became not only a proponent for black liberation but also of Ethiopianism to get there.

Leonard Howell was born in Jamaica in 1898. As a young man, he traveled the Caribbean and the United States, working on ships and in the Canal Zone. In the United States, he worked for the UNIA, but the US government deported him to Jamaica in 1932 after serving two years in jail on a theft conviction. He began studying the emerging anti-colonial movements in Africa in the first decades of the twentieth century, especially the Nyabinghi resistance movement in British-ruled Uganda. By the early 1930s, he joined other Garveyites and former workers from the diaspora—people like Robert Hinds, Joseph Hibbert, and Archibald Dunkley. Howell started preaching a new "Ethiopian" religion in the hills west of Kingston and then in the slums of Kingston itself. The religion centered on the third key figure in Rasta's rise: Haile Selassie.

In 1930, Selassie was the newly coronated emperor of Ethiopia, adopting several biblical titles: King of Kings, Lord of Lords, Descendant of King Solomon and King David, Lion of the Tribe of Juda. Born Tafari Makonnen, he took the name Ras ("Prince" in Amharic), becoming Ras Tafari. In Jamaica, Howell and the Nyabinghi "mansion" (the oldest of the three largest Rasta sects and whose name comes from the above-noted independence movement) looked to Ethiopia and Selassie's coronation, declaring Selassie the second coming of Jesus Christ who was now Earth's rightful ruler.

Jamaicans had long looked to the Bible for explanation and inspiration. For instance, Revivalist Baptist deacon Paul Bogle used the Book of Psalms to justify the Morant Bay Rebellion in 1865. Howell—a street preacher with a growing flock—found the source of Selassie's divinity in the Bible. Revelation 5:2-5 state, "And I saw a strong angel proclaiming with a loud voice: Who is worthy to open the book, and to loose the seals thereof?…And one of the elders saith unto me, Weep not: behold the Lion of the Tribe of Juda, the Root of David, hath prevailed to open the book, and to loose the seven seals thereof." Revelation 19:16 declares, "And he hath on his vesture and on his thigh a name written: king of kings, and lord of lords." Psalms offered more proof for believers. Psalms 68:31-32 proclaim, "A prince shall come out of Egypt; Ethiopia shall soon stretch out her hands unto God." Howell and his associates used Biblical verse to explain what was happening half a world away, believing God had returned to Earth as the emperor of Ethiopia and speaking Amharic—Jesus's language.

In the 1930s, Howell announced that Selassie was black Jamaicans' new monarch. In 1933, Howell preached, "If anyone has any grievance, he must write to Ras Tafari, the King of Kings and Lord of Lords," and when singing the national anthem "God Save the King," one had to "remember that you are not singing it for King George, but for Ras Tafari, our new King." And as to the British flag flying over Jamaica, "I am here to inform you," Howell stated, "that King George's flag is no flag for you. Yours is the Ethiopian flag—the green, yellow, and red flag, the robe of the Virgin Mary" (quoted in Lee 2003, pp. 65–66).

As urban laborers mobilized into labor movements and political parties in the 1930s and 1940s, Howell's followers took a different route to resist white colonial rule. Building on the idea that people needed their own land and modeled after maroon communities and nineteenth-century Baptist mission towns, Howell gained possession of a parcel of land west of Kingston in 1939 that he named "Pinnacle" where the poor and disenfranchised could worship. Residents called themselves "Ethiopian warriors." Pinnacle became a self-sufficient community largely financed by cultivating marijuana, which soon became an important sacrament in Rasta worship—something again finding Biblical justification in Psalms and Revelation.

Few outsiders knew much about Pinnacle's residents. Alexander Bustamante considered Howell dangerous, and the editors of Jamaica's *The Daily Gleaner* called Howell a monarch of a socialist colony. By the 1950s, authorities feared this was an extremist branch within an emerging anti-colonial movement. Police regularly raided Pinnacle, arrested Rastas, cut off their dreadlocks and beards, and tried to undermine Rasta to potential followers. By 1954, repression devastated Pinnacle, but the religion did not die. Instead, it spread around the island and especially to Kingston's slums where thousands of Jamaicans continued a decades-long migration from the countryside.

The government was correct to see Rasta as a form of anti-colonialism. To Rastas, all the West was where African peoples lived in Babylonian captivity awaiting liberation and repatriation to Zion. For many Rastas, repatriation to the motherland was essential. They unsuccessfully petitioned the government to finance their return to Africa, but in 1948 Selassie set aside 500 acres of Ethiopian land for African-descended people in the West. Hundreds of Rastas moved to Ethiopia. However, other Rastas began calling for liberation within

Babylon. From a Rasta worldview, the 1950s and 1960s proved that Babylon was falling: anti-colonial movements around the world, African independence movements, the civil rights movement in the United States, even the Cuban Revolution as an attack on the Babylonian United States. For Rastas, Zion was casting off Babylon.

In 1960, researchers at the University of the West Indies investigated the Rastas, concluding that they were not dangerous, and the government should "rehabilitate" them. In 1961, the government sent Rasta elder Mortimer Planno on an Africa fact-finding trip, where he met Selassie. Then, in 1965, Prime Minister Eric Williams of Trinidad conducted a nine-nation Africa tour and invited Selassie to the Caribbean. Jamaican officials believed that if Rastas saw the short, light-skinned emperor, they might question whether this could truly be the all-mighty black God of their faith. If the government hoped to undermine Rasta, their plan completely backfired. Following his visit to Trinidad, Selassie continued to Jamaica. In April 1966, as Selassie's planed taxied on the tarmac, the largest crowd ever for a foreign dignitary stormed police lines to greet Selassie.

Over the coming decades, Rasta morphed from just traditional religious groups calling for the fall of Babylon to more moderate and even secular forms of Rasta-inspired popular resistance. Radical students in Jamaica in the late 1960s celebrated Rasta's Afrocentric views but rejected Selassie's divination, while some Rastas joined left-wing organizations of workers, students, and political parties in the early 1970s. Rasta spread around the globe as well, becoming the first Caribbean religion to "conquer" the world.

Rasta and the Cultural Politics of Reggae Music in the 1970s

Reggae was key to this global conquest. Count Ossie (Oswald Williams) learned traditional Rasta drumming and played with the Rasta community in the 1940s and 1950s. His drumming style became central to Jamaican ska music which evolved into "reggae"—a term coined by "Toots" Hibbert of Toots and the Maytals. The Nyabinghi mansion rejected reggae music, though, believing that commercial appeal through technology and Babylon's capitalist markets failed to give due reverence to faith. They considered only Nyabinghi drumming and chanting as divine music. However, by the 1970s, some Rasta elders rethought the relationship between reggae and Rasta. Mortimer Planno, who had welcomed Selassie to Jamaica, encouraged Bob Marley to use reggae to spread Rasta globally.

Reggae music is associated with a happy, easy-living vibe—One love, one heart, let's get together and feel alright—that has become key to Caribbean tourist boards' efforts to market the islands. Yet, reggae always was a vehicle for Afrocentrism, anti-colonialism, black consciousness, and the masses' political empowerment. Roots reggae, from the 1970s to early 1980s, functioned as "conscious music" to awaken people to pursue their rights and justice in an unjust world. Jamaican reggae of this era commented on Jamaican reality while its transnational reach advocated for the world's marginalized peoples. Reggae inspired rebellious musical and political movements globally. This was liberation music to free people from captivity.

Though slavery ended over a century earlier and though many of the British West Indies were becoming independent, political leaders in the post-colonial era seemed to run things like before. The fight against Babylon was never-ending. Marley's 1973 song "Slave Driver" linked slavery and modern inequality, equating the brutality of the slave whip and slave ship with the brutalization of modern people's souls by a world focused on materialism and making money. Other songs by Marley, The Abyssinians, and Burning Spear challenged this ongoing colonial/neocolonial mentality in the independent Caribbean.

Ganja too had its political dimensions. Governments harassed Rastas over it. One of Peter Tosh's first hits, 1976's "Legalize It," called for the legalization of marijuana. For Tosh, people had to reject Babylon's treatment of God's holy herb. "Legalize It" was a revolutionary tune at a time when Kingston and Washington cooperated to eradicate marijuana fields and stop aerial shipments to the United States.

Reggae in the 1970s promoted Pan-Africanism. Burning Spear celebrated it in the song "Marcus Garvey." Marley's 1979 song "Africa Unite"—the title says it all—was a global anthem, especially by the early 1980s when South Africa's black majority increased its fight against apartheid, Afro-Cuban soldiers aided rebel groups in Angola and Namibia, and rebels in British Rhodesia fought for independence. When rebels in British Rhodesia won their 15-year guerrilla war and became Zimbabwe in 1980, the new government invited Marley to perform a concert following the ceremony that transferred power from Great Britain. It only made sense as not only did Marley's music reflect Pan-Africanism and anti-colonialism but also guerrilla forces had gone into battle listening to his songs and wearing Marley's image.

Reggae also focused attention on the fight against Babylon. Tosh's 1977 "Downpressor Man" celebrates the faithful who will watch as the oppressor (the downpressor) gets his due on Judgement Day. Marley was perhaps the best-known musical supporter and exporter of Haile Selassie's divinity. In songs and interviews, he praised Selassie as Earth's rightful ruler. His concerts prominently featured Selassie's image on stage. In 1973, Marley recorded "Iron Lion Zion" promoting Zion as the Biblical promised land and the antithesis to Babylon. The Lion was a central icon of the Ethiopian flag, and Selassie was the Lion of Juda. One cannot discuss the importance of Selassie in Marley's music without referencing his 1976 song "War" based on Selassie's 1963 speech to the United Nations.

Throughout the 1970s, Jamaica's JLP and the PNP political parties waged war with each other not just in electoral campaigns but also on the streets as each party armed supporters for urban warfare. Marley and others performed peace concerts to end the violence. However, many people thought the singer should stay out of politics. Before he was to perform in the 1976 Smile Jamaica peace concert on the eve of new elections, armed men entered Marley's compound, shot his wife Rita in the head and Bob in the arm and chest. Miraculously, both fully recovered and went on to play the concert. After touring the world, Marley returned to Jamaica in 1978 amid new political violence. He performed at the One Love Peace Concert, famously bringing to the stage leaders of the two rival parties—Edward Seaga and Michael Manley—and holding together the hands of all three men. The event exemplified just how political reggae music could be.

One would be remiss not to note one of the most important movies from Caribbean film history: 1972's "The Harder They Come," starring reggae legend Jimmy Cliff. The movie and soundtrack introduced many beyond Jamaica to reggae even before the name Bob Marley became known far and wide. The movie and the 1980 novel by Michael Thelwell explore the hard life of Jamaica's urban poor, the structural forces repressing them, and the challenges of resisting Babylon via the main character Ivanhoe Martin, aka Rhygin' (played by Cliff). The reggae-dominated soundtrack gave musical power to Ivan/Rhygin', who finds himself victimized by Christianity, petty street thievery, and a corrupt record business in league with corrupt cops who oversee the ganja trade. When Ivan shoots a policeman and battles corruption (i.e., attacks Babylon), he becomes a ghetto hero, making a mockery of police attempts to arrest him even as the Bablyonian record business begins making money off Ivan's song "The Harder They Come" because people demand to hear their hero. In the end, Ivan tries but fails to reach Cuba, where many Black Power advocates went into exile from the United States at that same time. He dies in a bloody shoot-out with Jamaican security forces.

AIMÉ CÉSAIRE, FRANTZ FANON, AND WALTER RODNEY: INTELLECTUAL ROOTS OF BLACK POWER

By mid-century, numerous Caribbean writers developed analyses of black consciousness and black power in both global and Caribbean contexts. As a member of the French Communist Party, Aimé Césaire participated in French and Martinican politics, serving as mayor of Fort-de-France and as a Martinican deputy to the French National Assembly. In 1950, Césaire published *Discours sur le colonialisme* (Discourse on Colonialism), which became a key text in a wave of 1950s–1960s anti-colonial literature. Colonizers liked to argue that peoples under colonialism benefited materially, politically, and culturally from European colonial rule. Césaire argued that through law enforcement, forced labor, and a colonial ideology of racial and cultural hierarchies, colonialism always benefited the colonizer, never the colonized. Colonizers always rationalized their rule by claiming they attacked backwardness and savagery. Yet, it was colonizers themselves who acted barbarically by stealing land, raping, killing, and then forcing an ideology that praised the supposedly "civilized" brutalizer:

"colonization works to *decivilize* the colonizer, to brutalize him in the true sense of the word, to degrade him, to awaken him to buried instincts, to covetousness, violence, race hatred, and moral relativism." Thus, colonization destroyed not only the colonized but also the supposed "civilizer" (Césaire 2000, p. 35).

Ultimately, European colonialism in Africa and the Caribbean was exploitative, racist, and dehumanizing. However, Césaire did not echo noiristes and argue that places like Martinique had to return to some African past. Rather, Afro-Caribbean peoples needed to focus on a forward-looking project of self-rule and self-determination: "For us, the problem is not to make a utopian and sterile attempt to repeat the past, but to go beyond. It is not a dead society that we want to revive....It is a new society that we must create, with the help of our brother slaves, a society rich with all the productive power of modern times, warm with all the fraternity of olden days"—and it would be the proletariat who guided the way (Césaire 2000, pp. 51–52). As Robin Kelley puts it, the *Discourse* was like "an act of insurrection" or a declaration of war (Kelley 2002, p. 181).

Césaire's Martinican comrade Frantz Fanon expanded this critique of colonialism's racial and class oppression. After joining Free French forces to fight Nazis, he became a prominent psychiatrist and author of two internationally influential books: *Black Skin, White Masks* (1952) and *The Wretched of the Earth* (1963). Both became prominent anti-colonial texts. Fanon believed Afro-Caribbean peoples lived two lives: one in the European world and another in the African world—a divided life created and perpetuated by colonialism. In the process, peoples of African descent lost their cultural identity and adopted a colonial identity. Black intellectuals like noiristes long had described mulattoes this way, but now Fanon turned to the black masses and said that they too had suffered this disruption in their identities. Marley sang about this when he urged people to "free yourselves from mental slavery"—the slavery of "free" people who identify with their colonizer. For too long, Caribbean peoples of African descent had imitated whites and Europe by valuing the colonial language, education system, capitalism, and more, thus thinking of themselves as "British" or "French" West Indians. The result was that by the 1950s and 1960s, black-skinned leaders walked around with white masks and became the "transmission line between the nation and capitalism," creating neocolonialism (quoted in Bogues 2009, p. 129).

Fanon stressed the multiple ways that colonialism violently violated the body, culture, identity, and mind of the colonized. Colonial rulers weaponized European culture to denigrate African and Afro-Caribbean cultures, taught only European history, and created laws privileging race and class. This was structural violence. So, if colonialism was violent, then anti-colonialism must be too. Fanon wrote that urban-based revolutionary intellectuals, hounded by colonial police, fled to the countryside where "they discover that the rural masses have never ceased to pose the problem of their liberation in terms of violence, of taking back the land from the foreigners, in terms of *national struggle* and armed revolt. These men discover a coherent people who survive in a kind of petrified state but keep intact their moral values and their attachment to the nation....The men from the towns let themselves be guided by the people and at the same time give them military and political training. The people sharpen their weapons. In fact, the training proves short-lived, for the masses, realizing their own muscles, force the leaders to accelerate events. The armed struggle is triggered" (Fanon 1963/1974, p. 79). This man from Martinique became a key intellectual influence in global anti-colonial struggles, especially Arab-Muslim Algeria's anti-colonial war against France in the late 1950s and early 1960s (he is buried in Algeria). His two books became required reading among Third World revolutionaries.

The third important mid-century intellectual in Caribbean black power was British Guiana-born Walter Rodney. After receiving his Ph.D. in African History in London in 1966, Rodney first taught in the new independent socialist Tanzania, then taught history at the University of the West Indies in Jamaica. From the start, he was controversial. Jamaica's education and political establishments did not like what he taught (Afrocentric history at a time when few did), and they did not like to whom he taught (not only university students but also poor and illiterate people in Kingston's ghettoes). Some of his talks were collected into the book *Groundings with My Brothers*—groundings referred to being at ground level speaking with people to discuss the root causes of problems; or, as he put it: "I have sat on a little oil drum, rusty and in the midst of garbage, and some black brothers and I have grounded together." Rodney argued Black Power and White Power (white supremacy) were not two sides of the same coin. Black Power sought to liberate the masses, while White Power dominated the masses and forced them into servitude. Violence (physical, cultural, structural, and psychological) of each could not be measured by the same yardstick since one advocated *black freedom* and the other advocated *black submission*.

In the West Indies, Black Power meant three specific things for Rodney. First, the West Indies had to completely break with imperialism. Second, because West Indian populations were majority black, those masses should be in power. This was democracy—majority rule. Third, West Indian culture had to be reconstructed to reflect the image of the masses, that is, privileging the culture and history of Afro-Caribbeans, not Europeans. It was not good enough that peoples of African descent rule, but they had to rule as "blacks" (not with a white mask, as Fanon put it). To this end, a Black Power government had to eliminate what the Marxist Rodney called "the lackeys of imperialism"—essentially black and brown people who ruled after their independence but did so in ways that allowed neocolonialism to take root via cultural penetration and capitalist domination. Black Power meant breaking these ties and bringing forth true independence in ways exemplified by Fanon.

Still, for Rodney, "black" was more than a color or race. It also was a class designation. Rodney incorporated mulatto and East Indian populations into his analysis. He suggested that because of how colonialism and imperialism racialized oppression, white oppressors considered mulattos and East Indians to be "black." Black Power movements should welcome mulattos and Indians if they chose to side with the black masses. In a sense, Black Power included all who were victimized by Tosh's "Downpressor Man." Thus, Black Power could be about both class and race liberation like the ABB had argued 50 years earlier.

BLACK POWER ACROSS THE CARIBBEAN

In 1966, 500 delegates from Africa, Asia, and the Americas attended the Tricontinental Conference in Havana. They sought transnational solidarity by creating a global Communist network to condemn capitalism, colonialism, and imperialism while seeking world revolution. They also attacked racism inherent in colonialism and imperialism, condemned white-minority rule in southern Africa, and supported the US Civil Rights movement. As Anthony Bogues puts it, the Tricontinental's "program of radical solidarity and internationalism marked a critical moment. At the global level, Black Power became connected to this internationalism" (Bogues 2009, p. 130).

West Indian governments increasingly viewed Black Power with alarm. Take the Henry Rebellion of 1960: Claudius Henry organized the first guerrilla movement in modern British Caribbean history, claimed Haile Selassie saw Jamaica as part of Africa, asked Cuba's Fidel Castro for support, and organized a First Africa Corps in New York to infiltrate Jamaica with weapons to arm Rastas who would be trained to seize power. In this atmosphere of Henry and the Tricontinental, Kingston banned black nationalist writings of people like Malcolm X and Stokely Carmichael. In October 1968, after attending a Montreal conference also attended by black consciousness advocates C.L.R. James and Carmichael, Walter Rodney returned to Jamaica, but authorities denied his reentry. This sparked a wave of demonstrations from the Caribbean to Canada, including the so-called Rodney Riots when some 2000 students, workers, and Rastas rebelled in Jamaica.

Meanwhile, Black Power movements spread across the Caribbean: the United Black Socialist Party Abeng in Dominica, Abeng in Jamaica, and others in Belize, Antigua, Guyana, and the Virgin Islands. Rodney's ideas gave voice to Jamaica's Rude Bwoys. Coming from the poorest sectors of unemployed society, these disaffected youth identified with Selassie, Garvey, Malcolm X, Che Guevara, and Rodney. They attended groundings and became for a time an armed wing of the Black Power cause. Jamaican Black Power advocates published the newspaper *Abeng*, which printed poetry, analyzed Afro-Caribbean culture, and covered the Black Power movement in the United States and African liberation struggles. *Abeng* offered a transnational Black Power perspective for readers, while editors linked themselves to broader resistance forces in Jamaica, especially trade unions, the PNP party, and Rastas.

The Black Beret Cadre in Bermuda focused on decolonization, and members created a liberation school to teach Rodney's ideas to youth. The government crushed the Cadre in 1972. However, it remained vigilant enough to assassinate the police commissioner who had repressed them, influenced the government to improve living standards for the island's population of African descent, and increased the visible presence of Afrocentric culture.

Meanwhile, after the Cuban Revolution, US tourists turned toward the US Virgin Islands, which saw a surge in hotels and tourism that led to privatization of many beaches. Beach access reflected social and racial inequality in the islands as "foreign" whites had access to beaches that "native" peoples of African descent did not. In the early 1970s, the Free Beach Movement (FBM) protested this condition through rallies, swim-ins, and letter-writing campaigns. The FBM's indirect challenge to US colonial rule in the Virgin Islands also questioned racial and class dimensions of tourism. Many of the FBM's rank-and-file members believed in Black Power. As Derick Hendricks argues, the FBM was an "example of black mobilization in a colonial Caribbean context" that emphasized "cultural self-determination and black solidarity" (Hendricks 2014, p. 219).

Black Power and the 1970 Trinidad Revolution

One of the most significant demonstrations of Black Power occurred in Trinidad in early 1970, with its roots in both Trinidad and Canada, its influence stretching to Guyana, and its aftermath leading to armed resistance. In February 1969, Canadian authorities arrested Caribbean university students who attacked and occupied the computer lab at Sir George Williams University in Montreal to protest racism and discrimination at the school. One of those arrested was the son of Guyanese political figures Cheddi and Janet Jagan. In Trinidad and Tobago, African- and Indian-descended peoples—especially from Trinidad's University of the West Indies campus—marched in protest. To mark the protests' first anniversary in February 1970, men and women formed the National Joint Action Committee (NJAC; Trinidad's most important Black Power organization), allied with steel bands and unions representing oil workers and sugarcane cutters, and took to the streets shouting, "Power to the People." NJAC's leader was Geddes Granger, known as Makandal Daaga—"Daaga" after a rebel within the British West Indies Regiment in Trinidad who mutinied in 1837 against the British, and "Makandal" possibly after the famous rebel in eighteenth-century Saint-Domingue. On 12 March 1970, Daaga and the NJAC led 40,000 protestors on a 26-mile "March to Caroni" for national unity.

Black Power women joined NJAC, serving on its Central Committee, distributing pamphlets, debating Black Power, and speaking at meetings and demonstrations. Several women challenged the movement's masculine nature. They advocated women's issues and pushed against any form of black male patriarchy within these movements because they had experienced not only racial and capitalist exploitation but also sexism. Sometimes Black Power leaders (women and men) glorified heterosexual motherhood but doing so risked excluding single and lesbian women. Many Black Power women also fought this exclusionary practice which—like all exclusionary, exploitative practices—had to be purged from society.

Since the 1970 Revolution occurred during Carnival season, annual festivities became politicized. Carnival marchers carried pictures of Carmichael, Malcolm X (whose mother was from Grenada and whose parents were Garveyites), and others. They marched with a picture of Prime Minister Eric Williams looking like a pig. The band King Sugar marched with a banner reading "Black blood, black sweat, black tears—white profits!" Demonstrators attacked the Williams government, Catholic Church, Canadian High Commission, and Royal Bank of Canada—believing all acted as "white" institutions repressing the masses. Violence erupted as people threw Molotov cocktails at banks, businesses, the Ministry of Education and Culture, and the US vice consul. Williams acquiesced and offered small reforms, but by late March and early April, protestors wanted radical action. In response, Williams declared a state of emergency and crushed the uprising (Fig. 8.1).

Black Power groups rarely resorted to armed violence, but Trinidad was different. As Brian Meeks puts it, the events of 1970 "could not simply end by proclamation" with Williams declaring the uprising over. Too many people had been radicalized and the military had mutinied (Meeks 2001, p. 50). Black Power activists grew disillusioned with the NJAC's retreat from confrontational politics. In response, some pursued armed struggle. Militants led by Jai Kernahan formed the National United Freedom Fighters (NUFF) and

Fig. 8.1   Black Power and the 1970 Trinidad Revolution (Creative Commons/Angelo Bissessarsingh)

relocated to the mountains to wage guerrilla warfare, rob banks, destroy a satellite uplink, ambush police, and shoot officials. They sought to purge the country of international capitalists and those who aided them with the goal of creating a Black Power, socialist, and anti-sexist unified Caribbean. Women like Beverley and Jennifer Jones joined the armed struggle, fighting on equal terms with men as NUFF considered revolutionary women vital to the struggle. Beverley died in action in 1973, becoming, as W. Chris Johnson puts it, "NUFF's slaughtered symbol…the nation's deviant daughter: a cross-dressing, ganja-smoking guerrilla girl who wanted to destroy capitalism and build a new nation in the hills" (Johnson 2014, p. 679). The Williams government defeated the NUFF in late 1973.

The Trinidad Revolution had ramifications throughout the Caribbean. It inspired the Caribbean Liberation Movement in Antigua and the New Jewel Movement in Grenada that in 1979 would lead a socialist revolution of that island (its leaders Maurice Bishop and Bernard Coard were in Trinidad during the 1970 rebellion). In Guyana, Forbes Burnham was prime minister when the Trinidad rebellion erupted. In February 1970, Burnham proclaimed Guyana a "cooperative republic," moved leftward, joined in alliance with Cuba, and began supporting African liberation movements. Burnham welcomed to Guyana many Black Power advocates banned in other islands, making him the only Caribbean leader other than Cuba's Fidel Castro to support Black Power. When Prime Minister Williams in Trinidad requested military assistance from Burnham to help suppress the rebellion, Burnham refused.

Burnham's support for Black Power in Trinidad was a tactical move, more about containing the movement in his own country than a reflection of his political views. By supporting Caribbean Black Power, Burnham hoped to bring Guyana's Black Power movement into his Afro-Guyanese power base and away from the political opposition in the country. Plus, Burnham's "Black Power" contradicted that of Walter Rodney. Now living in Guyana, Rodney duplicated Trinidad's Indian-Black coalition through his Working People's Alliance. While Burnham spoke of Black Power in racial terms, Rodney saw "Black" as a reflection of "the oppressed" and that exploited peoples of African descent and Indians could unite—an idea he advocated in groundings, talks, debates, scholarly writings, and children's books that he authored. Burnham's government eventually had enough with Black Power and the historian. In June 1980, they assassinated Rodney with a bomb.

Conclusion

Throughout the twentieth century, black consciousness ideas spread around the Caribbean and throughout the diaspora. The PIC sought political representation for Afro-Cubans. However, authorities saw the party as divisive and violating the spirit of José Martí's call of a "Cuba for all." They crushed it in 1912. The UNIA, the ABB, and Communist Parties pursued black consciousness agendas in the US and Caribbean, with the latter two blending black nationalism and Marxism that reflected the Bolshevik Revolution's impact. In Haiti, black consciousness noiristes came to political power while Rastas in Jamaica resisted governmental harassment to become a globally influential movement.

Rodney's Black Power ideas reflected a transnational resistance both in origins and in implications. Building on the black consciousness ideas of Garvey, Césaire, Fanon and the Rastas, this Guyana-born radical stirred up not only Jamaica but also the wider region as Black Power movements rose in the 1960s and 1970s to challenge neocolonial governments. Activists transferred Black Power, black consciousness, and Pan-Africanism around the region and throughout the diaspora via culture too. Novels, plays, short stories, and poetry from Harlem Renaissance, negrismo, and négritude writers developed a new way of looking and expressing the world from an Afro-Caribbean vantage point, challenging elites who held on to European cultural expressions. Reggae musicians took Rasta's messages to global audiences, bringing to the world's ears lyrical expressions of Pan-Africanism and challenges to neocolonialism from a distinct Afro-Caribbean perspective.

Black consciousness movements (literary, political, musical) confronted dominant cultures in the Caribbean, gave voice to oppressed peoples, and changed the conversation about Caribbean history. Yet, one might ask how successful they were in reshaping Caribbean power dynamics. Yes, school curriculums changed, Afro-Caribbean heroes became "national" heroes, and Afro-Caribbean cultural expressions became accepted and normalized. However, did they really change who ruled the region or how dependent the region remained on exports or tourism (which often meant marketing Afro-Caribbean culture to visitors)? As we scan the region, it is somewhat depressing to consider that the only black consciousness movement to achieve political power—the Duvalier regime in Haiti—also proved to be one of the most brutal, authoritarian governments in Caribbean history. This is not to say black consciousness and Black Power had embedded in them such barbarism. It is to suggest, though, that cultural-, ethnic-, and race-based resistance struggled to create a new power base around black consciousness ideas without governments and tourist boards absorbing and appropriating those ideas for different ends.

WORKS CITED AND FURTHER REFERENCES

A Hubert Harrison Reader (2001) J.B. Perry (ed.) (Wesleyan University Press).

G. Averill (1997) *A Day for the Hunter, A Day for the Prey* (University of Chicago Press).

L. Barrett (1987) *The Rastafarians* (Beacon).

A. Bogues (2003) *Black Heretics, Black Prophets: Radical Political Intellectuals* (Routledge).

———— (2009) "Black Power, Decolonization, and Caribbean Politics: Walter Rodney and the Politics of *The Groundings with My Brothers*," *boundary*, 2/36, 127–47.

———— (2014) "The *Abeng* Newspaper and the Radical Politics of Postcolonial Blackness" in Kate Quinn (ed.) *Black Power in the Caribbean* (University Press of Florida), 76–95.

G. Bonacci (2015) *Exodus, Heirs, and Pioneers: Rastafari Return to Ethiopia* (University of the West Indies Press).

T. Brunson (2019) "The Role of Women in the Partido Independiente de Color" in Aisha Finch and Fannie Rushing (eds.) *Breaking the Chains, Forging the Nation: The Afro-Cuban Fight for Freedom and Equality, 1812–1912* (Louisiana State University Press), 272–88.

H. Campbell (1987) *Rasta and Resistance: From Marcus Garvey to Walter Rodney* (Africa World).

M. Casey (2017) *Empire's Guestworkers: Haitian Migrants in Cuba during the Age of US Occupation* (Cambridge University Press).

A. Césaire (1939/2013) *Notebook of a Return to the Native Land* (Wesleyan University Press).

———— (2000) *Discourse on Colonialism* (Monthly Review).

B. Chevannes (1994) *Rastafari: Roots and Ideology* (Syracuse University Press).

R. Drayton (2014) "Secondary Decolonization: The Black Power Movement in Barbados, c. 1970" in Kate Quinn (ed.) *Black Power in the Caribbean* (University Press of Florida), 117–35.

F. Fanon (2008) *Black Skin, White Masks* (Grove).

———— (1963/1974) *The Wretched of the Earth* (Penguin).

M. Garvey (1920) *Declaration of the Rights of the Negro Peoples of the World: The Principles of the Universal Negro Improvement Association* http://historymatters. gmu.edu/d/5122/

A. Helg (1995) *Our Rightful Share: The Afro-Cuban Struggle for Equality, 1886–1912* (University of North Carolina Press).

D. Hendricks (2014) "Youth Responses to Discriminatory Practices: The Free Beach Movement, 1970–1975" in Kate Quinn (ed.) *Black Power in the Caribbean* (University Press of Florida), 219–38.

G. Heuman (2014) *The Caribbean: A Brief History* 2nd edition (Bloomsbury).

C. Høgsberg (2017) *Chris Braithwaite: Mariner, Renegade and Castaway* (Redwords).

W. James (2011) "Culture, Labor, and Race in the Shadow of US Capital" in Stephan Palmié and Francisco Scarano (eds.) *The Caribbean: A History of the Region and Its Peoples* (University of Chicago Press), 445–58.

———— (1998) *Holding Aloft the Banner of Ethiopia: Caribbean Radicalism in Early Twentieth-Century America* (Verso).

W.C. Johnson (2014) "Guerrilla Ganja Gun Girls: Policing Black Revolutionaries from Notting Hill to Laventille," *Gender & History* 26/3, 661–87.

R. Kelley (2002) *Freedom Dreams: The Black Radical Imagination* (Beacon).

———— (1996) *Race Rebels: Culture, Politics, and the Black Working Class* (Free Press).

V. Kutzinski (1993) *Sugar's Secrets: Race and the Erotics of Cuban Nationalism* (University of Virginia Press).

H. Lee (2003) *The First Rasta: Leonard Howell and the Rise of Rastafarianism* (Lawrence Hill Books).

R. Lewis (2014) "Jamaican Black Power in the 1960s" in Kate Quinn (ed.) *Black Power in the Caribbean* (University Press of Florida), 53–75.

B. Meeks (2001) *Narratives of Resistance: Jamaica, Trinidad, the Caribbean* (University of the West Indies Press).

——— (1996) *Radical Caribbean: From Black Power to Abu Bakr* (University of the West Indies Press).

M. Pappademos (2011) *Black Political Activism and the Cuban Republic* (University of North Carolina Press).

V. Pasley (2001) "The Black Power Movement in Trinidad: An Exploration of Gender and Cultural Changes and the Development of a Feminist Consciousness," *Journal of International Women's Studies* 3/1, 24–40.

J.B. Perry (2021) *Hubert Harrison: The Struggle for Equality, 1918–1927* (Columbia University Press).

J. Price-Mars (1928/1983) *So Spoke the Uncle* (Three Continents Press).

L. Putnam (2013) *Radical Moves: Caribbean Migrants and the Politics of Race in the Age of Jazz* (University of North Carolina Press).

K. Quinn (2014) "'Sitting on a Vocano': Black Power in Burnham's Guyana" in Kate Quinn (ed.) *Black Power in the Caribbean* (University Press of Florida), 136–58.

W. Rodney (2001) *The Groundings with My Brothers* (Frontline Distribution International).

B. Samaroo (2014) "The February Revolution (1970) as a Catalyst for Change in Trinidad and Tobago" in Kate Quinn (ed.) *Black Power in the Caribbean* (University Press of Florida), 97–116.

W.R. Scott (1993) *The Sons of Sheba's Race: African-Americans and the Italo-Ethiopian War, 1935–1941* (Indiana University Press).

T.D. Sharpley-Whiting (2000) "*Femme négritude*: Jane Nardal, *La Dépeche africaine*, and the Francophone New Negro," *Souls*, (Fall), 8–17.

M. Sheller (2000) *Democracy after Slavery: Black Publics and Peasant Radicalism in Haiti and Jamaica* (University Press of Florida).

M.J. Smith (2009) *Red & Black in Haiti: Radicalism, Conflict, and Political Change, 1934–1957* (University of North Carolina Press).

M. Stevens (2017) *Red International and Black Caribbean: Communists in New York City, Mexico and the West Indies, 1919–1939* (Pluto).

Q. Swan (2014) "I and I Shot the Sheriff: Black Power and Decolonization in Bermuda, 1968 1977" in Kate Quinn (ed.) *Black Power in the Caribbean* (University Press of Florida), 197–218.

"The Harder They Come" (1972) Perry Henzell (dir.) (International Films).

M. Thelwell (1994) *The Harder They Come: A Novel* (Grove).

M.-R. Trouillot (2000) *Haiti: State against Nation* (Monthly Review).

W. Zips (1999) *Black Rebels: African Caribbean Freedom Fighters in Jamaica* (Marcus Wiener).

CHAPTER 9

Hasta la Victoria Siempre: The Cuban Revolution Throughout the Caribbean, 1950s–1980s

In the 1960s, Trinidadian historian C.L.R. James included an update to his classic history of the Haitian Revolution *The Black Jacobins*, which contained an appendix titled "From Toussaint Louverture to Fidel Castro." James recognized the importance of the Haitian and Cuban revolutions shaping Caribbean history and their significance as Caribbean lightning rods shaping global history. Our penultimate chapter explores the Cuban Revolution's resistance to and victory over the dictatorship of Fulgencio Batista in the 1950s. We augment the well-known story of rural, bearded guerrillas in Cuba's eastern and central mountains with less-well-known accounts of men and women waging urban protests and warfare against Batista. Following Batista's defeat, the new government embarked on a nationalist project that also converted Cuba into the first Marxist country in the Americas. From its earliest years, the revolutionary government aided anti-dictatorial, anti-neocolonial guerrilla movements around the Caribbean. This transnational Marxism led to victories in 1979 in Grenada and Nicaragua—only to encounter US-backed resistance that overturned these two revolutionary experiments.

Our story tells other tales of resistance: transnational and domestic opposition to the Cuban socialist experiment. This resistance was sometimes violent, as with early armed attacks by domestic counterrevolutionaries in Cuba and armed opponents who had fled to exile in Miami. Domestic opposition emerged from numerous sources. Some resisted the lack of democratic rights and journalistic freedoms. Others disagreed with Sovietization and growing state control over many aspects of life. Still others resisted the revolution because they felt it did not go far enough in creating a free, egalitarian society. The rise of world-renown Cuban cinema fell between this dichotomy of support and opposition as movies helped to create Che Guevara's "new socialist" Cuban but also challenged the revolution.

© The Author(s), under exclusive license to Springer Nature Switzerland AG 2022
K. Shaffer, *A Transnational History of the Modern Caribbean*, https://doi.org/10.1007/978-3-030-93012-7_9

Urban and Rural Resistance Against
the Batista Dictatorship

Looking at aggregate statistics alone, one might think 1950s Cuba was one of the more economically advanced places in Latin America and the Caribbean. It had comparatively high literacy, more televisions and cars per capita, thriving tourism, and a stable trading relationship with the United States that enhanced economic growth. However, economic growth and economic development are very different concepts. While growth reflects trade, gross domestic product, and income per capita, development illustrates how the fruits of growth are distributed and enjoyed by the population for their benefit and improvement.

Cuba failed miserably at development under Batista's dictatorship following a military coup in 1952. Corruption blanketed the island. The US mafia colluded with Batista to run a drug-casino-prostitution trifecta. Cuba's economy completely depended on imports from and exports to the United States. Investment centered on large cities (especially Havana), resulting in massive rural poverty. All of this led to severe housing shortages, unemployment, underemployment, and high costs of living. Cuba was ripe for resistance.

Opposition emerged from the beginning of Batista's reign, erupting in the island's universities, among the middle class, and in the countryside. Women and men came together, disgusted by corruption and wanton violence. On 26 July 1953, revolutionaries led by Fidel Castro attacked the Moncada military barracks in Santiago de Cuba on the island's eastern end. This area long had been a bastion of revolutionary upheaval from the days of slave revolts following the Haitian Revolution to the wars for independence.

Castro's attack failed militarily but proved politically important in the anti-Batista struggle. At his trial, Castro defended his actions by painting a picture of corruption, exploitation, unending social problems, and brutal tyranny. He called for a largely reformist solution of improved living standards and a return to democracy. While the court sentenced Castro to prison, supporters published his trial defense as *La historia me absolverá* (History Will Absolve Me). Among other points in his defense, Castro asserted that the 1940 Cuban Constitution legitimized his armed uprising since Batista "betrayed" the Constitution and "deprived" Cubans of their rights. Thus, "the right to resist oppression and injustice" was the last remaining right because Batista had destroyed all others, pointing out that "the right of rebellion against tyranny, Honourable Magistrates, has been recognized from the most ancient times to the present day by men of all creeds, ideas and doctrines." In fact, "the right to rebellion is at the very roots of Cuba's existence as a nation" since Cuba was born from revolt against Spanish tyranny. Castro then listed a litany of anti-tyranny revolts from the ancient world to the French Revolution—though oddly not the Haitian Revolution (Castro 1968, pp. 94–100).

In May 1955, the Batista government issued a general amnesty, releasing Castro and numerous political prisoners. Fidel traveled to the United States to raise funds and then relocated to Mexico. There, he met the young Argentinian

Ernesto "Che" Guevara. In 1954, a leftist democratic government was in power in Guatemala when US-trained Guatemalan exiles overthrew the government of Jacobo Arbenz. Che Guevara was in Guatemala at the time, witnessing the US-backed assault against democracy and the imposition of military dictatorship. Che took the resulting hatred of imperialism with him to Mexico, where he became a key figure in Castro's thinking and eventually in the armed struggle versus Batista.

In November 1956, Castro's band of 82 men left Mexico, sailed across the Caribbean, and landed in eastern Cuba. The expedition from their base in Mexico continued a long history of Cuban exiles plotting the overthrow of a tyrannous government from across the Caribbean in Mexico: the Águila Negra in the 1820s, exiles in the 1890s, and leftists in the 1920s and 1930s. However, a tipped-off army unit attacked Castro's band, forcing survivors to scramble for their lives. Survivors included Fidel, his brother Raúl, Che, Juan Almeida, and Camilo Cienfuegos. They regrouped and formed the M-26-7 (July 27th Movement named after the date of the Moncada attack). Over the next two-and-a-half years, they expanded, gaining recruits from cities and support from small towns and villages around the Sierra Maestra mountains.

In 1957 and 1958, the rural campaign against Batista successfully spread west across Cuba. Not all guerrillas were Cuban. A US citizen—William Morgan—led one column of the rebel army, and after the revolution came to power he helped to defeat an armed uprising financed by Rafael Trujillo in August 1959. Women fought in the mountains with Fidel, including his soon-to-be longtime partner Celia Sánchez. Fidel created the Mariana Grajales Unit—an all-women's guerrilla unit named after the mother of Afro-Cuban independence general Antonio Maceo, killed in December 1896. In 1957, the mayor of Havana had named her the "Mother of Cuba."

Rebels waged rural guerrilla warfare against Batista's forces. As Che Guevara wrote later in his manual on guerrilla warfare, the rebels sought to turn their fight into a popular insurrection with "popular" being the key term. Rebels had to gain people's support, not by attacking schools, stores, and other targets that people needed to survive in their miserable lives. That would be terrorism and people would reject joining the armed struggle. Rather, rebels struck targets that oppressed the people. For Che, people would join the fight if rebels attacked police stations or taxing authorities—all dreaded institutions that made people's lives more wretched. The M-26-7 believed average people should benefit immediately from the armed struggle. Thus, rebels created schools, health clinics, and other services to benefit the poor in rebel-controlled zones. They usually paid for food and supplies they requisitioned from people—sometimes at better prices than people received on the open market. In this way, rebels generated trust with rural peoples. If all went right, then people would freely support the insurrection.

A less-well-known urban struggle accompanied the rural rebellion. Peaceful opposition to Batista emerged in cities throughout the 1950s. Between 1952 and 1955, all-women anti-Batista organizations staged plays by nationalist icon

José Martí with themes attacking the state of dependency and tyranny in Batista-run Cuba. Women students helped organize demonstrations at universities. Women also utilized the traditional realm of the home to organize against Batista. There, they wrote letters and surreptitiously dropped them off in movie theaters and other establishments, printed flyers, held clandestine meetings, and organized "stay at home day" boycotts that paralyzed the economy. In January 1957, over 10,000 mostly middle-class and often Catholic women (many of whom were mothers of children killed by the dictatorship) silently marched through Santiago de Cuba. They wore all black, carried banners with slogans like "Stop murdering our children," and held upside-down Cuban flags. Meanwhile, anti-Batista civic groups often led by Catholic, middle- and upper-class women mobilized as mothers. Like their counterparts in the Dominican Republic who battled Trujillo at the same moment, exploiting this maternal element gave Batista's opponents a moral upper hand.

Urban guerrillas waged armed struggle. Women served as decoys and planted bombs because authorities rarely suspected women of being bombers. Police often raided the anarchist Libertarian Association of Cuba headquarters for its anti-dictatorship positions. Some anarchists like Gilberto Lima, Luis Linsuaín, and Plácido Méndez joined the M-26-7 in the cities and then left to fight in the countryside. In Havana, university student and Catholic youth leader José Antonio Echeverría led the Directorio Revolucionario (Revolutionary Directorate, or DR). Frank País—a lower-middle-class, Baptist Sunday school teacher—organized the Acción Nacional Revolucionaria (Revolutionary National Action, or ANR). The ANR consisted of small cells of young students and workers in Santiago de Cuba. Both the DR and the ANR had coordinated with Castro for his armed landing in November 1956. Some 300 ANR militants attacked military and police installations in coordination with Fidel's landing, but Castro's yacht was delayed several days by bad weather, allowing authorities to put down the urban uprising and prepare for Castro.

The urban struggle was large but dangerous. In March 1957, Echeverría stormed Havana's presidential palace to assassinate Batista. Security forces killed Echeverría during the attempt. By mid-1957, the DR abandoned urban warfare to wage war in the countryside. Meanwhile, País regrouped urban fighters in the east. In July 1957, he, Castro, and political leader Raúl Chibás signed the *Sierra Manifesto* to coordinate urban and rural revolutionary uprisings against Batista. As Luis Martínez-Fernández writes, they "rejected the possibility of an electoral deal with Batista as well as any mediation in the conflict by third nations...and any form of transitional government by a military junta" (Martínez-Fernández 2014, p. 33). Only armed struggle could topple Batista and bring back democracy. However, two weeks after signing the manifesto, the military ambushed and killed País. Some 60,000 mourners attended País' funeral while strikes, protests, and sabotage brought the island to a halt. With Echeverría and País—two of the most popular young resistance leaders—dead, Fidel consolidated the M-26-7 around his leadership and away from other anti-Batista groups in exile and around the island. That same year, leading opposition groups signed the *Pact of Caracas*, agreeing to support Fidel as the revolution's leader. With that, most M-26-7 resources went to Fidel's rural insurgency.

In early 1958, the rebel army launched all-out war on the Cuban economy. Taking from the 1890s playbook, they torched cane fields and targeted mills, factories, railroads, and oil refineries. Batista could not stop it. Throughout the year, rebel victories siphoned away more support from Batista, first from the business class and eventually from the United States. Then in late 1958, US president Eisenhower ended US support for Batista. However, in reality the United States had secretly given funds to the rebels since mid-1958, hoping that if they were victorious, then the new rebel government would look favorably on Washington and US interests in Cuba. In late December 1958, Fulgencio Batista—one of the early heroes of the 1933 Revolution that brought down the dictator Machado—fled Cuba with $300 million (approximately $2.5 billion in 2020), going first to Trujillo's Dominican Republic before eventually finding protection under Portugal's fascist dictatorship. The rebels marched into Havana.

Building the New Socialist Cuba

Few in the anti-Batista opposition anticipated the dictator's fall would usher in a complete makeover of Cuban society. Communists (known at the time as the Popular Socialist Party) did not join the rebellion until near the end. No direction came from Moscow. Few in the M-26-7 or among their supporters were Marxists, though both Raúl Castro and Che Guevara were. By all expectations, the new government would be nationalistic and enact a series of social reforms and democratic principles.

The M-26-7 manifesto reflected many of the critiques and proposals Castro had announced in *History Will Absolve Me*: end latifundia (large, private estates), limit foreign ownership, establish cooperatives, nationalize public services, enact social legislation, expand education to all, and industrialize Cuba to end dependence on tourism and agricultural exports. What shocked the world was not these proposals. What shocked the world was that the revolutionary government began to carry them out, and go further by pushing a Marxist agenda that came into the open following Washington's failed attempt to overthrow the revolution during the Bay of Pigs invasion of CIA-trained Cuban exiles in April 1961. On May Day 1961, Fidel announced a Marxist-Leninist direction for the revolution, and Che Guevara began proposing what it would take to create a new socialist Cuban.

How does one create a revolutionary, egalitarian society in an underdeveloped country long built on exploitative capitalist relations promoting self-interest? One cannot just pass laws and say the next day that "we're all socialists now so behave like it." Initially, the government used "material incentives" to build the material foundations of Cuban socialism. For instance, the government sought to improve the material conditions of women across the island.

Women flocked to new women's organizations, while the government launched the Federación de Mujeres Cubanas (Cuban Women's Federation, or FMC) led by Vilma Espín, a guerrilla fighter married to Raúl Castro. These organizations, especially the FMC, sponsored women's healthcare, day care for working mothers, education, and efforts to reform prostitutes while seeking sexual equality.

Governments long had neglected rural Cuba, making the countryside less well-off compared to cities. The new government redistributed millions of acres of land, ended the cycle of underemployment between sugar harvests, granted government aid to private farmers (though farms soon were collectivized under the state), and built new towns that provided medical clinics, schools, electricity, movie theaters, and more. The policies materially benefited rural peoples and slowed their migration to crowded cities. In the corrupt, vice-filled, housing-shortage plagued cities, the government converted abandoned mansions into apartment complexes, slashed rents, provided free bus and telephone services, closed casinos and brothels, and began anti-alcohol and drug campaigns. Meanwhile, volunteers working on a construction crew or in the fields could be rewarded with extra food, electronics, or other material items.

Yet, to Che, material incentives merely "bought off" the individual to do the revolution's work. Che argued that there had to be a corresponding change in people: how they thought, how they behaved, what they valued, what they were willing to do for the benefit of the whole and not just themselves. To do this, he proposed using "moral incentives." Acknowledgment, honors, and especially education would create a new morality, which would increase production and efficiency as well as personal satisfaction.

Che outlined ideas to create a new socialist person in his essay "Socialism and Man in Cuba." The new socialist Cuban "begins to free his thinking of the annoying fact that he needs to work to satisfy his animal needs....Work no longer entails surrendering a part of his being in the form of a labor power sold, which no longer belongs to him, but represents an emanation of himself, a contribution to the common life in which he is reflected, the fulfillment of his social duty" (Guevara 2013, p. 339). One should work because it benefitted all, not as a means for individual survival and enrichment. One worked hard for the success of the revolution, not because they received a toaster.

Che believed people should prioritize community needs over their own wants and desires. Capitalism led individuals to pursue everything for one's own benefit—greed, if you will—and in the process one became alienated from the larger community. The key was to help individuals develop a new consciousness privileging the community. When the community prospered, then individuals were less likely to feel alienated and better able to achieve their goals in the context of the rest of society benefiting. To do this, individuals had to avoid mechanically following orders to change society and instead become conscious agents of revolutionary transformation. By participating, people changed themselves as they changed society and built socialism in Cuba.

As Che put it, "The new society in formation has to compete fiercely with the past. This past makes itself felt not only in the individual consciousness...but also through the very character of this transition period [from capitalism to communism] in which commodity relations persist. The commodity is the economic cell of capitalist society. So long as it exists, its effects will make themselves felt in the organization of production and, consequently, in consciousness" (Guevara 2013, p. 338). Thus, using "things" to reward work to develop socialism retarded creation of a socialist economy and a socialist mentality.

RESISTING THE REVOLUTION: COUNTERREVOLUTIONARY VIOLENCE

By the mid-1960s, Che grew disillusioned with Cuba's growing reliance on economic and military aid from the Soviet Union. He feared this and the resulting top-down Sovietization of Cuba smothered the masses' revolutionary potential. Che—never abandoning Marxism—increasingly resisted the Cuban state's subservience to Soviet dictates. He left Cuba to lead revolutionary activity in Africa and Latin America, before dying in Bolivia in 1967. Throughout the revolution's first decade, many average Cubans also opposed the revolution's policies, centralized state control, and the state's opposition to dissent which violated the M-26-7's own calls for return to democratic institutions. Some Cubans picked up arms.

In January 1959, Fidel's former brother-in-law living in exile in New York organized the first anti-Castro exile force: La Rosa Blanca. La Rosa Blanca's leadership was rumored to have allied with Rafael Trujillo, who in the summer 1959 organized the Anticommunist League that invaded Cuba to topple the new government. Both failed. Within a few months of the revolution coming to power, 200,000 Cubans had fled to Florida, where many organized to oppose the revolution. In 1960, the US CIA brought together five Miami-based exile groups to form the Revolutionary Democratic Front. In March 1961, the US-based Revolutionary Council began training Cuban exiles in Florida and Central America to invade Cuba. Exiles expected Washington's military support. In what came to be known as the Bay of Pigs/Playa Girón affair, Washington failed to support the invasion at the last minute. The Castro-led military rebuffed the invasion, captured over 1200 exile fighters, and jailed thousands of dissidents on the island who the government believed supported the invasion. Over the coming decades, other armed efforts to topple the government arose, largely based out of Miami. These included assassinations of Cuban officials, bombing of a Cuban airliner over Barbados in 1976, and terrorist attacks on Cuban hotels. In the 1980s, less violent opposition organizations emerged, led by the Cuban American National Foundation (CANF). Founded by Bay of Pigs veterans, the CANF became a powerful lobbying organization in Washington, using its influence and Cold War rhetoric to strengthen

US policies against Cuba. In 1983, Washington launched Radio Martí (and TV Martí in 1990) to beam opposition messages into Cuba.

Armed opposition also emerged on the island. In March 1960, saboteurs blew up the French ship *La Coubre* in Havana's harbor, killing nearly 100 people. By late 1960, armed guerrillas—dubbed "bandits" by the new government—sprouted in the El Escambray Mountains of central Cuba. William Morgan—the North American guerrilla leader during the anti-Batista struggle—grew disillusioned with the revolution's direction and began running arms to the El Escambray rebels. Government militias eliminated most, but survivors regrouped and continued to fight. Meanwhile, the government captured and executed Morgan in March 1961—just weeks before the Bay of Pigs. Other armed groups secretly organized in preparation for the Bay of Pigs. They planned to spearhead an armed popular insurrection to coincide with the exile landing. On the eve of invasion in mid-April 1961, urban counterrevolutionaries bombed the popular Havana department store El Encanto.

Small farmers also grew disillusioned with the revolution's agrarian reforms. While they benefited from initial policies, those early benefits disappeared, and local peasants lost autonomy to bureaucratic state decision-makers. In 1961, peasants in western Cuba launched a four-year armed uprising and sabotage campaign against collectivization and new government labor policies. The CIA supported some, but others acted independently, burning fields, assassinating officials, and destroying property. Meanwhile, independent fishermen resisted government takeover of the fishing industry. To supporters, these peasants and fishermen were true revolutionaries, not bandits like the government labeled them. They believed the revolution had promised reform and state aid. Instead, the government was taking them over and destroying their autonomy—yet another version of the state versus the nation, as some would see it.

Other forms of resistance emerged. Exiles fueled rumors that Fidel and government leaders ate well while the masses stood in ration lines for a sliver of meat and a few eggs. Exile propaganda campaigns targeted housewives and mothers standing in these lines, leading to the 1961–1962 "Cacerolas" demonstrations. In these protests, women took to the streets, banged pots and pans, and protested food shortages.

RESISTING REVOLUTIONARY POLICIES: THE POLITICS OF CHILDHOOD IN THE EARLY 1960s

Perhaps the most famous policy reforms designed to create an egalitarian, nationalist society centered on education. Education from primary school to university cost no money (though critics argued it cost academic freedom and freedom of thought). Beyond this, the government aimed to eliminate traditional divisions between rural and urban, wealthy and poor. Thus, the government called 1961 the "Year of Education," launching a campaign to eliminate illiteracy and develop a new sense of what it meant to be "Cuban." High school and university students in cities left for the countryside to teach basic literacy. During the day, young teachers worked alongside their rural students. The goal: teach basic literacy while building a rural-urban, rich-poor understanding of what other Cubans' lives were like. The government believed this new egalitarian nationalism was essential to create socialism.

Meanwhile, both the revolution and opposition politicized children and youth. Childhood especially became a rallying point for those resisting government policies. Anita Casavantes Bradford describes how the government saw young Cubans as "recipients of its earliest social justice initiatives" because youth were essential to build a new society. The opposition resisted growing state interference in private education, school curricula, and forced mobilization of children into campaigns and demonstrations. They saw children as primarily the responsibility of the family. This "battle between revolutionary and counterrevolutionary nation-making projects was destined to play itself out through a struggle for control of the meanings attributed to childhood—and for control over the bodies and minds of flesh-and-blood Cuban children" (Casavantes Bradford 2014, pp. 49, 91).

This fight between two different wings of what had been the anti-Batista opposition (one socialist and increasingly Soviet-leaning and the other more middle class and religious) began as early as September 1959 during a Cuban Catholic Youth Day mass where children praised independence heroes Antonio Maceo and José Martí but not the revolution's leaders. Amid the early 1960s' exile invasions and rural resistance, Catholic parents and church officials deployed youth in sabotage campaigns, Catholic student strikes, and bombings of public schools. As this unfolded, youth supporting the revolution helped to repel the Bay of Pigs invaders and their island supporters.

In the United States, exiles and US policy makers portrayed the revolution as brainwashing children. Just as the 1950s opposition depicted Batista destroying Cuban families and killing Cuban kids, the new opposition continued that message against the revolution. As Michelle Chase writes, the opposition at home and abroad accused the government of displacing "the rights and duties of parenthood and the patriarchal family onto an authoritarian state" while linking anti-Castroism to "defense of the family, traditional gender roles, and Catholicism" (Chase 2015, pp. 170, 173). This led in part to Operation Pedro Pan between 1960 and 1962 when Cuban parents sent 14,000 children alone to the United States to be with relatives and friends—a sort of childhood marronage. For some, it was better that their children live abroad without parents than be indoctrinated by the Cuban state.

THE REVOLUTION DIDN'T GO FAR ENOUGH: BEING TOO RADICAL FOR THE REVOLUTION

While many anti-Batista centrists and rightists turned against the revolution, others confronted and resisted the revolution from the political left. They attacked the state for its shortcomings in creating a truly egalitarian society with more freedom. Anarchists, young people caught up in the youth culture of the 1960s, young women, and Afro-Cubans challenged the revolution—not for its radicalism, but for not being radical enough.

After 1959 and especially after the Bay of Pigs in 1961, Marxists gained control of the revolution's institutions. Anarchists resisted what they saw as an authoritarian state bent on controlling society and destroying the individual. In 1959 and 1960, anarchists condemned government tribunals and firing squads for people convicted of political crimes. While anarchists continued supporting the revolution's goals of creating a new society from the grassroots, they issued a declaration in 1960 condemning Communist influence, militarization of the population, and centralizing control of the revolution in the state, not the nation. As the declaration concluded, the revolution was for all Cubans, but it was being taken over by "authoritarian tendencies that surge in the breast of the revolution" (quoted in Fernández 2001, pp. 75, 86). Communists disliked such dissent and expelled anarchists from unions and organizations.

In response to the government labeling them as counterrevolutionaries, some anarchists published clandestine bulletins attacking Communism. Others armed themselves and fought in the western and central mountains. One anarchist—Luis Linsuaín—attempted to assassinate Raúl Castro. Some anarchists were executed. Others like Linsuaín ended up in Cuba's ever-expanding prison system. Still others fled to the United States where they created the Movimiento Libertario Cubano en el Exilio (Cuban Libertarian Movement in Exile, or MLCE). The MLCE resisted Cuban Communism, anti-Castro capitalists in Miami, the Soviet Union, US foreign policy, and leftist groups around the world who supported the Cuban Revolution.

Other Cubans criticized leaders for failing to live up to the revolution's goals and promises. The government mobilized millions of people to perform various tasks to build a new revolutionary society: labor and sugarcane-cutting brigades, rallies and marches, the literacy campaign, and more. Many Cubans participated willingly, believing their actions would create a better society for themselves and future generations. However, as Lillian Guerra notes, mobilizations and heightened expectations "inadvertently spawned dissent as younger revolutionaries contested the tiers of authority and demanded accountability" (Guerra 2012, p. 14). When aspirations failed to meet expectations, youth challenged the Communist state.

Many young Cubans felt alienated from the global youth culture of the 1960s. Around the world, young people found freedom of expression and promoted revolutionary causes. However, the Cuban government prohibited Cuban youth from engaging with this global youth culture that often idolized them. The government banned rock music and long hairstyles in men, even though the victorious rebel army marched into Havana in January 1959 with flowing hair and scraggily beards. Youth tried listening to smuggled rock music. They fought to be expressive, creative, and join the international youth movement but found state-imposed obstacles at every turn. Many sought freedom to love whomever they wanted, even if it was another man or another woman, but the government condemned homosexuality, saw gays and lesbians as counterrevolutionaries, and sent homosexuals to reeducation camps. Afro-Cuban youth and young women showed how racism and sexism were still rampant, countering the government's grand narratives that these were being extinguished. While the state often labeled dissenting youth as counterrevolutionary, the reality is that often they were more revolutionary than the revolutionary state. They believed the government was not listening to the nation. As Guerra concludes, these were "unintended dissidents who were too radical for Fidel's Revolution" (Guerra 2012, p. 275).

AGAINST THE REVOLUTION, NOTHING: CUBAN CINEMA AND REVOLUTIONARY POLITICS

Few cultural outlets existed for dissent in the revolution's first decades. However, Cuba is famous for its *choteos*—humor and jokes mocking those in power, and which long have been a popular form of everyday resistance. Guerra calls the *choteo* a tool that "subverted the state's use of language" and that was carried along Radio Bemba (Lip Radio) from person to person, neighborhood to neighborhood (Guerra 2012, pp. 202–204). Martínez-Fernández adds that jokes "allowed common citizens to channel frustrations to create temporary alternative realities in which they turned hierarchies upside down. They were not unlike those created by slaves and their descendants, whose jokes, stories, and sayings mocked masters and overseers" (Martínez-Fernández 2014, p. 210).

Another form of cultural dissent was built into the revolution: cinema. The government utilized film to build a new society. Mobile cinema units toured the island, showing films on outdoor screens. In line with Che's notions of putting people front and center in making the revolution, directors put movie cameras in people's hands so they could document their own lives. This gave voice to the previously voiceless and helped build a new national identity as people around Cuba heard voices and stories from the previously unheard.

The government also poured money into professional filmmaking, launching one of the most ambitious experiments in what became known as Third World Cinema. For directors and theorists working in the Instituto Cubano del Arte e Industria Cinematográfica (Cuban Institute of Cinematographic Art and Industry, or ICAIC), movies should entertain, educate, and inspire. They imagined revolutionary cinema as cultural resistance to Hollywood, where they said movies were only about making money since film was a capitalist commodity to be consumed. In ICAIC's eyes, film was "popular culture," reflecting the perspectives and culture of the people, that is, the popular classes.

They also believed film should criticize the revolution, and here the movies walked an ideological tightrope enunciated by Fidel in his "Words to the Intellectuals" speech in 1961: "Within the revolution, everything. Against the revolution, nothing." Films produced through ICAIC should help people see what the revolution had accomplished while acknowledging shortcomings— critique and challenge the revolution without calling for its demise: criticism within, not against, the revolution.

The 1966 comedy *La muerte de un burócrata* (Death of a Bureaucrat) follows the unnecessarily difficult task of a widow getting her dead husband's labor card (which was buried with him by mistake) so she can claim his death benefits. In the film, Cuba's state bureaucracy is the brunt of the joke, making fun of how red tape and unsympathetic bureaucrats made ordinary Cubans' lives more difficult. The director—Tomás Gutiérrez Alea—replicated this critique of an omnipotent and incompetent Cuban bureaucracy in his last film in 1995 titled *Guantanamera*. Little had changed it seemed, and even Fidel Castro publicly chastised the latter film for criticizing the revolution's aging leadership as being out of touch and unable to adapt to necessary changes.

Cuban cinema addressed racism and sexism. Gutiérrez Alea's 1976 film *La última cena* (The Last Supper) portrayed a 1790s Cuban enslaver reenacting Jesus's last supper (the owner is Jesus, his enslaved workers the disciples). The supper spurs those same men to revolt. This harsh look at race, slavery, and capitalism portrays enslaved rebels as heroes against the racist, capitalist owner. Humberto Solás' *Lucía* from 1968 explores gender roles and political resistance in three eras of Cuban history: the 1890s war for independence, the battles against Machado, and the 1960s literacy campaign. Each chapter centers on a young woman named Lucía, highlighting Cuban struggles against tyranny: first versus Spain, then versus dictatorship, then versus post-1959 sexism. The third chapter is key as a young student from Havana arrives to teach literacy to the young married Afro-Cuban Lucía. Her jealous white husband locks her away, refusing to let her be educated. This boorish behavior is no way for a new socialist man to behave, and his comrades let him know it. In the end, Lucía flees her husband as she takes the reigns of self-liberation. The film held up the problem of sexism that had to be resisted and overcome to create an egalitarian socialist society, but sexism did not disappear, and filmmakers regularly returned to the topic. In Pastor Vega's 1979 movie *Retrato de Teresa* (Portrait of Teresa), a working mother deals with a husband who refuses to help around the house, has an affair, and then is put in his place when Teresa asks him why she cannot have an affair too—wouldn't it be equal? Despite government laws requiring men to share equally in household duties and efforts to promote gender equality, cinema was called on again with the 1983 Gutiérrez Alea film *Hasta Cierto Punto* (Up to a Certain Point) that centers on an affair between a single mom who is a leader among dockworkers (a traditional male domain) and a theater director who needs his machismo checked.

None of these films called for overthrowing Cuban Communism or the revolution. They celebrated the good from the revolution (overthrowing capitalism, battling racism and sexism, and the goal of sexual equality). However, they also critiqued the revolution, highlighting remaining problems (bureaucracy, incompetence, and sexism) needing fixed.

Though exiles left the island beginning in 1959, exile cinema did not emerge for almost 20 years. In 1965, the government created the infamous Unidades Militares de Ayuda a la Producción (Military Units to Aid Production, or UMAP), which were "re-education" camps designed to imprison "undesirables," homosexuals and other "deviants," including dissident culture makers. Filmmakers and culture producers began leaving Cuba. Movies like *El Super* (The Building Superintendent 1979) and *La Otra Cuba* (The Other Cuba 1985) focused on dilemmas and traumas of life in exile and, by extension, condemned Communist Cuba and Fidel Castro for forcing people to flee their homes and country. Other films from the 1980s took strong anti-Castro viewpoints. *Improper Conduct* (1984) exposed human rights violations waged by the state against homosexuals, poets, and dissidents in the UMAP camps and beyond. While Cuban cinema used critique to advance revolutionary goals, exile movies were blatant "resistance films."

Spreading Revolution

Cuba's revolutionary leaders believed revolution against capitalist imperialism had to be global. Immediately, Havana sought allies in Africa and Latin America. Cuba sent weapons to Algeria after its victory over French colonial rule in 1962. Algeria became a trans-Atlantic ally of Cuba in pursuit of Third World revolution with both serving as guerrilla training sites for African and Latin American leftists. One recalls, too, that Che Guevara had left Cuba to spread revolution on both continents.

Cuba especially tried to expand its influence in the Caribbean. Fidel denied Cuba "exported revolution" though. Rather, as he put it in "The Second Declaration of Havana" in 1962, "revolutions are not exported, they are made by the people. What Cuba can give to the people, and has already given, is its example…that revolution is possible, that the people can make it, that in the contemporary world there are no forces capable of halting the liberation movement of the peoples" (quoted in *The Caribbean Reader* 2013, p. 337). As others have noted, the Cuban Revolution "provided a relevant and a seemingly more practical model [than the Russian or Chinese Revolutions]. The Cuba example seemed both more appropriate to the region and more palatable" (May et al. 2018, pp. 148–149).

During the 1950s, Nicaraguan students supported the anti-Batista struggle, seeing it as a transnational battle against dictators: their own Somoza and Batista. In 1960, Nicaraguans from the Sandino Revolutionary Front went to Cuba, met other regional leftists, and began training in guerrilla warfare. Cuba also aided leftist rebels in Colombia who first arrived in Havana in the 1960s.

Cuba supported Puerto Rican nationalists too. In fact, nationalists had allied themselves with Cuban M-26-7 organizations in New York during the late 1950s. In the 1960s, Puerto Rican nationalists moved operations to Cuba, while Havana aided leftists in the Dominican Republic. In the 1970s, pro-Cuban socialist governments emerged in the Caribbean. In Jamaica, Michael Manley's Peoples National Party came to power in 1976 on a platform of democratic socialism and maintaining friendly relations with Cuba while Cuba aided socialist governments in Guyana. By the 1980s, Cuba supported revolutionary movements in El Salvador, Grenada, Guatemala, and Nicaragua, and then sponsored Marxist governments that came to power in 1979 in Grenada and Nicaragua.

The Grenadian Revolution, 1979–1983

In 1974, Eric Gairy led Grenada to independence, but soon lost support among workers, the middle class, and the intelligentsia. Meanwhile, a radical political element emerged originally centered around Black Power. In 1982, Maurice Bishop—the Dutch Aruba-born Grenadian prime minister—reflected on how the Black Power Movement transformed Caribbean politics "largely because so many of its adherents later continued to develop politically" so that "progressive forces of the Caribbean are comrades who first became engaged in political struggle through their involvement with the Black power movement" (Bishop 1984, p. 198).

When Black Power failed to provide material benefits, Grenada's Black Power advocates leaned toward Marxism, organizing around class, not race. Radicals like Bishop formed the New Jewel Movement (NJM) in 1973. The NJM wanted a socialist society different than the Cuban model. The Cubans created a strong, centralized state pushing reforms from the top-down. The NJM sought a popular, municipal-based socialism with local communities (not a centralized state) guiding development and managing Grenada's resources. On a small island like Grenada, this seemed feasible and completely in line with the long history of Caribbean peoples seeking more autonomy away from a centralized state apparatus. The NJM also wanted to end the British parliamentary system and replace it with People's Assemblies. By the late 1970s, the NJM gained support from labor unions, teachers, and nurses—even though the Gairy government's security forces regularly used violence to repress the NJM. Still, Bishop persisted and even served with the opposition in parliament beginning in 1976.

In March 1979, the NJM and sympathetic military supporters—and with wide local backing—toppled the Gairy government. International organizations supported revolutionary initiatives like literacy programs, promotion of creole language, and economic development without massive amounts of debt. Cuba sent doctors, nurses, and teachers, as well as material and personnel to build a new international airport runway to accommodate larger aircraft and more tourists.

Throughout the revolutionary era, Bishop regularly referenced Caribbean history to situate the Grenadian Revolution in a broader historical and political context. In a March 1982 speech, he noted that slavery only ended because enslaved peoples took action themselves. Such slave-initiated struggles reflected a larger reality: "human rights have always come only after struggle....the truth of the matter is that every single important right under the law...came after a struggle by the ordinary working people" (Bishop 1984, p. 116).

Such struggles by everyday people had transnational implications as Bishop's government sought to create a free, united Caribbean. In late 1982, Grenada hosted a series of conferences bringing together workers, educators, intellectuals, and others from across the Caribbean to explore similar concerns "of sovereignty." On the one hand, organizers designed the conferences to show broad Caribbean support for the revolution; on the other hand, they sought to create regional solidarity and identity to resist transnational capitalism's impact on the region. "Comrades," Bishop announced, "the people of the Caribbean are concerned about this international capitalist crisis which causes the prices of our goods to keep dropping every day...yet every week when we buy items such as cars, trucks, tractors, food in cans, fertilizer and so on, all of the things that we do not produce, those prices keep going up" (Bishop 1984, pp. 181, 184). It did not matter where you lived; the same capitalist forces crushed the people. Regional unity also meant making it cheaper to travel between countries or to buy cheaper drugs and goods in bulk from abroad for regional distribution—all strategies of unity to resist transnational capitalist pressures as well as Cold War challenges from the United States. "Our duty," Bishop concluded in a 1982 speech, "is to continue to struggle to have our Caribbean Sea declared a zone of peace, independence and development in practice" (Bishop 1984, p. 194).

In the summer 1983, Bishop invoked the concept of Pan-Americanism at a speech in Washington, recalling how "the destiny of our English-speaking Caribbean is inextricably linked with our Spanish-speaking brothers and sisters" (Bishop 1984, p. 229). Yet, in the same city at the exact same time, the Reagan Administration was planning the overthrow of the New Jewel government. Washington feared this expansion of socialism in its backyard. The new Reagan Administration did not believe Grenada's extended runway was for tourism. Instead, Reagan claimed it would be used to accommodate Soviet and Cuban military aircraft in some global Communist plot to export revolution throughout the hemisphere.

In 1983, internal problems also began eating away at the revolution. The masses benefitted little from the government's economic policies. New membership requirements meant fewer people were joining the New Jewel party. People then channeled discontent into protests, which the government countered with violence and imprisonment of political prisoners. Then, on 19 October 1983, a disastrous rivalry erupted between two of the revolution's leaders: Bishop and Bernard Coard. Coard led a coup against his old ally, arresting Bishop, but Bishop had popular support. Civilians stormed the jail and released him. Soldiers loyal to Coard confronted them. The resulting violence left Bishop and numerous supporters dead.

To the Reagan Administration, the chaos and resulting instability justified what came next. On 25 October 1983, the United States invaded Grenada on the pretext of protecting US citizens studying at the island's medical school. However, the larger context was the ramped-up Reagan Administration's opposition to the presence of any Marxist regime in the Caribbean. The invasion succeeded with cooperation from various Caribbean governments associated with the Organization of Eastern Caribbean States. Grenada was a major setback for Castro. Twenty-four Cubans died in the operation, and Cuba lost a partner. It also coincided with US efforts to topple another Cuban ally in the region: Nicaragua's Sandinistas.

The Sandinista Revolution, 1979–1990

Since the early 1960s, armed groups had fought the US-backed Somoza dynasty that ruled Nicaragua since the 1930s. As noted earlier, students in the Nicaraguan opposition moved to Cuba to train for revolution beginning in 1960. In 1961, Fidel Castro brought together several Nicaraguan opposition groups to form the Frente Sandinista de Liberación Nacional (Sandinista Front for National Liberation, or FSLN) named after the 1920s-era anti-imperialist Augusto César Sandino. In the early 1970s, the FSLN engaged in small skirmishes and attempted to win the people to its side—essentially following Che Guevara's strategy of fighting a popular war.

In 1972, an earthquake devastated the country. International aid relief poured into Nicaragua. Somoza and his allies siphoned away most of it, outraging unions, newspapers, human rights organizations, peasant and student organizations, and Catholic liberation theologians. The anti-Somoza opposition grew. In 1978, the Sandinistas attacked Nicaragua's national palace. Rebels spread throughout the country, claiming one victory after another. Somoza's national guard began collapsing. By July 1979, the FSLN surrounded the capital city of Managua while Somoza ordered planes to bomb Nicaraguan cities. International outrage and FSLN pressure eventually forced Somoza to surrender and flee ultimately to exile in Paraguay.

Victory led to building a new revolutionary society. Marxists and non-Marxists comprised the FSLN leadership, which created a mixed economy with both public and private ownership of property. The Sandinistas launched a literacy campaign with Cuban teachers arriving to help. Cuban doctors and advisers also moved to Nicaragua. Meanwhile, international solidarity groups in Europe and the Americas offered support to the Sandinistas and resistance to Washington's growing attempts to overthrow the revolution.

Originally, the Sandinista Revolution was largely "nationalist," focusing on developing Nicaragua. However, Sandinista leaders had larger transnational goals. They had just toppled a dictatorship that abused human rights for decades. Why wouldn't they want to spread their messages of liberation, anti-dictatorship, human rights, and anti-imperialism to neighbors who likewise suffered under authoritarian rule? As a result, just as Cubans aided revolutionary movements in the region, the Sandinistas began too as well. Cuba sent arms and advisers to Nicaragua, which could better send aid and supplies to rebels fighting a military dictatorship in Guatemala and an authoritarian regime in El Salvador.

Not everyone was happy with these developments, and many resisted the Sandinistas. Some Sandinista leaders and supporters saw too much Cuban and Marxist influence. Many deserted and joined counterrevolutionaries known as the Contras with bases originally in Costa Rica and Honduras. Other Contras were veterans of Somoza's national guard. As the Reagan Administration in Washington began its campaign against Grenada, it also stepped up funding for the Contras, who waged guerrilla war and sabotage against the Sandinista Revolution. CIA operatives also mined Nicaragua's harbors.

Other Nicaraguans resisted the Sandinistas. Opposition groups that included large numbers of Miskito Indians on the Caribbean coast aided the Contras against the FSLN. The Contras and a US-economic embargo undermined the FSLN's ability to economically develop Nicaragua. Many Nicaraguans grew frustrated with the Sandinistas. The FSLN never created a one-party political system like the Cubans did. They continued to allow a multiparty system where opposition candidates challenged FSLN dominance. In 1990, the FSLN-dominated government stood for reelection. They lost to Violetta Chamorro, who took over the government on promises she and her party could end the Contra War, which they could since Washington backed both the Contras and the Chamorro campaign.

The 1990 Sandinista loss and the 1983 US invasion of Grenada were major blows to Cuba's anti-American foreign policy. Since coming to power, the Cuban government had followed a radical transnationalism to help revolutionary allies. Yet, by the early 1990s, this foreign policy unraveled, and it did so just as Cuba's domestic socialist experiment began collapsing. In 1989, Soviet Bloc countries in Eastern Europe rebelled against Communist Party rule and Moscow, culminating in November's opening of the Berlin Wall. Over the coming years, the USSR drastically reduced oil supplies, aid, and subsidies to Cuba. In December 1991, the USSR ceased to exist, and Cuba drifted into uncharted territory. We explore some of those dimensions in our final chapter.

Conclusion

During the 1950s, the anti-Batista opposition mobilized people against the dictatorship. The rural struggle of bearded revolutionaries led by Fidel and Che was born transnationally from Mexico where the two met. The urban struggle was equally vital as it brought together mothers horrified by the killing of their children, university students, and workers from across the political and religious spectrum who demonstrated and waged warfare against Batista.

The Cuban Revolution ushered in the first Marxist, anti-capitalist Caribbean government. Havana encouraged Caribbean revolutionaries to challenge US neocolonialism and authoritarian leaders. Such resistance created a backlash as the United States countered with its own resistance to Havana's foreign policy. Domestically, the revolution went far in advancing the conditions of women and rural populations, as well as the educational, health, and material needs of Cuba's masses. Che's new socialist Cuban was to play a role creating a revolutionary society to resist capitalism's deep roots on the island while building an alternative socialist world.

However, thousands of Cubans resisted government policies. Many from middle-class, Catholic backgrounds condemned the government's youth policies. They sent away their children or fled as families into exile. Some revolutionaries became disillusioned when the government adopted Soviet-style strategies and Soviet norms rather than return to 1940s-era liberal democracy. Some anti-Batista revolutionaries picked up arms against the new government; others went into exile.

Many who stayed in Cuba from the 1960s to the 1980s continued to resist and challenge the government. Youth, women, Afro-Cubans, and intellectuals grew frustrated that the revolution did not go far enough or fast enough. Sometimes acts of defiance emerged in Cuban cinema, which itself was designed to both celebrate the revolution's achievements and point out its shortcomings. If challenges did not call for overthrowing the revolution, Fidel said they were fine. However, that interpretation could be fuzzy, and it was always up to the state to determine when the nation crossed the line.

WORKS CITED AND FURTHER REFERENCES

J. Arboleya (2000) *The Cuban Counter-Revolution* (Ohio University Press).

M. Bishop (1984) *In Nobody's Backyard: Maurice Bishop's Speeches 1979–1983: A Memorial Volume* (Zed Books Ltd.).

A. Casavantes Bradford (2014) *The Revolution Is for the Children: The Politics of Childhood in Havana and Miami* (University of North Carolina Press).

F. Castro (1968) *History Will Absolve Me* (Johathan Cape Ltd.).

M. Chanan (1985) *The Cuban Image* (British Film Institute).

M. Chase (2015) *Revolution within the Revolution: Women and Gender Politics in Cuba, 1952–1962* (University of North Carolina Press).

"Death of a Bureaucrat" (1966) Tomás Gutiérrez Alea (dir.) (ICAIC).

L. Dubois and R.L. Turits (2019) *Freedom Roots: Histories from the Caribbean* (University of North Carolina Press).

"El Super" (1979) León Ichaso and Orlando Jiménez Leal (dirs.) (Max Mambru Films).

F. Fernández (2001) *Cuban Anarchism: The History of a Movement* (Sharp).

G.A. Geyer (1991) *Guerrilla Prince: The Untold Story of Fidel Castro* (Little, Brown, and Company).

"Guantanamera" (1995) Tomás Gutiérrez Alea (dir.) (ICAIC).

L. Guerra (2012) *Visions of Power in Cuba: Revolution, Redemption, and Resistance, 1959–1971* (University of North Carolina Press).

E. Guevara (1998) *Guerrilla Warfare* (University of Nebraska Press).

——— (2013) "Man and Socialism in Cuba" in Nicola Foote (ed.) *The Caribbean History Reader* (Routledge), 337–40.

"Improper Conduct" (1984) Néstor Almendros and Orland Jiménez Leal(dirs.) (Les Films du Losange).

C.L.R. James (1963) *The Black Jacobins: Toussaint L'Ouverture and the San Domingo Revolution* (Vintage).

G.K. Lewis (1987) *Grenada: The New Jewel Despoiled* (The Johns Hopkins University Press).

A.M. López (1993) "Cuban Cinema in Exile: The 'Other' Island," *Jump Cut: A Review of Contemporary Media*, (June), 51–9.

"Lucía" (1968) Humberto Solás (dir.) (ICAIC).

L. Martínez-Fernández (2014) *Revolutionary Cuba: A History* (University Press of Florida).

R.A. May, A. Schneider, R. González Arana (2018) *Caribbean Revolutions: Cold War Armed Movements* (Cambridge University Press).

B. Meeks (2001) *Caribbean Revolutions and Revolutionary Theory: An Assessment of Cuba, Nicaragua, and Grenada* (University Press of the West Indies).

L.A. Pérez (1995) *Cuba: Between Reform & Revolution* (Oxford University Press).

"Portrait of Teresa" (1979) Pastor Vega (dir.) (ICAIC).

D. Sheinin (2011) "The Caribbean and the Cold War: Between Reform and Revolution" in Stephan Palmié and Francisco Scarano (eds.) *The Caribbean: A History of the Region and Its Peoples* (University of Chicago Press), 491–503.

T. Szulc (2000) *Fidel: A Critical Portrait* (Harper Perennial).

The Caribbean History Reader (2013) Nicola Foote (ed.) (Routledge).

"The Last Supper" (1976) Tomás Gutiérrez Alea (dir.) (ICAIC).

"The Other Cuba" (1985) Orlando Jiménez Leal (dir.) (Connoisseur/Meridian).

"Up to a Certain Point" (1983) Tomás Gutiérrez Alea (dir.) (ICAIC).

D. Wood (2009) "Tomás Gutiérrez Alea and the Art of Revolutionary Cinema," *Bulletin of Latin American Research*, 28/4, 512–26.

M. Zeuske (2011) "The Long Cuban Revolution" in Stephan Palmié and Francisco Scarano (eds.) *The Caribbean: A History of the Region and Its Peoples* (University of Chicago Press), 507–22.

CHAPTER 10

Masses vs. Massa: The Ongoing Antiauthoritarian Struggle

Resistance remained a feature of Caribbean political culture in the last decades of the twentieth century and into the first decades of the new millennium. In the 1980s and early 1990s, militancy erupted against the Duvalier dictatorship in Haiti, US colonialism in Puerto Rico, and the Surinamese and Trinidadian governments. Leftist guerrillas continued a civil war in Colombia dating to the early 1960s. Hugo Chávez's government in Venezuela forged alliances across the Caribbean to confront Washington as Chávez embarked on policies to build a "twenty-first century socialism" against US-led neoliberal capitalism.

Meanwhile, people resisted other forms of repression and neglect resulting from economic, political, and natural disasters. In the 1990s, Cuba entered what the government called the "Special Period" in which the government asked people (they had few choices in the matter) to make material sacrifices to continue building socialism. However, many activists, Afro-Cubans, hip-hop and rap musicians, journalists, bloggers, and more openly defied Communist one-party rule. French West Indians fought continued exploitative labor conditions. Natural disasters struck the Caribbean, leading Haitians to take control of their own lives following the 2010 earthquake while Puerto Ricans struggled against lazy, corrupt responses by island and US authorities in the wake of Hurricane María in 2017.

Identity issues shaped another form of resistance at the turn of the century. Indigenous movements reasserted their identity and quest for justice as the world remembered the 500th anniversary of Columbus's arrival in the Caribbean. Lingering gender inequality propelled people to attack sexual harassment, sexual assault, and victim-shaming. By the 2010s, LGBTQ movements challenged conservative societies and governments. In the late 2010s, activists campaigned for reparations to Afro-Caribbean peoples for the lingering structural violence resulting from slavery. In these struggles against tyranny, imperialism, corruption, and injustice, the human, democratic impulse to shape one's own destiny lived on.

© The Author(s), under exclusive license to Springer Nature Switzerland AG 2022
K. Shaffer, *A Transnational History of the Modern Caribbean*, https://doi.org/10.1007/978-3-030-93012-7_10

FALL OF THE DUVALIERS AND TRANSITION TO PEOPLE'S RULE IN HAITI, 1980s–1990s

In Haiti, the dictator François "Papa Doc" Duvalier died in 1971. His son Jean-Claude (Baby Doc) succeeded as ruler and brutalizer of the nation. The government had crushed leftist opposition in 1968, and survivors joined others fleeing into exile in the United States and Canada. The Haitian diaspora soon launched a liberation struggle from abroad. Waves of anti-Duvalier popular music created a lyrical score for anti-Duvalier activists. They incorporated elements of peasant culture with Vodou lyrics and symbols, giving birth to the *kilti libète* (freedom culture). Traditional musical styles and Vodou drums blended with rock-oriented electric guitar. Reggae musician Bob Marley influenced the band Boukman Eksperyans' Lolo Beaubrun, who wanted to replicate what Marley and reggae had done for inspiration and liberation in Jamaica. As Gage Averill notes, with one million Haitians in the diaspora, the "transnational circulation of ideas…and the availability of the diaspora as a free space for political, cultural, and intellectual activities, proved over the long run to be a powerful antidote to Duvalierism" (Averill 1997, p. 110).

Throughout the 1970s and 1980s, the kilti libète recorded protest music onto cassette tapes. People smuggled them into Haiti, then copied and distributed them widely. Music did what Duvalier himself had done to achieve and maintain power: exploit symbols of peasant culture and Vodou. This time, though, the opposition stressed the peasants' desire for freedom, autonomy, and antiauthoritarianism central to rural life while also promoting Vodou's emancipating dimensions. In short, the kilti libète liberated the nation's symbols and religion from the state.

By 1983, Baby Doc's authority began crumbling. That year, Pope John Paul II declared that Haiti had to change and supported priests pushing for social justice. The army and Catholic Church began breaking with Duvalier. The Church split between traditionalists seeking to maintain order and new leftist liberation theologians like Jean-Bertrand Aristide calling for end to dictatorship, elimination of poverty, and power to the people. In 1984, slum dwellers in Gonaïves shouting "Down with poverty!" and "Down with Duvalier!" sacked warehouses looking for donated food aid. National protests erupted following the murders of four children in late 1985. With Carnival preparations in early 1986, opposition elements grew bolder and the government more worried. Influenced by growing leftist Catholics and their station Radio Soleil, the masses rebelled. The military broke completely from Duvalier, and the combination of pressures from the people, the army, and Washington forced Duvalier to flee into exile in February.

The next decade did not bring peace. In the wake of Duvalier's exile, the masses sought vengeance. Popular rage led people to hunt and kill Tonton Macoutes in what became known as *Opération Dechoukaj* (Operation Uprooting). However, the late 1980s witnessed one military coup after another, all ensconced in violence with no benefit for the poor masses. As

Aristide noted, "We're glad Duvalier is gone....But this is not the end of the affair, by a long shot....We have a warning to issue to this new government. If the people were willing to expose themselves to the regime's bullets to cry, 'Down with Duvalier,' they will surely do the same with the new government, which is, after all, the *same* government. What we have now is Duvalierism without Duvalier" (quoted in Wilentz 1989, p. 55).

As a leftist priest, Aristide urged Haiti's youth to take up the mantle and create a socialist country. Drawing on the allusion of a bicycle rider, he railed against corrupt forces who steered the bicycle to the right. "But we the youth of Haiti, in the name of our faith, say no! to that right-hand turn. We say yes! to a turn toward the left, a historic turn to the left. Freely, voluntarily, and in the name of our faith, we refuse this right-wing curve of corruption. Instead, we shall advance toward the left, where our real faith, our unshakable belief, can build a socialist Haiti. For only in a socialist Haiti will...*all* people be able to eat...will *all* people be able to find justice...will *all* people be able to live in liberty...will the lives of *all* people be respected" (quoted in Wilentz 1989, p. 221).

In 1990, tired of endless coups and "Duvalierism without Duvalier," the now-former priest Aristide ran for president. People poured out to support his *Lavalas* (Flood) social movement and easily elected Aristide with 67% of the vote. His government investigated human rights abuses and brought Tonton Macoutes to trial. He tried to bring the army under civilian rule. He battled corruption by banning the departure of wealthy Haitians until the government investigated their bank accounts. Not all were happy with his social democratic reforms to reign in the elite, business community, and military. In September 1991, the military overthrew Aristide, driving him into exile, and colluding in its own dechoukaj against Aristide supporters. However, Aristide returned to Haiti in October 1994 in one of those odds twists of history. The United States—which had supported tyrants in Haiti and elsewhere, undermined democracy around the region, and had a history of imperialistic intervention—invaded Haiti and returned Aristide to power. The US invasion accomplished what the Caribbean Legion in the 1940s could have only dreamed of doing.

PUERTO RICAN NATIONALISTS, 1970s–2000s

In the 1970s, the Puerto Rican nationalist El Ejército Popular Boricua (Popular Boricua Army, aka Los Macheteros) continued to attack the United States. Filiberto Ojeda Ríos accused Washington of destroying Puerto Rican people's national identity and keeping the island subservient by denying Puerto Rico its own self-sustaining economy. The Macheteros' analysis reflected what by the early 2000s became a central critique of neoliberal capitalist globalization: corporations controlled the world; the US president served as their "chief of staff"; and US-led corporate capitalism created poverty, environmental destruction, and diminished human and democratic rights. How to resist? The Machetero program was clear: revolutionary violence.

In the 1970s and 1980s, Los Macheteros attacked US sailors and military bases. They rose to the top of the FBI's Public Enemies list after robbing a Wells Fargo bank in the United States in 1983, making off with $7 million ($18.4 million in 2020) to fund further independence actions. The US government responded with mass arrests in August 1985. Ojeda Ríos fled in 1990 and claimed responsibility for bombings in 1998 during a general strike on the island. Meanwhile, he became a symbol of Puerto Rican resistance to the US navy bombing range on the small Puerto Rican island of Vieques. Anti-navy campaigns continued until 2003 when Washington agreed to end military use of the island. Two years later, the FBI tracked Ojeda Ríos to a small city in western Puerto Rico and killed the independence fighter in a shootout. His death sparked outrage, even among islanders not sympathetic to independence. The popular Puerto Rican reggaetón band Calle 13 memorialized his death while calling for Puerto Rican liberation in their song "Querido FBI" (Dear FBI) released within hours of the shooting. The death marked the possible end to *violent* resistance against US neocolonial rule in Puerto Rico, but, as we will see later, it did not mark the end of resistance.

THE MAROON WAR IN SURINAME, 1986–1992

In 1975, the Netherlands granted independence to Suriname. The country's political system then became entrenched in what Anthony Maingot calls "the politics of ethnic patronage and special dealing" as ethnic-based political parties dominated the country and awarded government spoils to their ethnic supporters (Maingot 2011, p. 525). In 1980, a Surinamese sergeant, Desi Bouterse, led a military coup that quickly lost support when in 1982 the government tortured and executed businessmen, artists, and intellectuals. Soon, armed opposition to Bouterse emerged.

In 1984, the military demoted one of Bouterse's former bodyguards, the Maroon Ronny Brunswijk. He returned to his village and began organizing young Maroons. Since the 1980 coup, select Maroons benefited from military appointments and access to consumer goods previously out of their reach. However, soon the military elite blocked these goods from reaching Maroons like Brunswijk, who in response seized trucks importing luxury items. Bouterse sent soldiers after Brunswijk, strip-searched Maroons, desecrated community shrines, and committed massacres. As repression increased, Maroons joined Brunswijk and openly revolted against Bouterse.

With support from Suriname's largest Maroon communities and transnational support from exiles in the Netherlands, Brunswijk's men formed the Jungle Commando. They waged guerrilla war against government forces and attacked corporations like the Suriname Aluminum Company, which had collaborated with the government to build a hydroelectric dam that flooded Maroon territory. Maroons robbed banks too, distributing some of the money to maroon villages. Brunswijk undertook "these actions to support those 'who had nothing' and to protest against the enrichment of the army's elite." In return, "enthusiastic villagers gave Brunswijk the nickname 'Robin Hood'" (Thoden van Velzen 1990, p. 166). For two-and-a-half years, the Jungle Commando fought the military and Bouterse, paralyzed Suriname's bauxite and alumina export industry, and, in April 1987, proclaimed an independent Maroon state covering one-fourth of the country. Ultimately, such pressure forced the government to hold new elections in 1987. Bouterse lost overwhelmingly, ending the rebellion.

However, this was not the end for either Bouterse or Brunswijk. In 2019, a military court convicted Bouterse of murder for fifteen executions in 1982. For Brunswijk, INTERPOL issued an international arrest warrant resulting from earlier Dutch convictions *in absentia* for drug trafficking. Yet, by 2020, Brunswijk was free, owned several gold concessions in Suriname, and won election as speaker of Parliament. He then surrendered the speakership to be elected Vice President—the highest elected position for any Maroon in Suriname's history.

Abu Bakr and Trinidad's Muslim Revolt, 1990

Islam arrived in Trinidad with enslaved Africans. A new wave of Islam arrived with East Indian indentured servants in the 1800s. Today, Muslims comprise around 5% of the island's population. In 1990, a small cohort of Muslim converts decided that Trinidadian society was so corrupt and the urban masses so discontented that only a popular armed revolt led by Muslim activists could save the country.

Lennox Phillips was a former Black Power activist from Trinidad's 1970 Revolution. While some Black Power activists abandoned the cause and converted to Marxism, Phillips retained his race analysis and merged it with Islam. Taking the name Yasin Abu Bakr, he claimed that only through Islam could peoples of African descent successfully break from exploitation. In the 1970s, Abu Bakr and his followers traveled to Libya for commando training. Upon returning to the island in 1982, he formed the Muslim group Jamaat al Muslimeen and purchased weapons in Florida. On 27 August 1990, Abu Bakr launched an uprising with 125 armed men.

As Brian Meeks notes, the uprising might have been as much about perceived government abuse as about "whitey" and his lackeys in Trinidad. Abu Bakr claimed that former prime minister Eric Williams granted his group control of a piece of land on the capital's outskirts. Over time, people moved to the land, built shops and homes, and constructed a mosque. Some urban residents supported Abu Bakr, especially when he led campaigns against drug dealers. For many in Port of Spain's shanty towns, he was a "larger than life Robin Hood" (Meeks 1996, p. 74).

However, the new government of Prime Minister A.N.R. Robinson refused to recognize Abu Bakr's control of the land and Trinidad's high court ruled for the government. At this point, the group launched the uprising, demanding control of the land, elimination of certain taxes, and new elections. For three days, they captured and held the Parliament, Robinson, his Cabinet, and a television station. Despite his popularity in some urban shanty towns, the bulk of Port of Spain's urban population refused to join the revolt. The government soon crushed it, and Abu Bakr served two years in jail.

Colombian Revolutionaries, 1960s–2010s

Colombian leftists waged revolution from the mid-1960s to the signing of a peace deal in 2016, making it the longest war in the history of any Caribbean land. The Fuerzas Armadas Revolucionarias de Colombia (Revolutionary Armed Forces of Colombia, or FARC) and smaller leftwing groups had claimed they were fighting for the country's vast poor population against the dominant two-party system they believed was corrupt and ignored the masses' material needs. These organizations attacked not only the government but also international corporations like foreign oil companies. Drug cartel carnage waged by the Medellín and Cali cocaine cartels in the 1980s compounded the violence. At times, guerrillas attacked not only the government but also cartels and vice versa.

With the cartels' demise in the late-1990s, the FARC became involved in cocaine trafficking by protecting cocaine producers, facilitating transit of drugs through its territory, and collecting "taxes" from drug producers. Revenues financed continued armed struggle. More money, the government's surrendering of large tracts of land to the FARC, and growing discontent with governmental corruption led to a surge in leftist violence in the early 2000s—violence countered by right-wing death squads that attacked mostly civilian peasant and human rights organizations perceived as friendly to guerrillas. Meanwhile, Washington sent more military assistance to Colombia than any other country in the Western Hemisphere. After the 2001 terror attacks in the United States, the US State Department dubbed the FARC a "narco-terrorist" organization.

By the late 2010s, guerrilla organizations saw desertions, lost territory, and flagging support from Venezuelan and Cuban backers. In 2016, the government and the FARC negotiated a peace agreement, though many sectors within Colombia rejected the agreement. By 2020, segments of the FARC returned to armed struggle, accusing the government of reneging on the treaty.

Transnational *Chavismo* and the Multipolar Axis Against Washington

In the 1980s, falling global oil prices, declining income, and economic instability wrecked Venezuela's economy. By accepting International Monetary Fund assistance, the government in 1989 made things worse by imposing IMF austerity measures like reducing spending on social programs and ending price controls. Food, transportation, and gasoline prices soared by as much as 100%. In February, people protested, marched, and looted. The resulting government crackdown killed 2000 people.

A dissident faction within the armed forces plotted a coup against the government. In 1982, Hugo Chávez and fellow military officers had formed the Movimiento Bolivariano Revolucionario—200 (Revolutionary Bolivarian Movement—200, or MBR—200), taking the name from independence leader Simón Bolívar, who was born 200 years earlier. In 1992, the MBR—200 (with apparent Cuban assistance) staged an unsuccessful coup. Authorities arrested Chávez. After being released from prison in 1994, Venezuelans elected him president in 1999. Chávez led Venezuela toward "Twenty-First Century Socialism" by using Venezuela's vast oil wealth to fight poverty, control prices, and expand livelihoods of Venezuela's poor. Cuban teachers and doctors poured into Venezuela to support these efforts.

Chávez's Bolivarian Revolution was also anti-Washington. In his famous address before the United Nations in 2006, where he referred to US president George W. Bush as the "Devil," Chávez condemned US-led neoliberal capitalism and US foreign policy not just in the Caribbean and Latin America, but globally: "Imperialists see extremists everywhere. No, we are not extremists, what is happening is that the world is waking up, and people are rising up…against North American imperialism….Yes, they call us extremists and we are rising up against the Empire….The President of the United States addressed the people of Afghanistan, the people of Lebanon and the people of Iran. Well, one has to wonder, when listening to the U.S. President speak to those people: if those people could talk to him, what would they say? I am going to answer on behalf of these peoples because for most of them, I know their soul well, the soul of the Peoples of the South, the downtrodden peoples. They would say: Yankee Empire, go home!" (quoted in *Latin America and the United States* 2011, pp. 398–399).

Chávez and his regional allies did more than just speak. They organized the Alianza Bolivariana para los Pueblos de Nuestra América (Bolivarian Alliance for the Peoples of Our America—or ALBA). ALBA began with two leftist Caribbean partners (Venezuela and Cuba) but expanded to include 11 Caribbean countries by 2012 (Antigua and Barbuda, Cuba, Dominica, Grenada, Haiti, Nicaragua, St. Kitts and Nevis, St. Lucia, St. Vincent and the Grenadines, Suriname, and Venezuela). ALBA sought to share resources, trade, and a regional currency to resist US political and economic pressures and reliance on the US dollar—in many ways a new version of Maurice Bishop's goals during Grenada's revolution. Venezuela sold cheap oil (and even gave free oil) to countries, especially those facing severe hardships. A news media service (TeleSUR) provided ALBA-friendly alternative perspectives to Western corporate media. However, plummeting oil prices led to political and economic instability in Venezuela, especially after Chávez's death from cancer in 2013 and as several leftist governments in the hemisphere fell from power. Still, ALBA demonstrated the transnational ability to pull together likeminded countries to resist US-led capitalist globalization.

Dissent during Cuba's "Special Period," 1990s–2010s

When the Soviet Union ceased to exist in 1991, Cuba lost its most important ally. Facing this new reality, the Cuban Communist Party launched a series of religious and political reforms: people could openly practice religion, one could express their faith while still being a Communist Party member, one did not need to be a party member to run for election, and elections increasingly were done by secret ballot. This was Cuba's "democratic" opening. There was also a "capitalist" opening. The government legalized the US dollar to acquire hard currency. Money flowed into Cuba from relatives abroad and through a new tourist boom as the government created joint tourism ventures with foreign corporations. Foreign currency circulated throughout the economy as Cubans with dollars bought food and supplies from people who had access to them. The revolution survived due to "dollarization."

Yet, it came with a cost. Tourism led to more prostitution. Cars and rationed gasoline were diverted for the interests of tourists, and people struggled any way possible to survive. Because tourists usually stayed in cities or beach resorts, dollarization's material benefits rarely reached rural areas. Many tourists stayed in private homes, paying dollars to their hosts. However, nicer homes tended to be in whiter parts of cities, so dollars were unevenly distributed between races. Material inequalities grew, creating what some called "dollar apartheid."

By 1994, Cubans had suffered over two years of extreme privation. Young people had never experienced Batista-era shortages; this challenged everything their teachers and political leaders had taught. By summer, 5000 people had fled the island on makeshift rafts and boats—yet another maritime marronage. In August, several thousand people in Havana marched along the Malecón sea wall shouting "Freedom" and "Down with the Castros." The short-lived and heavily repressed march known as the *Maleconazo* convinced the government to allow anyone to leave who wanted. Some 35,000 Cubans joined the exodus to Florida.

Grassroots campaigns then made waves on the island. In 1995, the Concilio Cubano formed, comprising over 130 civil society groups. The government regularly repressed the organization, especially after the exile group Hermanos al Rescate (Brothers to the Rescue) intensified its propaganda and armed attacks on the island at the same time. The government charged that the Concilio worked with exiles and Washington. Meanwhile, the government had amended the Cuban Constitution in 1992, allowing for referenda on issues receiving 10,000 valid signatures. In 1998, Oswaldo Payá and the Christian Liberation Movement launched the Varela Project calling for freedom of speech, freedom of assembly, and release of political prisoners. By 2002, they gathered over 11,000 signatures and submitted the petition to the National Assembly. However, instead of recognizing the petition and holding a referendum, the government claimed many signatures were invalid and the project was sponsored by Washington—constituting international subversion of the revolution. In March 2003, the government cracked down on all dissident groups, jailing 75 journalists, librarians, and human rights activists in what protesters called the Black Spring. In response, spouses and family members of political prisoners organized as the Ladies in White. After Sunday mass, dressed in white for peace and wearing buttons with pictures of their loved ones in jail, they silently walked through streets to draw attention to human rights violations.

By 2020, activists for causes ranging from free speech to animal protections to LGBTQ rights mobilized via social media. Independent journalists reported news suppressed by state-run media. The internet, though heavily restricted and with limited access, allowed bloggers to challenge state versions of reality. One of the most famous bloggers was Yoani Sánchez, who was 16 when the USSR vanished, and Cuba entered a tailspin. In 2004, she and friends began an online journal and the blog *Generación Y*. They bemoaned Cuba's situation, lack of free speech and press, and human rights abuses. Government censors often blocked articles but many were picked up abroad and distributed across the internet. These "Cuban Digital Revolutionaries" (or "Cyber Mambises" as Anastasia Valecce calls them) continued the long tradition of dissent and resistance with the tools of the day.

Other groups emerged like the *Red Barrial Afrodescendiente* (Afrodescendant Neighborhood Network, or RBA) in 2012 comprised of Afro-Cuban women who were educators, activists, scientists, and artists from across Cuban governmental and nongovernmental sectors. The RBA explored ways to overcome racial, gender, and sexual discrimination in Cuba, empower working-class peoples, and forge economic ties of solidarity across communities. The RBA supported intersectionality through solidarity and consciousness-raising events around the Afro-Cuban LGBTQ community. Educational workshops tackled femicide, sexuality, and race and gender concerns, allowing people to express opinions as equals where each learned from the other. The RBA's initiatives and its relations with other groups reflected a rejection of top-down state socialism approaches. Instead, the RBA embraced horizontal networking in line with libertarian democratic socialism while remaining committed to the Cuban Revolution's ideals.

People used culture to express political discontent. Cubans developed a thriving hip-hop and rap music scene that merged the US-originated genre with Cuban-centered themes and instrumentation to criticize the revolution's inability to abolish racism, racial inequality, and lingering Eurocentrism in much Cuban culture. The Aficionados Artistic Movement was, as Tanya Saunders writes, a "grassroots artistic movement" playing alternative music that democratized the arts scene. During the first decade-plus of the Special Period, the Cuban Underground Hip Hop Movement deployed explicit, racially charged lyrics "that radically challenges Cuban society to recognize and critically address the way in which a crucial issue like 'race' continues to oppress and marginalize Cuban citizens" (Saunders 2015, p. 76). As cinema had done earlier, Cuban hip-hop activists created music that critiqued the revolution's lingering shortcomings. However, in 2018, a new law regulating the arts restricted sales and banned the use of national symbols against the country or the revolution. In 2020, many in Cuba's culture and arts community took to the streets or launched hunger protests against government control and arrests of Cuban artists. In 2021, frustrated by COVID spread, food shortages, and limitations on freedoms, thousands networked through social media and took to streets across the island to protest government shortcomings.

The 2009 Labor Uprisings in the French West Indies

During the height of tourist season in early 2009, an island-wide general strike erupted in Guadeloupe and spread to Martinique. In Guadeloupe, the Lyannaj Kont Pwofitasyon (Alliance against Profiteering, or LKP)—an umbrella group of 48 organizations—led the strike. They protested the high cost of living for residents dependent on tourism and imported consumer goods. Even though both islands are technically part of France, people's salaries fell far below those of workers in France, and unemployment figures were almost double the French rate. In both islands, protesters demanded price freezes, tax cuts, and wage increases.

Strikes turned violent in Guadeloupe in February when protestors and police shot at each other while looters decimated businesses. In March, Paris acquiesced to most of the LKP's demands. Meanwhile, French Guianan workers proclaimed solidarity with the strikes and demanded wage increases too. The general strike illustrated départmentalization's lingering neocolonial tentacles attaching the French Caribbean to France, but it also demonstrated how working peoples fought back transnationally to improve their lives.

Resistance to Political and Natural Disasters in Haiti and Puerto Rico

On 12 January 2010, a 7.0 earthquake devastated Haiti, killing 230,000 people. Known colloquially as *Goudougoudou* (The Event), the disaster ushered in international relief aid that went mostly to 11,000 nongovernmental organizations around Haiti, companies whose headquarters were in donor countries, graft, and corruption. Little money fell into Haitians' hands. Meanwhile, tens of thousands of people poured into makeshift relief camps where women and girls faced sexual assault. In response, women teamed with international groups to support abuse victims and help identify and report rapists.

Camp residents condemned the attacks as well as widespread shortages of supplies and essential services, especially since there was so much international aid arriving in Haiti. With no coordinated rebuilding or relief efforts by 2012, protests erupted. In Port-au-Prince, homes in the poor suburb of Jalousie teetered on collapsing onto homes of wealthy Haitians in the neighboring suburb of Pétionville. In response to the government bulldozing Jalousie homes, 2000 people marched to the National Palace (itself a heap of rubble) to protest the demolitions.

Elsewhere, 200,000 people formed a new community. Refusing to wait for help that many suspected would never come, Haitians built the new city of Canaan on uninhabited land 30 minutes' drive from Port-au-Prince. Canaan quickly grew into Haiti's third largest metro area, with houses, restaurants, football fields, schools, a health center, and pharmacies. This autonomous community lived apart from the machinery of the state—continuing the concept of a "maroon nation"—as residents did not create a local government or police force, paid no taxes, and did not vote.

In 2017, Hurricane María devastated Dominica, St. Croix, and Puerto Rico, killing over 3000 people. For a decade leading to the hurricane, Puerto Ricans had dealt with deteriorating economic and political situations. In 2010, students at the University of Puerto Rico declared a strike against the government, which had violated the university's autonomy, raised tuition costs beyond reach of many, and reduced government assistance. Student groups from Mexico, New York, Spain, and the Dominican Republic aided the Puerto Rican cause. Students pressed their demands through blogs and their own radio station. Though courts ruled largely in favor of students and most campus student groups voted to accept a negotiated settlement, tensions continued. In March 2011, protesters physically attacked university officials for their perceived complicity in these actions. Things got worse in 2016 when Washington created a nonelected financial oversight board to manage the island's crumbling finances. Residents protested yet another example of US colonialism whereby the board implemented austerity measures cutting healthcare, pensions, and education to pay off the island's immense debt. A year later, Hurricane María ripped apart the island, devasting much of the island's housing, water supply, and electrical grid just as the government implemented austerity measures. US government relief aid only haltingly arrived, and the island government seemed incapable of helping people.

In response, activists formed the Ricky Renuncia Project (Ricky Resign) in 2019, forcing the island's governor, Ricardo Rosselló, to resign over his use of sexist and homophobic language toward islanders and corruption for withholding aid to people in the hurricane's wake. Central to the movement were island rap music artists like Bad Bunny, whose song "Afilando los Cuchillos" (Sharpening the Knives) energized anti-Rosselló demonstrators. Meanwhile, local, decentralized resistance arose as people acted autonomously to solve their own problems. Transnational activists, volunteer organizations, and poor vulnerable communities cooperated to create municipally controlled water and micro-grid electric supplies while seeking ways to enhance food sovereignty and not rely on imported goods. People mobilized to tackle the impact of fiscal mismanagement, economic austerity, political chicanery, and climate change. As Joaquín Villanueva and Marisol LeBrón put it, "Abandoned by the state, communities organized to restore their lives, build networks of solidarity, and reconstruct their communal spaces. Unintentionally, governmental neglect helped sow the seeds of a political culture that eventually grew to oust the governor and some of his accomplices from office" (*The Decolonial Geographies* 2019).

INDIGENOUS PEOPLES' RESISTANCE

By the 1800s, most indigenous Caribbean island peoples had died from starvation and genocide, fled, been incorporated biologically with whites or maroons, or been forcibly relocated. Despite depopulation throughout the Caribbean, there was some survival. Indigenous populations and cultures on the mainland Caribbean survived, though under the repression of Spanish colonialism. Ethnic Maya lived along the Caribbean coast of today's Mexico, Belize, and Guatemala for millennia and had a long history of resistance. In 1639, the Maya in modern Belize revolted against Franciscan missionaries. From 1847 to 1901, Mayan peoples in the Yucatán peninsula and Mexico's Caribbean coast revolted in the Caste War against the ruling Mexican elite who dominated the region. Numerous examples of everyday resistance including cultural retention continued among these people who formed (and still form) an important population on the Western Caribbean.

Fugitives from slavery escaped to St. Vincent's mountains, living and having children with surviving indigenous peoples. In 1797, colonizers deported them to British Honduras (Belize). In the 1930s, Caribs in Dominica rebelled, seeking return of a king they believed the British had removed. A compromise resulted with Caribs authorized to elect their own king. By 2015, Dominica Caribs—the largest indigenous population in the Eastern Caribbean with 3000 people—officially became known by their original name "Kalinago."

In 1992, Guatemalan Maya activist Rigoberta Menchú won the Nobel Peace Prize for advancing indigenous people's rights. Menchú's Nobel Peace Prize turned the international spotlight on the long history of indigenous resistance. The emerging pan-indigenous movement swept the Americas, leading to indigenous revitalization projects. One of the largest of these focused on the Taíno, who dominated the Greater Antilles when Columbus arrived. Mixed-race descendants of native peoples led cultural survival efforts, preserved and asserted indigenous cultural traits, and refused to allow Taíno history to be erased by Eurocentric history or a focus on peoples of African descent at the exclusion of native peoples. The Taíno movement also challenged mainstream historical accounts that native islanders did not survive European conquest. Some used the image of the Taíno for political agendas. Many modern-day Puerto Rican Taínos acquired their identity in the United States to symbolically resist US colonialism in Puerto Rico. Meanwhile, nationalists appropriated Taíno symbols "as a central emblem of their nation," a "first root" of Puerto Rican identity, and thus a symbol of resistance to Spanish and then US colonialism (Duany 2001, p. 56). Samuel Wilson concludes, "the Indians are powerful symbols of Caribbean identity, national identity, and resistance to colonialism" (Wilson 1997, p. 206).

Today's indigenous peoples are more than just symbols of resistance; they resist too. Colonial and national forces long pitted Belizean Garifuna (exiled descendants of St. Vincentian deportees in the 1790s) and Maya peoples against each other. By the 2010s, they joined forces to solve issues facing both communities. Indigenous women forged alliances to learn from and share with each other in collective action, labor, and resistance. These long-exploited peoples realized that they required mutual aid and cooperation to fight for cultural, land, and political rights. Meanwhile, the 2007 United Nations Declaration on the Rights of Indigenous Peoples granted "indigenous" recognition to Rastafarians. They used the designation to fight for "traditional" lands like the site of the original Pinnacle community. One of Bob Marley's granddaughters and sons of Leonard Howell sought possession of the land to prevent it from succumbing to commercial development.

RESISTING SEXUAL VIOLENCE

Across the Caribbean, women and girls face high rates of sexual harassment and assault. A 2017 United Nations report identified the Bahamas, Jamaica, and Barbados as among the world's top ten countries with the highest incidence of rape. A third of Caribbean women were victims of domestic abuse, and as many as 30–50% of murders in the Caribbean resulted from domestic abuse. Men especially targeted young women as reflected in a popular refrain stating that "Anything after 12 is lunch"—a reference to the idea that any girl who had reached puberty was fair game for sexual targeting. In fact, by the 2010s, UNICEF estimated that between 20 and 45% of Caribbean children were sexually assaulted.

Caribbean women fought back, launching grassroots campaigns using social media to challenge long-standing government and social indifference to harassment, exploitation, and rape. Activists discussed gender-based violence, sharing across the region what turned out to be common experiences. For instance, many women chose to wear leggings—popular, comfortable, practical pants. Officials too often dismissed complaints of assault and harassment by saying that women wearing leggings "asked" to be assaulted. In 2017, the Life in Leggings campaign exploded across British Caribbean social media. Activists worked in solidarity with another anti-gendered violence organization—the Tambourine Army in Jamaica. They argued violence against women and children differed little from violence against indigenous, African, and other subjugated peoples in Caribbean history where abusers treated individuals as little more than property to be exploited. Together, they protested sexual violence, sought to awaken a new understanding of women's rights, and worked to change the culture from shaming victims to blaming perpetrators of violence.

LGBTQ RESISTANCE TO HOMOPHOBIA AND INJUSTICE

Throughout most of the Caribbean, same-sex relations and marriage remained illegal into the twenty-first century, reflecting the legacy of conservative religious ideas and colonial-era laws criminalizing same-sex behavior. However, a strident LGBTQ movement arose across the region pushing for anti-discrimination laws and changes in societal attitudes. In 2014, young Caribbean men and women gathered in Trinidad as "Generation Change," demanding the end to social and legal discrimination against LGBTQ communities. Human rights campaigns helped eliminate laws criminalizing same-sex relations in Belize and Trinidad & Tobago in 2016. Activists launched campaigns in Jamaica, Barbados, and elsewhere while filing a case with the Inter-American Commission on Human Rights. Then, in 2019, the Being LGBTI in the Caribbean project launched a regional, multilingual "Proudly Caribbean" campaign. Using social media, art, theater and more, the campaign promoted respect for human rights in the British West Indies, the Dominican Republic, and Haiti.

Cuba was the first country to address such concerns. During the 1960s and 1970s, Cuba's government labeled homosexuals "counter-revolutionaries," sending them to work camps to "purge" them of their ways and turn them into new socialist Cubans. Then in 1981, the government declared homosexuality was natural, and homophobia (like sexism and racism) was a prerevolutionary trait needing eradication. Police harassment of homosexuals declined, and state publishing houses printed homosexual material. Then, as Cuba embarked on the Special Period, the government lifted its ban on homosexuals serving in the military, Fidel took personal responsibility for persecution in the 1960s, and in 1993 Tomás Gutiérrez Alea directed his international hit movie *Fresa y chocolate* (Strawberry and Chocolate), in which the hero is a gay artist and dissident while the villain is an anti-homosexual Communist militant. The following decades saw the government not only provide open space for LGBTQ culture but also call for periodic arrests and crackdowns, making for an unstable freedom.

Meanwhile, same-sex marriage freedom in the Caribbean evolved. Mexico's state of Quintana Roo, home to Cancún's Caribbean resorts, legalized same-sex marriage in 2012. In 2013, France legalized same-sex marriage, applying the law to the French West Indies. Aruba, Bonaire, and Curaçao—as parts of the Kingdom of the Netherlands—recognized same-sex marriages but were not required to perform them. In 2015, it became constitutionally protected in the United States and thus in Puerto Rico and the US Virgin Islands. Bermuda legalized same-sex marriage in 2017—only to reverse it later. Costa Rica legalized it in 2020, but the Dominican Republic made it unconstitutional. Meanwhile, the Cuban effort to legalize same-sex marriage was led by the head of Cuba's National Center for Sex Education, Mariela Castro, daughter of former president Raúl Castro and Vilma Espín (founder of the Cuban Women's Federation). In a 2019 referendum, Cubans repealed language in the constitution defining marriage as between a man and woman, paving the way for future same-sex marriages.

REPARATIONS

We end our history of resistance in the modern Caribbean with the transnational struggle to win reparations for descendants of enslaved peoples. The modern reparations campaign brings us full circle to the era of slavery and its abolition at the beginning of this book. The call for reparations is not new and had been enunciated (somewhat differently) since emancipation in the 1800s after some white enslavers received compensation at the end of slavery. Frantz Fanon, Walter Rodney, Rastas, and others called for reparations and/or repatriation for slave descendants. As they and others argued, wealth generated by enslaved peoples in the Caribbean built modern capitalism. British banks and European industries would have been impossible without profits derived from unpaid Caribbean workers. Advocates for reparations sought to right this historical injustice.

In 2001, the United Nations World Conference against Racism, Racial Discrimination, Xenophobia and Related Intolerance (aka, the Durban Conference) met in South Africa. The resulting document recognized colonialism, the slave trade, and slavery played central roles in creating long-term poverty. Delegates called for local, national, and international actions to combat racism and xenophobia. The document's Declaration 166 "Urges States to adopt the necessary measures, as provided by national law, to ensure the right of victims to seek just and adequate reparation and satisfaction to redress acts of racism, racial discrimination, xenophobia and related intolerance" (*Durban Declaration* 2001, p. 52).

Two years later, Haiti's president Aristide demanded $21 billion from France. After the Haitian Revolution, Haiti paid France 90 million francs for the loss of both French property and their enslaved peoples. Aristide sought the money back at current rates. In 2007, Guyana's president Bharrat Jagdeo demanded Europe pay reparations. In 2011, Antigua and Barbuda did too. In 2012 and 2013, Jamaica and Barbados established commissions to explore reparations.

In 2013, the Caribbean Community (CARICOM) sued Great Britain, the Netherlands, and France in the International Court of Justice over reparations. However, no former colonial power recognized the court's jurisdiction in matters before 1974 (Great Britain), 1921 (the Netherlands), or at all (France). Later that year, CARICOM issued a "Ten Point Action Plan" demanding formal apologies from European governments, repatriation and resettlement programs, "Psychological Rehabilitation," an "African Knowledge Program," and financial programs like debt cancellation, technology transfers to the Caribbean, and programs to enhance culture, education, and health. As Claudia Rauhut puts it, this was compensation "to address the living legacies of the crimes committed against indigenous populations and enslaved Africans and their descendants" (Rauhut 2018, p. 137).

Caribbean countries kept up the pressure. Private institutions began acknowledging their historic roles in slavery. For instance, in 2019, the

University of Glasgow conceded that wealth earned in the slave trade and slavery was instrumental in the university's growth. The university committed money for research and development with the University of the West Indies to seek solutions related to economics, health, and identity in the British Caribbean as well as scholarships for West Indian students. That same year, Harvard University entered negotiations with Antigua and Barbuda, recognizing that profits from Antigua's Isaac Royal plantations helped fund the creation of Harvard Law School. These efforts were miniscule, but they were a beginning.

In mid-2020, the global COVID-19 pandemic swept the world. Amid psychological and economic turmoil unleashed by the pandemic, protests and demonstrations erupted around the United States after police killed a man of African descent—George Floyd. Uprisings spread around the world, including among Caribbean populations both at home and in the diasporas. In fact, the seeds of this transnational activism linking US and Caribbean efforts went back over a century to when Afro-Cubans attended the Tuskeegee Institute and returned home with a larger transnational identity, the Harlem Renaissance that linked New York and the Caribbean artistically, musically, and politically, Garvey's UNIA, and more.

This time it took shape as a global Black Lives Matter (BLM) movement. BLM built off nearly two centuries of civil rights activism in the United States. Organizers originally founded BLM in 2013 following acquittal of a white man who shot the unarmed teenager Trevon Martin in 2012. The movement grew in response to a wave of police and white supremacist murders of people of African descent in the United States in the following years. By 2016, BLM spread to Canada, France, and Great Britain. During the summer 2020, in response to the Floyd murder, BLM protests spread across the United States in waves of both peaceful and violent demonstration against police abuse and historic structural violence against communities of color. Protests quickly proliferated throughout Caribbean diaspora communities and the Caribbean as well. In these communities, protestors explicitly linked BLM's attacks against systemic racism to growing transnational cries for slavery reparations. This was a multipronged push for justice. During this global uprising, various banks, firms, and churches apologized for profiting from slavery. They did little else.

While massa apologized, the masses took matters into their own hands, toppling statues of people linked to slavery, genocide, and exploitation. Statues dedicated to enslaved peoples and slave resistance exist in Barbados, Cuba, Curaçao, Guadeloupe, Guyana, Haiti, Jamaica, Martinique, and Puerto Rico. However, there also was no shortage of monuments and place names of enslavers and their allies. In 2020, amid calls for reparations and global BLM demonstrations, protestors toppled statues of Confederate generals and Christopher Columbus in the United States. In Puerto Rico, activists—some dressed as Taíno—demanded removal of a gigantic Columbus statue erected in San Juan in 1998. In the US Virgin Islands, activists questioned the lingering existence of Danish-era street names and a statue of Danish king Christian IX in St. Thomas's Emancipation Gardens. Other activists tore down a statue of a West

Indian slave trader, rolling it into Bristol Harbor in Great Britain. In Barbados, the government bowed to popular pressure and removed the statue of British naval commander Horatio Nelson from National Heroes Square. On 22 May 2020—Martinique's Emancipation Day—protestors toppled and destroyed two statues of Victor Schoelcher, the man who prepared a decree abolishing slavery in the French Caribbean. Activists shouted "Schoelcher is not our savior." They reframed history from an official version that glorified French abolitionists to one celebrating the abolitionist resistance of average people. Though Schoelcher might have ushered in the legal end to slavery, it was the rebellious enslaved peoples and their unending quest for freedom that created conditions leading to slavery's demise. That legacy persisted as common people continued waging struggles for justice from below. Transnational acts of resistance in the twenty-first century, rooted in Caribbean history.

Works Cited and Further References

A.L. Araujo (2017) *Reparations for Slavery and the Slave Trade: A Transnational and Comparative History* (Bloomsbury).

J-B. Arisitide (1991) *In the Parish of the Poor: Writings from Haiti* (Orbis).

G. Averill (1997) *A Day for the Hunter, A Day for the Prey* (University of Chicago Press).

H. McD. Beckles (2013) *Britain's Black Debt: Reparations for Caribbean Slavery and Native Genocide* (University of the West Indies Press).

A. Dávia (2001) "Local/Diasporic Taínos: Towards a Cultural Politics of Memory, Reality, and Imagery" in Gabriel Haslip-Viera (ed.) *Taíno Revival: Critical Perspectives on Puerto Rican Identity and Cultural Politics* (Markus Wiener), 33–53.

G. de Laforcade and D. Springer (2019) "The *Red Barrial Afrodescendiente*: A Cuban Experiment in Black Community Empowerment," *Souls*, 21/4, 339–46.

J. Duany (2001) "Making Indians Out of Blacks: The Revitalization of Taíno Identity in Contemporary Puerto Rico" in Gabriel Haslip-Viera (ed.) *Taíno Revival: Critical Perspectives on Puerto Rican Identity and Cultural Politics* (Markus Wiener), 55–82.

Durban Declaration (2001) World Conference against Racism, Racial Discrimination, Xenophobia and Related Intolerance https://www.un.org/WCAR/durban.pdf

R. Fernández (1987) *Los Macheteros: The Wells Fargo Robbery and the Violent Struggle for Puerto Rican Independence* (Simon & Schuster).

H. García Muñiz (2011) "The Colonial Persuasion: Puerto Rico and the Dutch and French Antilles" in Stephan Palmié and Francisco Scarano (eds.) *The Caribbean: A History of the Region and Its Peoples* (University of Chicago Press), 537–51.

N.L. González (1997) "The Garifuna of Central America" in Samuel M. Wilson (ed.) *The Indigenous People of the Caribbean* (University Press of Florida), 199–205.

F. Guridy (2010) *Forging Diaspora: Afro-Cubans and African Americans in a World of Empire and Jim Crow* (University of North Carolina Press).

G. Heuman (2014) *The Caribbean: A Brief History*, 2nd edition (Bloomsbury).

M. Jiménez Román (2001) "The Indians Are Coming! The Indians Are Coming!: The Taíno and Puerto Rican Identity" in Gabriel Haslip-Viera (ed.) *Taíno Revival: Critical Perspectives on Puerto Rican Identity and Cultural Politics* (Markus Wiener), 101–38.

G. Joseph (1997) "Five Hundred Years of Indigenous Resistance" in Samuel M. Wilson (ed.) *The Indigenous People of the Caribbean* (University Press of Florida), 214–22.

Latin America and the United States: A Documentary History (2011) R.H. Holden and E. Zolov (eds.) (Oxford University Press).

T.B. Lindsey and J.M. Johnson (2014) "Searching for Climax: Black Erotic Lives in Slavery and Freedom," *Meridians: Feminism, Race, Transnationalism* 12/2, 169–95.

A.P. Maingot (2011) "Independence and Its Aftermath: Suriname, Trinidad, and Jamaica" in Stephan Palmié and Francisco Scarano (eds.) *The Caribbean: A History of the Region and Its Peoples* (University of Chicago Press), 523–35.

B. Meeks (1996) *Radical Caribbean: From Black Power to Abu Bakr* (University of the West Indies Press).

M.J. Newton (2017) Presentation at Indigenous Geographies and Caribbean Feminisms Symposium, University of the West Indies, St. Augustine. https://www.youtube.com/watch?v=8JzuDmR9BM

———— (2013) "Return to a Native Land: Indigeneity and Decolonization in the Anglophone Caribbean," *Small Axe*, 17/2, 108–22.

C. Rauhut (2018) "Caribbean activism for slavery reparations: An overview" in Wiebke Beushausen et al. (eds.) *Practices of Resistance in the Caribbean: Narratives, Aesthetics, and Politics* (Routledge), 137–50.

A. Rosa (2018) "*Una Universidad Tomada*: Resistance performances in the (re)construction of spaces of resistance and contention during the first wave of the 2010–2011 University of Puerto Rico student movement" in Wiebke Beushausen et al. (eds.) *Practices of Resistance in the Caribbean: Narratives, Aesthetics, and Politics* (Routledge), 169–93.

T. Saunders (2015) *Cuban Underground Hip Hop: Black Thoughts, Black Revolution, Black Modernity* (University of Texas Press).

"Strawberry and Chocolate" (1994) Tomás Gutiérrez Alea (dir.) (ICAIC).

Ten Point Action Plan (2013) CARICOM Reparations Commission. https://caricom-reparations.org/.

The Decolonial Geographies of Puerto Rico's 2019 Summer Protests: A Forum (2019) Joaquín Villanueva and Marisol LeBrón (eds.) https://www.societyandspace.org/forums/the-decolonial-geographies-of-puerto-ricos-2019-summer-protests-a-forum.

H.U.E. Thoden van Velzen (1990) "The Maroon Insurgency: Anthropological Reflections on the Civil War in Suriname" in Gary Brana-Shute (ed.) *Resistance and Rebellion in Suriname: Old and New,* 159–88.

M.-R. Trouillot (1990) *Haiti: State against Nation* (Monthly Review).

A. Valecce (2020) "(In)visible Cuba(s): Digital Conflict, Virtual Diasporas, and Cyber *Mambises*" in Héctor Fernández L'Hoeste (ed.) *Digital Humanities in Latin America* (University Press of Florida), 74–88.

S.M. Wilson (1997) "The Legacy of the Indigenous People of the Caribbean" in Samuel M. Wilson (ed.) *The Indigenous People of the Caribbean* (University Press of Florida), 206–13.

A. Wilentz (1989) *The Rainy Season: Haiti since Duvalier* (Touchstone).

W. Zips (1999) *Black Rebels: African Caribbean Freedom Fighters in Jamaica* (Marcus Wiener).

Index[1]

A

Abolition, 10, 12, 19, 25, 32, 37, 41, 42, 46, 48–49, 51, 52, 58, 60–62, 75, 80–82, 128, 187

Abortion, 10, 41–43

Abu Bakr, Yasin (Trinidad 1980s 1990s), *see* Muslim Revolt (Trinidad 1990)

Acaau, Jean-Jacques (Haiti 1840s), 59

Acción Feminista Dominicana (1940s), 111

Acción Nacional Revolucionario (ANR, Cuba 1950s), 156

Active *vs.* passive resistance, 4, 5, 9, 10

Aficionados Artistic Movement, *see* Cuban Revolution

African Blood Brotherhood (ABB, New York 1910s-1920s), 134–135, 146, 149
  and the Comintern, 134

Afro-Cubans, 14, 67, 80–82, 127–129, 132, 135, 142, 149, 155, 162, 163, 170, 173, 181, 188

Agency, 1, 19

Albizu Campos, Pedro, 115, 116
  See also Anti-colonialism; Puerto Rican nationalists

Alianza Bolivariana para los Pueblos de Nuestra América (ALBA), 179

Almeida, Juan (Cuba 1950s), 155

Anancy, 45

Anarchists
  and anti-imperialism, 96
  in Cuban Revolution 1950s, 15, 162
  and Cuban War for Independence 1890s, 83, 84
  exiles in Florida, 162
  and opposition to Cuban Revolution, 162
  and opposition to US rule in Cuba, 92
  Panama Canal Zone, 105
  in Puerto Rico, 13, 92

Anti-Batista resistance
  anarchist opposition, 162
  armed opposition, 160
  Catholic opposition, 170
  middle-class opposition, 156, 161
  motherhood and opposition, 156, 169
  transnational opposition, 165

Anti-Castro resistance, *see* Cuban Revolution

[1] Note: Page numbers followed by 'n' refer to notes.

K. Shaffer, *A Transnational History of the Modern Caribbean*, https://doi.org/10.1007/978-3-030-93012-7

1.1   1,3,4,8,10,11,14, 15, 16, 18

not < 1.2   1,3,7,11,13

focus 1.3   1,3,5,9,10,11,13,14, 15, 17,19, 20, 21

2.1   3,4,5,11, 15, 17,20

2.2   1,3,6,7,10

2.3   1,3,6,7,10

Made in the USA
Las Vegas, NV
01 May 2024

89382987R00125